Chronicling Westerners in Nineteenth-Century East Asia

SOAS Studies in Modern and Contemporary Japan

SERIES EDITOR:
Christopher Gerteis (SOAS, University of London, UK)

EDITORIAL BOARD:
Stephen Dodd (SOAS, University of London, UK)
Andrew Gerstle (SOAS, University of London, UK)
Janet Hunter (London School of Economics, UK)
Barak Kushner (University of Cambridge, UK)
Helen Macnaughtan (SOAS, University of London, UK)
Aaron W Moore (University of Edinburgh, UK)
Timon Screech (SOAS, University of London, UK)
Naoko Shimazu (NUS-Yale College, Singapore)

Published in association with the Japan Research Centre at the School of Oriental and African Studies, University of London, UK.

SOAS Studies in Modern and Contemporary Japan features scholarly books on modern and contemporary Japan, showcasing new research monographs as well as translations of scholarship not previously available in English. Its goal is to ensure that current, high-quality research on Japan, its history, politics and culture, is made available to an English-speaking audience.

Published:

Women and Democracy in Cold War Japan, Jan Bardsley
Christianity and Imperialism in Modern Japan, Emily Anderson
The China Problem in Postwar Japan, Robert Hoppens
Media, Propaganda and Politics in 20th Century Japan, The Asahi Shimbun Company (translated by Barak Kushner)
Contemporary Sino-Japanese Relations on Screen, Griseldis Kirsch
Debating Otaku in Contemporary Japan, edited by Patrick W. Galbraith, Thiam Huat Kam and Björn-Ole Kamm
Politics and Power in 20th-Century Japan, Mikuriya Takashi and Nakamura Takafusa (translated by Timothy S. George)
Japanese Taiwan, edited by Andrew Morris
Japan's Postwar Military and Civil Society, Tomoyuki Sasaki
The History of Japanese Psychology, Brian J. McVeigh
Postwar Emigration to South America from Japan and the Ryukyu Islands, Pedro Iacobelli
The Uses of Literature in Modern Japan, Sari Kawana
Post-Fascist Japan, Laura Hein
Mass Media, Consumerism and National Identity in Postwar Japan, Martyn David Smith
Japan's Occupation of Java in the Second World War, Ethan Mark
Gathering for Tea in Modern Japan, Taka Oshikiri
Engineering Asia, Hiromi Mizuno, Aaron S. Moore and John DiMoia
Automobility and the City in Japan and Britain, c. 1955–1990, Simon Gunn and Susan Townsend
The Origins of Modern Japanese Bureaucracy, Yuichiro Shimizu (translated by Amin Ghadimi)
Kenkoku University and the Experience of Pan-Asianism, Yuka Hiruma Kishida
Overcoming Empire in Post-Imperial East Asia, Barak Kushner and Sherzod Muminov
Imperial Japan and Defeat in the Second World War, Peter Wetzler
Gender, Culture, and Disaster in Post-3.11 Japan, Mire Koikari
Empire and Constitution in Modern Japan, Junji Banno (translated by Arthur Stockwin)
A History of Economic Thought in Japan, Hiroshi Kawaguchi and Sumiyo Ishii (translated by Ayuko Tanaka and Tadashi Anno)
Haruki Murakami and the Search for Self-Therapy, Jonathan Dil
Japan's Empire of Birds, Annika A. Culver
Chronicling Westerners in Nineteenth-Century East Asia, Robert S. G. Fletcher and Robert Hellyer (eds.)

Chronicling Westerners in Nineteenth-Century East Asia

Lives, Linkages, and Imperial Connections

Edited by

Robert S. G. Fletcher and Robert Hellyer

BLOOMSBURY ACADEMIC
LONDON • NEW YORK • OXFORD • NEW DELHI • SYDNEY

BLOOMSBURY ACADEMIC
Bloomsbury Publishing Plc
50 Bedford Square, London, WC1B 3DP, UK
1385 Broadway, New York, NY 10018, USA
29 Earlsfort Terrace, Dublin 2, Ireland

BLOOMSBURY, BLOOMSBURY ACADEMIC and the Diana logo are
trademarks of Bloomsbury Publishing Plc

First published in Great Britain 2022
Paperback edition first published 2024

Copyright © Robert S. G. Fletcher and Robert Hellyer, 2022

Robert S. G. Fletcher and Robert Hellyer have asserted their right under the Copyright,
Designs and Patents Act, 1988, to be identified as Editors of this work.

Cover image: Nagasaki University Library

All rights reserved. No part of this publication may be reproduced or transmitted
in any form or by any means, electronic or mechanical, including photocopying,
recording, or any information storage or retrieval system, without prior
permission in writing from the publishers.

Bloomsbury Publishing Plc does not have any control over, or responsibility for,
any third-party websites referred to or in this book. All internet addresses given
in this book were correct at the time of going to press. The author and publisher
regret any inconvenience caused if addresses have changed or sites have
ceased to exist, but can accept no responsibility for any such changes.

A catalogue record for this book is available from the British Library.

A catalog record for this book is available from the Library of Congress.

ISBN:	HB:	978-1-3502-3890-9
	PB:	978-1-3502-3893-0
	ePDF:	978-1-3502-3891-6
	eBook:	978-1-3502-3889-3

Typeset by Integra Software Services Pvt. Ltd.

To find out more about our authors and books visit www.bloomsbury.com
and sign up for our newsletters.

Contents

Illustrations	vi
Tables	vii
Contributors	viii
Foreword	xiii
Acknowledgements	xv
Notes on Conventions	xvii
Map of Principal Locations	xviii

Introduction   William Alt and Charles Richardson:
Family, fortune and fortuity in nineteenth-century East Asia
Robert S. G. Fletcher and Robert Hellyer   1

1. Disturbed reciprocity: Rutherford Alcock's diplomacy and merchant communities in China and Japan *Sano Mayuko*   21
2. George S. Morrison and Japan's first British consulate at Nagasaki *Brian Burke-Gaffney*   43
3. Making safe the settlement: The British troops at Yokohama and their influence on foreign and Japanese society *Nakatake (Hori) Kanami*   61
4. Between trade and diplomacy: The commercial activities of the Swiss silk merchants Siber and Brennwald in late Edo and early Meiji Japan *Fukuoka Mariko and Alexis Schwarzenbach*   83
5. Afterlife of the wealthy: The burial of mercantile communities in nineteenth-century colonial Hong Kong *Bobby Tam*   105
6. *Charlotte Jane*: National symbol and global reality *Annette Bainbridge*   125
7. Dreams of expanding the British Empire: The life of George Windsor Earl *Ranald Noel-Paton*   145

Notes	166
Bibliography	203
Index	221

Illustrations

I	Map showing principal locations featured in this book	xviii
1	Charles Lenox Richardson	3
2	William John Alt, *c.* 1864	3
3	Sir Rutherford Alcock K.C.B. Her Brittannic Majesty's Minister in Japan, by Felice Beato	23
4	Royal Marines Light Infantry, Parade Ground, Huts, Yokohama, 1864–5	63
5	Hermann Siber, as a young man (undated)	85
6	Caspar Brennwald as a young man (undated)	85
7	Cemetery, Happy Valley, Hong Kong. Photograph from a negative by John Thomson (1837–1921), *c.* 1868	106
8	The Charlotte Jane. James Edward Fitzgerald, watercolour on paper, 1850	127
9	Captain and Mrs Lawrence	131
10	George Samuel Windsor Earl, *c.* 1860	147

Tables

1	British and French Regiments stationed at Yokohama between 1863 and 1875	66
2	Troop strengths and movements	67
3	Table of Brennwald's negotiations over Weapons in 1866–7	94
4	Imports of the Sendai domain from Siber & Brennwald and Textor & Co. (August to November 1868)	96
5	Schedule of fees for interments in the cemetery in 1854	110

Contributors

Annette Bainbridge was born in Christchurch, New Zealand. She received her Bachelor of Arts degree from the University of Canterbury. She then began her teaching career at a small school in rural Japan. This inspired her to return to academia and complete a first-class honours degree and teaching diploma at the University of Waikato in New Zealand's North Island. After teaching for several years she then took time off to go travelling and start a family. In 2014 she returned to academia, completing a Master's degree in colonial women's history at the University of Waikato. She then worked as a tutor and lecturer at the university on topics ranging from war and social history to environmental history. She has also published in the field of computing and the humanities. She has since presented, both in New Zealand and internationally, on topics from her thesis and is currently beginning the first year of a PhD at Victoria University of Wellington that will expand on her previous research themes and delve more into New Zealand's environmental history. She is a member of the Hamilton Garden Research Committee which is based at the international award winning Hamilton Gardens and promotes research into all aspects of New Zealand garden history.

Brian Burke-Gaffney was born in Winnipeg, Canada, in 1950 and came to Japan in 1972, going on to train for nine years as an ordained monk of the Rinzai Zen sect. He moved to Nagasaki in 1982. He is currently Professor of Cultural History at the Nagasaki Institute of Applied Science and also honorary director of the historic preservation facility Glover Garden. He earned a PhD in 2007 for research related to the former Nagasaki Foreign Settlement, and received the Nagasaki Prefecture Citizens Award in 1992 and the Nagasaki Shimbun Culture Award in 2016. He has published several books in both Japanese and English, including *Starcrossed: A Biography of Madame Butterfly* (EastBridge, 2004) and *Nagasaki: The British Experience 1854–1945* (Global Oriental UK, 2009). He launched Flying Crane Press in 2015 to publish information related to Nagasaki.

Robert S.G. Fletcher is Professor of History and Kinder Professor of British History at the University of Missouri. He grew up in East Anglia and read Modern

History at Magdalen College, University of Oxford. He lived in Tokushima prefecture as a participant on the Japan Exchange and Teaching Programme before returning to Oxford to complete his doctoral studies, and has previously held positions at the Universities of Exeter and Warwick. Robert works in the fields of imperial and global history, with a focus on Britain's experiences of empire. His first book *British Imperialism and 'The Tribal Question'* (Oxford University Press, 2015) examined British relations with the Bedouin in the deserts of the Middle East. His second *The Ghost of Namamugi* (Amsterdam University Press, 2019) was an exploration of mercantile ambition and imperial power in mid-nineteenth-century China and Japan. Robert has been the Principal Investigator on a number of research projects supported by the UK Arts and Humanities Research Council, including *Science in Culture* awards on the international campaign against the desert locust. His current research examines Britain's historic relationship with the world's desert environments.

Fukuoka Mariko is Associate Professor of Early Modern Japanese History at the National Museum of Japanese History and the Graduate University for Advanced Studies in Japan (Sokendai). She has researched the diplomatic history of the transitional period between early modern and modern Japan (the Meiji Restoration period), with a focus on relations between Japan and Western nations (especially German-speaking regions and the United States). She completed her PhD thesis at the University of Tokyo on 'The Prussian East-Asian Expedition and Japanese Diplomacy in the Late Edo Era', which was awarded the University of Tokyo Nanbara Shigeru Publication Prize, and published in 2013 by The University of Tokyo Press. The book also received the 2014 Prize of the Japanese Society of German Studies (Nihon Doitsu Gakkai). Following several publications on the diplomatic and commercial activities of German-speaking actors in the Meiji Restoration period, especially the Prussian diplomat Max von Brandt and the Swiss silk trading firm Siber & Brennwald, she is now preparing her second book on Townsend Harris, the first US Consul General (later Minister Resident) in Japan, and who played a critical role in the 'opening' of Japan.

Robert Hellyer is Associate Professor of History at Wake Forest University (USA). He grew up in Tacoma, Washington, and first developed an interest in Japanese history while teaching in Yamaguchi prefecture as a member of the Japan Exchange and Teaching Programme. He later served on the faculty of the University of Tokyo and taught at Allegheny College before beginning his current position at Wake Forest in 2005. A historian of early modern and modern Japan, Hellyer has explored foreign relations from the seventeenth to the nineteenth centuries, research presented in *Defining Engagement: Japan and Global Contexts, 1640–1868* (Harvard, 2009). He co-organized a multi-year, global project that examined Japan's Meiji Restoration surrounding the 150-year anniversary in 2018, an initiative that resulted in Robert Hellyer and Harald Fuess, eds., *The Meiji Restoration: Japan as a Global Nation* (Cambridge, 2020). He is also the author of *Green with Milk and Sugar: When Japan Filled America's Tea Cups* (Columbia, 2021) which explores Japan's role in the global tea trade of the late nineteenth and early twentieth centuries, a project supported by Smithsonian, Japan Foundation, Hakuhodo Foundation, Sainsbury Institute and NEH fellowships.

Nakatake (Hori) Kanami received her MA in international relations from Tsuda University, Tokyo, in 1982. She has been Curator and Senior Curator at the Yokohama Archives of History since 1982. Her work focuses on researching, collecting and arranging historical records on the modern history of Yokohama, the largest cosmopolitan city in Japan in the second half of the nineteenth century and the early twentieth century. Her main research theme is that of Western political and cultural influences – especially those of Britain and France – upon the government and local society in Yokohama. She has written papers and published joint books, including 'Bakumatsu-Ishinki no Yokohama Eifutsu chūtongun no jittai to sono eikyō: Igirisu gun o chūsin ni' (The Conditions Surrounding the Stationing of British and French Troops in Yokohama and Their Influence – A Focus on the British Troops), *Yokohama Archives of History Review* (1994), *Yokohama Eifutsu chūtongun to gaikokujin kyoryūchi* (The British and French Troops Stationed in Yokohama and the Foreign Settlement), Tokyo-dō shuppan, 1999, and *Yokohama to gaikokujin shakai* (Yokohama and Foreign Societies in the Early Twentieth Century), Nihon Keizai Hyōronsha, 2015. She was also recognized as a Certified Archivist by the National Archives of Japan in 2021.

Ranald Noel-Paton was born in Bombay in 1938. Growing up after the Second World War in Scotland and England, he was educated at Rugby School and McGill University. He spent twenty-one years in the airline industry and served overseas in West Africa and the Asia-Pacific region; in Hong Kong as General Manager Far East for British Caledonian Airways. He returned to the UK in 1986 to be Group Managing Director of John Menzies PLC. In 1991, he was awarded an honorary doctorate by Napier University in Edinburgh. He and his wife have been married for forty-five years and they now live in Scotland. Ranald Noel-Paton is a direct descendant of George Windsor Earl.

Sano Mayuko is Professor at Kyoto University where she pursues research on the 'Cultural History of Diplomacy'. After working for the Japan Foundation, UNESCO, the International Research Center for Japanese Studies and other organizations, she assumed her current position in 2018. She holds an MPhil in International Relations from the University of Cambridge, and a PhD from the University of Tokyo. Her publications include *Orukokku no Edo: Shodai Eikoku koshi ga mita Bakumatsu Nihon* (Alcock's Edo: Japan in the Bakumatsu Period, as Seen by the First British Minister) Chūōkōron-shinsha, 2003; *Bakumatsu gaikō girei no kenkyū: Ōbei gaikōkan tachi no shōgun haietsu* (Diplomatic Ceremonial in the Bakumatsu Period: Western Diplomats' Castle Audiences with the Shogun) Shibunkaku, 2016; and the edited volume, *Banpakugaku: Bankokuhakurankai to iu, sekai o haaku suru hōhō* (Expo-logy: Expos as a Method of Grasping the World) Shibunkaku, 2020.

Alexis Schwarzenbach was born in Zurich in 1971. He read Modern History at Balliol College in Oxford obtaining a BA in 1994 and held a PhD scholarship at the Department of History and Civilisation at the European University Institute in Florence. After completing his doctorate in 1997, he worked in publishing and began to write books and curating exhibitions as a freelance historian. From 2009 to 2011 he was Senior Curator at the Swiss National Museum in Zurich. In 2012 he became a lecturer and in 2015 a professor at the School of Art and Design at Lucerne University of Applied Sciences and Art. In 2021 he founded the history studio filanda della storia in Thalwil/Zurich. His research focuses on nineteenth- and twentieth-century European cultural history with a special focus on transnational material culture. He is currently working on a history of the Zurich silk industry since 1800 which is scheduled for publication in German and English in 2022. He lives in Zurich.

Bobby Tam is a PhD candidate in the History Department at the University of Warwick. He received his BA and MPhil from the University of Hong Kong. During his MPhil, he wrote a thesis on how death was managed in colonial Hong Kong from 1841 to 1913. His current PhD research focuses on the history of death from an emotional perspective, exploring emotional expressions around death in multiple British colonial contexts in nineteenth-century China. He explores how emotions of death were expressed and discussed in a context where cultural norms were actively contending. This includes looking into emotional expressions from both public collective and private individual perspectives. Bobby is broadly interested in the history of emotions, memory studies, the nineteenth-century British Empire, and Late Imperial and Modern China.

Hans van de Ven, educated at Leiden and Harvard Universities, is Professor of Modern Chinese History at Cambridge University. His most recent works are *The Chinese Communist Party: A Centenary in Ten Lives, China at War: Triumph and Tragedy in the Birth of the New China* (Profile, 2017), and *Breaking with the Past: The Chinese Maritime Customs Service and the Global Origins of Modernity in China* (Columbia, 2014).

Foreword

Reading *Chronicling Westerners* is like receiving postcards from a relative or a friend travelling to new parts of the world – in a different age. We are treated to essays on a ship, *Charlotte Jane,* as she sailed from Britain to New Zealand, Australia, Shanghai and elsewhere in the middle of the nineteenth century; to ethnically inflected competitions for cemetery spaces in Hong Kong; to the activities in Japan of the Swiss silk merchants Caspar Brennwald and Hermann Siber as they exploited the destruction of Europe's silk growing fields by the pebrine parasite, and learned to trade in ships, arms and people; to the fights for equity and justice of consul and later diplomat Rutherford Alcock, who built new governance systems based on still fresh notions of sovereignty first in Shanghai and then Japan; and to George Windsor Earl's empire buccaneering and still valuable scholarly treatises of Australia and Indonesia. This is a rich offering.

Connecting these varied stories are two men, William Alt (1840–1908) and Charles Richardson (1833–62). Their correspondences to family and friends form the basis of this book of postcards from a distant, far-away age. Richardson is mainly known because his killing in 1862 led to the bombardment of Japan's Satsuma domain by a squadron of British warships in 1863. Alt, like Richardson, began his career in Shanghai but built a fairly successful business in Nagasaki. Collectively the essays allow us to reconstitute in our own minds the world in which they lived and which they helped shape, and to see the many connections that existed between these realities, which are usually kept apart. Just one example is that George Windsor Earl's daughter, Annie, fell in love with Alt while both were on a ship sailing from Singapore to Adelaide.

We do not yet have a good word for this world really. Geographically it encompassed European settlements in East and Southeast Asia (but not India), but its territorial scope was in flux. Earl, for instance, led an Admiralty effort to establish a base in north Australia and incorporate it into the British Empire, but he failed. Politically it was just as uncertain. The middle of the nineteenth century was a period of deep changes, for instance about the separation of government and commerce. Rutherford Alcock battled with British merchants in order to create stable relationships with Japanese authorities, but Brennwald made sure to be a Swiss consul in Japan so that he could use its privileges, including residence in Edo, to gain commercial advantages. Most travel still happened in sailing vessels, but the *Charlotte Jane* delivered train carriages to Southland in New Zealand. British power grew rapidly because the Royal Navy genuinely ruled the waves, but the Dutch in Indonesia, which only in this period gained its name, still were often in their way. This book makes clear how embryonic this world then still remained.

We must be grateful to Robert Fletcher and Robert Hellyer for putting this unique volume together. It offers a fresh perspective on issues and places usually studied as part of national histories or in terms of political structures such as empire. They have done us a real service in reminding us that for many these categories were not necessarily all that relevant and also for giving due prominence to the personal and the emotional. Enjoy.

Hans van de Ven
7 March 2021

Acknowledgements

As befitting of a historical study focused on personal connections, this book became a reality thanks to transcontinental familial and professional ties. Tessa Montgomery laid the foundation for this project first by kindly allowing Robert Hellyer, a historian of Japan and her distant cousin, to research the letters of William Alt, penned during his days on board *Charlotte Jane* as well as in Shanghai and Nagasaki in the 1850s and 1860s. She later generously donated the letters to the Sainsbury Institute for the Study of Japanese Arts and Cultures in Norwich. Meanwhile, in London, Michael and Marigold Wace had kindly granted permission to Robert Fletcher, a historian of the British Empire, to research the personal correspondence of Charles Richardson: another British merchant who, like Alt, lived and worked in Shanghai in 1850s and 1860s before his infamous murder near Yokohama in 1862.

Thanks to the introduction of Robert Bickers at the University of Bristol, Hellyer subsequently learned of Fletcher's research. Realizing the shared themes and intriguing overlaps of their projects, the two developed plans for a conference at which scholars researching topics with links to Alt and Richardson could present papers and share ideas on how to cross geographic, temporal and thematic borders.

In June 2017, a symposium, 'Documenting Westerners in Nineteenth-Century China and Japan: New Sources and Perspectives', at which most of the contributors to this volume presented papers, was convened at the Sainsbury Institute. Fletcher and Hellyer especially thank the Sainsbury Institute, particularly the then executive director, Mami Mizutori, for funding this event. The Daiwa Anglo-Japanese Foundation, the Global History and Culture Centre at the University of Warwick, and the Wake Forest University Department of History also provided support to allow scholars from the UK, Germany, the United States and Japan to attend. Hans van de Ven of Cambridge University, who offered insightful comments on the entire symposium, generously contributed the foreword to this book. Following the conference, Simon Kaner, the current Executive Director of the Sainsbury Institute (who also served a discussant at the symposium), remained supportive by offering additional funding as this project moved forward to publication.

The editors also thank Christopher Gerteis, editor of the SOAS Studies in Modern and Contemporary Japan series, as well as Rhodri Mogford and Laura Reeves of Bloomsbury for their assistance. Seth Kannarr of the University of Missouri designed the book's map. Three anonymous readers provided valuable feedback and suggestions, which helped to improve this book in many ways.

Notes on Conventions

Romanization

Japanese words, names, titles and place names are spelled using the modified Hepburn system. Japanese words include macrons, except for commonly used ones, such as 'shogun' and 'Tokyo', which appear in standard English dictionaries.

Chinese words, proper names and place names are spelled according to the pinyin system except in some book titles and in cases, such as Canton (Guangzhou), where the older romanization is more familiar to English-language readers.

Proper Names

Chinese and Japanese names appear in the original order, with the family name first, followed by the given name, except for citations in English-language works where the author's name appears in Western order.

Dates

Except for those included in direct quotations from sources, dates of the Japanese calendar (used until 1873) have been converted into the Gregorian calendar. Months referred to by name (e.g. 'June') are Gregorian dates, while references by number (e.g. 'the fifth month') are dates according to the Japanese calendar.

Map of Principal Locations

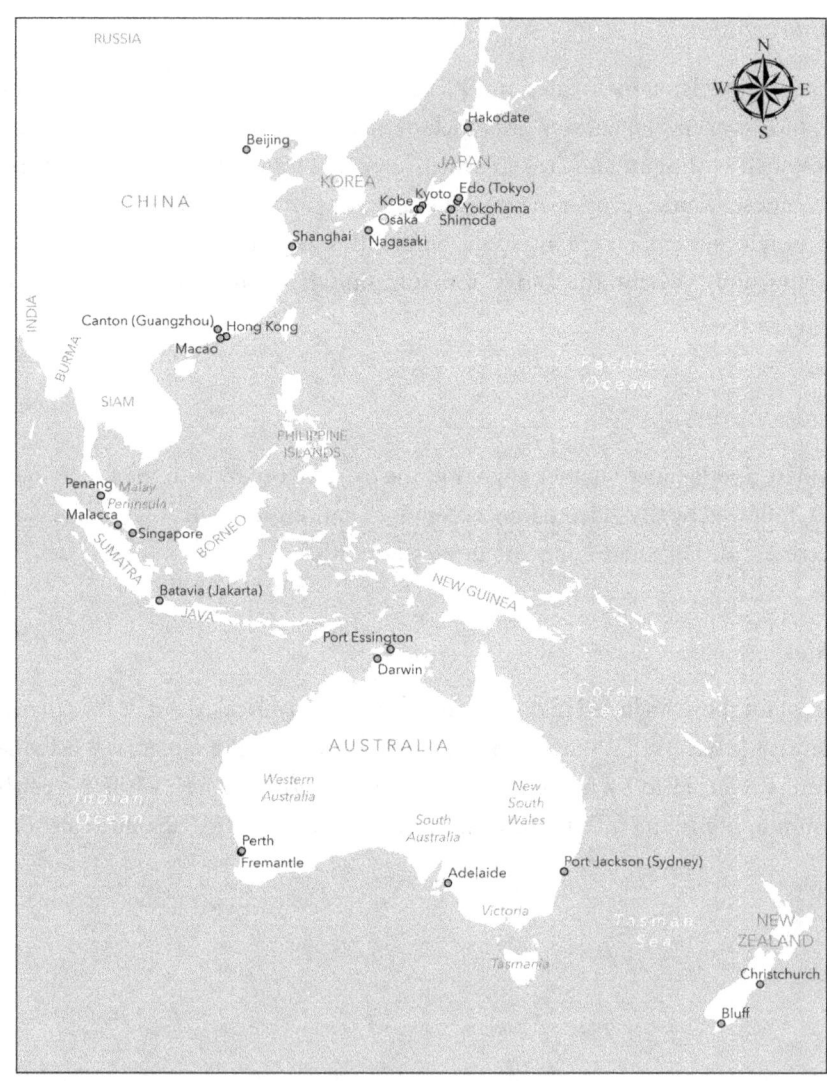

Map I Map showing principal locations featured in this book.

Introduction

William Alt and Charles Richardson: Family, fortune and fortuity in nineteenth-century East Asia

Robert S. G. Fletcher and Robert Hellyer

This volume is a contribution to the literature on a favoured subject in the study of East Asia: the world of the treaty port. As both place and process, the treaty port has loomed large in our new global histories of the region, and of the great forces that have rocked it, from imperialism and nationalism to capitalism and globalization. These forces can seem somewhat impersonal at times, and individual lives and trajectories can get pushed from centre stage by the drama and consequence of the changes around them. Worse still, they can become obscured behind caricature and myth, falling foul of hagiography on the one hand, and scapegoating on the other. Yet reconstructing the world of the treaty ports (and the world they made) ought also to be a matter of sensitively tracing and connecting lives and experiences. Doing so not only reveals the myriad pathways and exchanges connecting East Asia's treaty ports with one another, and with diverse sites beyond the region; it is also a timely reminder of the human element that went into the '-isms' of history.

Two transformations of the 1850s and 1860s have informed the writing of this book: the dramatic change in Britain's position in and knowledge of East Asia, on the one hand, and the Victorian 'revolution in letter writing', on the other. This book emerged from a desire to explore these phenomena in parallel, and to ask the following question: how can collections of personal correspondence help us gain new perspectives on East Asian history? Two British men living and working in nineteenth-century East Asia have inspired our own research projects, but the similarities and connections between them have pushed us to examine how such individuals, and the private correspondence they left behind, can add nuance, texture and complexity to our renderings of the treaty port world. Charles Lenox Richardson (1833–62) wrote one group of letters across a decade working as a merchant in Shanghai in the 1850s and 1860s. Although spending most of his time in China, Richardson gained lasting historical note with his death in Japan in 1862 at the hands of retainers of the Shimazu, the clan ruling the southern Kyushu domain of Satsuma. William John Alt (1840–1908) penned the other batch of letters beginning with his time as a crewman on *Charlotte Jane*, a British merchant ship, as well as during two years in Shanghai. Alt subsequently made a significant mark as a trader in Nagasaki, an experience chronicled in letters sent home to family in Britain during the early 1860s.

The two men were young when they entered the treaty ports and witnessed tumultuous events in the so-called 'openings' of China and Japan. Both struggled to find – and to narrate – 'success'. Both offer a window onto the new connectivities being made at this time between East Asia, Britain, its empire and the world: personal, familial, political and economic. Both give historians much to consider in terms of the place of letter writing, non-state actors and neglected private sources in writing our histories of European expansion and the region. As one of its main threads, this book offers fresh insights on the individual experiences of these two men and others like them. It also charts personal aspirations and disappointments, to broaden discussions of the role of Westerners in mid-nineteenth-century East Asia.

Historians have long used the letters, company records and official missives penned by Westerners as sources to explore the development and progression of the treaty port system initiated in China following the First Opium War (1839–42).[1] The Treaty of Nanjing (1842) and subsequent pacts signed between the Qing Empire and Britain, along with other European nations and the United States, allowed Western signatory states to establish commercial enclaves in select ports on the China coast (initially Canton, Shanghai, Ningbo, Xiamen (Amoy) and Fuzhou). The treaties also set specific tariff rates that the Qing regime could not freely revise. In addition, Westerners enjoyed extraterritoriality, the right to be governed by the laws of their own countries even when in China. In 1858, a US diplomat, Townsend Harris, helped to bring the treaty port regime to Japan, incorporating these core features into treaties signed between the United States and the Tokugawa shogunate (*bakufu*), Japan's central authority. The following year, Western merchants began to reside and trade at enclaves established in the ports of Nagasaki, Hakodate, Yokohama and, beginning in 1868, Kobe.[2]

Because of the trade that surged through them, historians have focused on the treaty ports as lenses to consider the national economic and political

Figure 1 Charles Lenox Richardson.
Source: J.C. Fraser album, Yokohama Archives of History.

Figure 2 William John Alt, *c*. 1864.
Source: David Carmichael album. Courtesy of David Carmichael.

trajectories of Japan, which had treaty ports until 1899, and China, where they remained in place until 1943.[3] Many have also been interested in questions of extraterritoriality, as well as the legal issues that arose with Westerners possessing land in treaty ports.[4] In addition, historians have explored the treaty ports' physical spaces with an eye to their landscapes and architecture, which presented particular challenges in governance and administration.[5] Because of the broad range of scholarly interest in them, and their significant roles in the course of modern China and Japan, compendiums of research on, and details about, the treaty ports have also been assembled.[6] Finally, scholarship has taken up issues surrounding health and the daily lives of Westerners, and used letters and other personal correspondences to craft new profiles of prominent individuals in the treaty ports in the late nineteenth century.[7]

This book builds on these approaches to develop multiple, new insights by employing people as 'connectors', focusing on individuals linked in surprising ways by their families, activities, correspondence and consequences to seemingly disparate historical figures and events within, through and beyond treaty-port East Asia. Although not the sole connectors profiled in this volume, Alt and Richardson are the most prominent, and their lives featured numerous familial and personal ties with other individuals mentioned and explored in this volume. Alt connected through family relations, notably as the son-in-law of George Windsor Earl, an English adventurer, ship captain and early scholar of Southeast Asia. Richardson intriguingly connected many through his murder, which triggered the dispatch of British soldiers to Yokohama who established a range of new social and cultural connections with the residents of that treaty port.

In addition, this book examines avenues in which connectors – Alt and Richardson most prominently, but also other individuals introduced in this volume, from British diplomats Rutherford Alcock and George S. Morrison to the Swiss merchants Caspar Brennwald and Hermann Siber – demonstrate the insufficiency of historical frameworks that encapsulate events within national borders. In that vein, this volume takes a more expansive, East Asian approach by showing how Shanghai, Nagasaki, Yokohama and other Chinese and Japanese treaty ports were linked in personal, commercial, diplomatic, political and societal ways.[8] In tracing these connections, the book draws on the work of David Lambert and Alan Lester and the methodology of 'imperial careering'. By following the movements of individuals like Richardson, Alt, Morrison, Alcock, Brennwald and Siber along and beyond the networks of empire, we can see new ideas, attitudes, identities and practices being formed in motion.[9] As such, the book seeks to add a more personal, human focus to recent attempts by historians to illustrate the myriad circuits and flows connecting discrete treaty ports in this period of expanding world trade and national transformation. Collectively, the chapters in this volume remind scholars of East Asia of the value of bringing personal, regional, imperial and global dynamics into dialogue, for a fresh perspective on the specific sites, events and phenomena they study.

As part of this approach, the book will also reveal how correspondences and experiences, as well as familial and personal connections, offer entrées to consider anew aspects of British expansion in not only nineteenth-century East Asia but outside the region as well. While historians such as Alan Lester and Zoë Laidlaw have demonstrated the importance of a networked conception of empire, there has been surprisingly little work on British emigrant communities themselves, especially outside the ranks of the formal colonial service or the military, and outside the white settler world.[10] There is still much that we do not know about Britons who migrated to the towns and cities of Britain's informal empire in East Asia, and even less about those, like Richardson, who worked initially as humble clerks, and who met with something less than unequivocal success. Nationalist historiography has tended to erase individual colonists as figures of study; metropolitan literature, too, would sometimes reduce them to caricature in the era of decolonization. And yet, as Robert Bickers and John Darwin have noted, it is not necessary to sympathize with British expatriates to find them interesting, or to acknowledge their importance.[11] In treaty-port East Asia, where the power of the British state to intervene was often circumscribed, the private business and daily interactions of people like Charles Richardson and William Alt formed the stuff of empire. By expanding its geographical scope, the volume examines the maritime commercial ties that linked East Asia to Australasia as well as to global networks extending to Europe and the Americas.

Chronicling Westerners therefore additionally explores the global reach of British commerce, influence and power, including detailed examinations of several diplomats and officials acting to advance imperial interests in East Asia and beyond. In illustrating this theme, the examples of Alt and Richardson are again instructive. While neither man ever held official, military or diplomatic positions in the British imperial system, they were nonetheless linked in numerous ways to the British imperial enterprise in Asia – in life and, for Richardson at least, in death. Moreover, they had only loose affiliations with the large firms that have typically held historians' attention, such as Jardine, Matheson & Co., and which became key, informal arms of British expansion. In the same vein, other chapters also focus on individuals not officially connected with British military and imperial enterprises, such as the two Swiss merchants, Brennwald and Siber. In so doing, the volume underscores the importance of other Europeans (and Americans), and of lesser-known figures and the sources they left behind, in understanding East Asian foreign trade and diplomacy in the late nineteenth century.

Together, the volume aspires to allow readers to explore nineteenth-century international commercial intercourse, state formation and imperial agendas as shaped by a fluid process of events moving between individual/personal history to national and regional levels, and at various times intersecting with the global.

Connected lives: William Alt and Charles Richardson in nineteenth-century China and Japan

The year 1858 offers a useful temporal starting point to highlight the individual, regional and global threads running through this volume. Employing again the examples of William Alt and Charles Richardson, we note that on an individual level, 1858 was the first full year in which Alt, then eighteen, and Richardson, then twenty-four, resided in the same city: Shanghai. At the time, the city was growing rapidly amid British and Western imperial forays along the China coast, a series of conflicts that historians have dubbed the Second Opium War (1856–60). One of the war's more significant battles unfolded on 27 December 1857 when British naval and army units, fighting alongside French forces, moved into the southern Chinese port city of Canton. Tensions between the Qing and British had been brewing throughout that year. In January, a Chinese baker in nearby Hong Kong had delivered arsenic-laced bread to the British community, poisoning around 400 residents including George S. Morrison, the British diplomat profiled by Brian Burke-Gaffney in Chapter 2 of this book.[12] British troops also skirmished with Qing forces in and around Canton. Nonetheless, British commanders held off from launching a full-scale assault on the city until sufficient numbers of troops had arrived, delayed by the need to deploy increased forces to suppress the Indian Rebellion (Mutiny) that had erupted earlier in the year.

On 1 January 1858, British and French leaders could proclaim their control of Canton, capturing the Qing provincial governor in the process (he later died in custody in India). In the early summer of that same year, British, French and other representatives of Western nations followed up military victories in northern China by pressing the Qing to sign a series of agreements that collectively came to be known as the Treaty of Tianjin. Among other points, the treaty allowed Britain and several Western nations to base diplomatic envoys permanently at Beijing, and increased the number of treaty ports throughout China.

Sherard Osborn, an officer on a British warship involved in the war, rationalized the use of force to press Britain's claims against the Qing. 'We always come to this in the long-run in China – the sword or the threat of the sword, has invariably decided every dispute, however trivial, with these people.' Describing his ship's entry into Shanghai in 1858, he boasted that the British navy had served as 'pioneers of a new order of things', helping to make the city 'a magnificent European colony', the 'queen of Central China', in the scant sixteen years since the Treaty of Nanjing had inaugurated the treaty port system. To illustrate, Osborn provided a summary of trade through Shanghai the previous year. All told, it amounted to roughly 26 million pounds sterling in total value – 16 million in general trade, 5 million in opium and another 5 million in bullion and copper coins.[13]

Osborn's account makes plain the geopolitical context that frames our discussions in this volume, most notably Britain's liberal use of military force to pursue its imperial and commercial goals in China. Richardson's death in Japan would see components of this system brought there, too – although the resultant military action (the bombardment of Kagoshima, better-known in Japan as the *Satsuei-sensō*, or Anglo-Satsuma War) proved less decisive than its proponents had hoped. As in the case of the aforementioned Battle of Canton, these interventions demonstrated British military prowess, but also revealed the very real limitations of imperial manpower and resources. British military and political leaders, often acting on incomplete, delayed and partial information, struggled to weigh calls for action in East Asia against the competing demands of other parts of the British world system. Nonetheless, and in line with a refrain common in the treaty-port presses of the time, Osborn brashly attributed a thriving Shanghai's commercial success to British initiative, with scant regard for the contributions of the majority Chinese population in the city.

In any case, Alt and Richardson were drawn to Shanghai because of its burgeoning role in international trade. And there, in some respects, their careers parted ways. Alt left Shanghai after an unsatisfying two-year stint as a clerk (in both private firms and for several months in the Qing Customs House), and sailed to Nagasaki late in 1859. There, he achieved greater success, establishing a trading firm that profited from the sale of ships (many obtained in Shanghai) to Japanese lords and the Tokugawa shogunate. He retired to England in 1871. Richardson spent a difficult decade at Shanghai as a clerk and merchant, before his investments in real estate began to pay off. In 1862 the lure of new opportunities also drew Richardson to Japan, only to famously meet his end in a violent incident on the Tōkaidō, the thoroughfare that connected the cities of Edo and Kyoto. For all the differences in the personalities and prospects of Alt and Richardson, it is the similarities that strike us most. A parallel examination of their lives and careers provides insights on a number of issues explored in many of the contributions to this volume, and indicates how the twin practices of comparison and connection reward the examination of Westerners' lives from East Asian, imperial and global historical perspectives.

First, it is striking just how young Richardson, Alt and so many of these Westerners were when they decided to make their lives and fortunes in mid-nineteenth-century East Asia. Both men were prompted to leave Britain due to family financial concerns. Richardson was nineteen when he set sail for China, and he did so, in large part, to meet the wants of his parents and sisters at home. Richardson's father seems to have been a particular liability – as the recipient of most of the letters Charles sent back from China, his debts and regular requests for assistance were a recurrent worry across ten years of correspondence.[14] Alt was no older than thirteen when he left Britain to start a life on the seas. Although not explicitly stated in his letters, like Richardson, financial strains within his family (following the death of his father, an army officer) appear to have prompted him, as the eldest son, to leave home at such a young age, to make a living and assist his widowed mother and siblings.[15]

Thus, a second related theme running through both men's lives and experiences is the importance of home and familial networks. Replete with references to home, and thoughts about it, Richardson's correspondence illustrates how home guided his personal and professional passage into the treaty port world. His family had some experience in trade. His grandfather and his uncle had captained merchant vessels; another uncle, John Lenox, had experience in trading Shanghai silk in London, and it seems to have been through him that the young Charles got his first position as an assistant to Mackenzie Brothers and Company. The Mackenzie brothers were certainly known to Richardson's father – through their correspondence, father and son followed the movements of the brothers between Shanghai and England, giving each other notice of where they were going to be, so as to be sure to call in and give thanks for the kindnesses they had shown Charles.

By contrast, Alt's immediate family seems to have been one where the military was an accepted vocation. In the footsteps of their father, Alt's younger brothers, Balser and Harry, joined the British army. Alt probably chose a different course – a position on a merchant ship – in order to take advantage of maternal family connections in the shipping industry. Letters he penned from London in 1853 suggest that the Hellyer family, to whom his mother was related through marriage, aided in his job search. Many Hellyers worked in the shipbuilding industry, and therefore were no doubt acquainted with various ship captains.[16] Extended family mattered in Richardson's story, too, for Richardson had an especially fraught relationship with his maternal uncle, John Lenox. It seems that Lenox had refused to help his brother-in-law, Richardson's father, with a request for money, and instead encouraged Charles to go to Shanghai to support him from there, 'a subject which I am still rather sore upon altho' I say nothing', Richardson wrote home. As Eileen Cleere has shown in her work on avuncularism in nineteenth-century English culture, uncles could play important economic and political roles in Victorian families, opening connections and acting as alternative sources of status and authority.[17] This was an important relationship, then, and another reason for the prominence of what Richardson called 'Home News', particularly in the early years of his letters. Alt's letters do not mention maintaining any strong connections with an uncle or another male elder in his family in Britain (only two of his letters are to an uncle). But Captain Russell of Alt's ship, the *Charlotte Jane*, seems to have fulfilled something of this avuncular role, and taken the young Alt under his wing. As Annette Bainbridge explores in detail in her chapter, Russell looked after his young crewmember's personal and spiritual well-being, such as instructing him to read his bible daily.[18]

Beyond business, Richardson seems to have genuinely appreciated and needed the emotional support provided by correspondence as a link to home. 'You can have no idea how welcome these nice little notes are & with what pleasure I look forward to the arrival of every mail', he wrote; 'I can assure you that it is one of the greatest pleasures I have.'[19] Alt maintained strong emotional ties with his mother, an aunt and sisters. He often lamented not receiving more correspondence from them, a complaint voiced in a note sent to his aunt in late 1857. In it, he asked about the likenesses (perhaps photographs or small portraits) of his family members that he had earlier requested.[20] He clearly cherished such mementos as the following year, he queried his mother about them, and described their importance. 'When I have you all to look [at], I really do think I shall not be able to do any wrong although there is a frightful deal of temptation to be withstood in this country where every lady does as they like.'[21] Alt also penned a number of letters to his sister, Emma, during his time on *Charlotte Jane* and after his move to Shanghai. In addition he often wrote to his brother, Balser (whom he called Bolly), or asked his mother to relay news to him. Writing from Adelaide when *Charlotte Jane* stopped there in 1854, Alt asked his mother to tell Balser of the curios – especially the shark's heart preserved in rum – he was bringing home.[22] He also kept track of his brothers' efforts to join regiments in the British army, including congratulating Balser on his appointment to the 1st West Indian Regiment in March 1863.[23]

Richardson was particularly close to his sisters, and wrote to them with striking tenderness. He sent them silk, dresses, money for a watch and endless quantities of tea; he thanked his sister Minnie for the locket 'with her hair most exquisitely put in'. He sent yet more dresses for a wedding, and became annoyed at the prospect that they might not arrive in time. As Leonore Davidoff has shown, in the long nineteenth century siblings shared material fortunes and social and emotional circles with an intensity matched at no other time.²⁴ For Richardson, his sisters kept a vital link with the parental home alive. 'I'd like to drop down in England just now and have a look at you,' Richardson wrote in 1855, 'but it is no good thinking of that after only being away 18 months'.

Nothing shows the prominence of 'home' in Richardson's thoughts more, however, than remittances. As mentioned often in his letters, Richardson only ever intended to stay in Shanghai long enough to restore the family finances; he never sought to make a home for himself in China, and never felt truly comfortable in the foreign settlement (themes and tensions explored further in Bobby Tam's chapter, below). From the beginning, Richardson had planned to send money home regularly, but often struggled to do so. 'I would do anything on earth to make my Mother and Sisters comfortable', he assured his father in 1859, but 'I have little or no money of my own... and unless I look sharp may rot out the rest of my existence in this infernal hole'. The subject forms a thread that runs throughout the whole correspondence; in time, it would see Richardson taking on a growing responsibility for the family's overall finances, managing them remotely from a distance of almost 6,000 miles – settling bills, purchasing shares, providing allowances for his sisters, liaising with solicitors. One of his final letters home alludes to a wholesale family retrenchment scheme which he looked to implement on his return to England, and which, he hoped, would see the family right once and for all. Remittance, then, lay at the heart of the webs of personal and financial responsibility that linked sojourners like him with their families at home. It made the Richardson family itself – as Esme Cleall, Laura Ishiguro and Emily Manktelow have explored in different contexts – 'a site of economic strategy and capital accumulation'.²⁵

After he began working in Shanghai in late 1857, Alt also regularly sent funds home to assist his family.²⁶ Like Richardson, he seemed focused on achieving personal wealth to allow him to eventually return permanently to Britain, a point which brings us to a third theme in the lives of the two men: success, or its absence. What did 'success' look like to our protagonists, and how might we account for their varied record? Sometimes, we can get carried away by Westerners' descriptions of the stirring events of mid-century East Asia. (These include Alt's observations of the unfolding domestic processes towards what would result in the Meiji Restoration in 1868, and Richardson's descriptions of the battles around Shanghai of the Taiping Rebellion.) Nonetheless we cannot forget that making money – fast – was often their abiding preoccupation.

Alt remained focused, almost obsessed, with achieving long-term financial success. In letters to his mother, he often described his anticipated profits as well as his estimated personal fortune, which in 1863 he gauged to be around £70,000 in total assets.[27] Overall his correspondences reveal a man who saw his time in East Asia as a means to an end – an opportunity to gain enough wealth upon which to retire and return to live in Britain.

In Richardson's case, a close examination of his business affairs works to unsettle claims made at the time of his death about his commercial success (including by Alt, which we will explain below). In fact, for much of his time at Shanghai, Richardson scraped by while his trades were disrupted by violence: in the Crimea and India, within the Qing Empire, and by the Second Opium War. ('The whole 7 years I have been out here', he wrote home in 1860, 'there has always been some infernal row going to take place somewhere'.) This consistently frustrated his plans to send money home. 'Much do I regret my inability to assist you materially', he apologized in 1855; 'you may rest assured had it laid in my power you should not have had to have asked for it, but the end of last season sadly crippled me'. And again in 1862, at the start of his final year in China: 'what kind friend has been putting it into your head that I am a millionaire? If such was the case – or a portion of one – I should not stop in this abominable country long.' In the end, it was not trade at all, but property that brought Richardson a measure of success.[28] As a merchant, Richardson's record is an important reminder of the risks, insecurity and contingency attending every treaty port 'success story'.

A fourth theme concerns the importance of locating our subjects at the interface of multiple connectivities. These justify a more expansive concept of an East Asian treaty port world even as they exceed its boundaries. Both Alt and Richardson started out in Shanghai before setting their sights on Japan (with greater success, in Alt's case).[29] In this, their experiences illuminate a wider phenomenon: many foreign merchants operating in Japan during the closing days of the shogunate (termed by historians the *bakumatsu* period) had cut their teeth on the China coast, including Kenneth Ross Mackenzie (of Shanghai's Mackenzie Bros. & Co.) and William Gregson Aspinall (co-founder of Aspinall, Cornes and Co. of Kobe and Yokohama). Shanghai sent forth the capital, expertise and shipping on which numerous exploratory trades in Japan relied. Alt founded his firm in Nagasaki thanks to connections and financial support gained during his time in Shanghai. The captain of the vessel that transported him to Nagasaki provided seed capital. In addition, Alt used severance pay received from the Qing Customs House, which had made him redundant in 1859. To expand his business, he also benefited from a letter of introduction provided by the 'head of the House of Jardine, Matheson Co.' to the firm's Nagasaki agent.[30] During his time in Nagasaki, Alt often posted letters home from Shanghai and Hong Kong describing his business activities in both port cities.

Richardson and Alt were also embedded in private, mercantile and political relationships that connected their endeavours in East Asia to other parts of the world in unexpected ways. The Richardson family, for example, had connections in the West Indies that ran in tandem with Charles's labours at Shanghai. His father, in happier times, had worked for Ellice, Kinnear & Company, a well-connected firm under the merchant-politician Edward Ellice, with interests in the fur and sugar trades in North America and the West Indies.[31] Charles's uncle Henry (b. 1799) had been a planter in Demerara; in 1853 his sister Georgie was married to another planter, and Charles keenly followed the news of her move out to Trinidad. But by the late 1850s, this connection had increasingly become a liability. Facing mounting debts, Charles's uncle took to borrowing from his father – indeed, his father attributed his own financial predicament to the declining fortunes of the family in the West Indies. In that sense, Charles Richardson's life and death in Asia and the family's links to the West Indies were intimately connected: it may very well have been to make good those West Indian losses that Charles had gone out to Shanghai in the first place.

Alt did not possess the same family connections to merchant endeavours in other parts of the British Empire. He did, however, develop indirect ties with the US market. During his time at Nagasaki, Alt built a tea processing factory which refined green tea shipped, by other US and British firms, almost exclusively to the United States.[32]

A fifth theme concerns our subjects as writers, and the place of letter writing in treaty port life. This is how Richardson and Alt come down to us as historians, of course, but the records of both men spur us into thinking about Western merchants and diplomats *as writers*, narrating and seeking to explain the world around them. In the early 1860s, Alt would often update his mother about events in Nagasaki and Japan overall, particularly related to attacks on Westerners that arose as a movement to forcibly expel foreigners from Japanese soil gained supporters. In late September 1862, he shared news of Richardson's murder a few weeks before. Choosing words to suggest that the two had met, Alt lamented that 'poor Richardson was a fine fellow. He made his fortune in Shanghai and came to look [and] see Japan before going home. "In the midst of life we are in death." What sad news for his poor friends at home.'[33]

Taken together, Alt's letters also allow us to see how without formal schooling, a young British man developed his writing skills that he would later use in business and personal affairs. We can speculate that Captain Russell pressed his crewman to perfect his writing as part of his overall studies as Alt's letters written on *Charlotte Jane* show a distinctive progression in form and clarity over the course of his five-year stint on the ship. After he established his firm in Nagasaki, Alt alluded to the time devoted to 'mail work' and to crafting official letters as part of his company's business.[34] As his firm gained more success, he toyed with the idea of inviting his brother Balser to 'give up soldiering' and join his firm in Nagasaki. Yet Alt showed some reservation, concluding that Balser 'would have to at least [spend] a year in an office at home and above all things improve his hand writing which at present is worse than mine'.[35]

For Richardson letter writing was pleasurable, if exhausting work. When the mail was due it could dominate his day from eight in the morning until six in the evening; in humid Shanghai summers he described himself as 'wet through' from the effort. During his first years at Shanghai, in particular, Richardson wrote to a wide range of friends and relations in England. It was his father who urged him to keep this up; he would need these contacts, he was reminded, on his eventual return home to England. Most of Richardson's personal letters home seem to have been written in periods of down time, when trade was slack – a fact which may account, if only in part, for their often downbeat tone about his commercial prospects. With his parents, he discussed friends and relations, the turmoil in China, and news of the progress of the war in Crimea, the Indian Rebellion (Mutiny) and the US Civil War. This emphasis on world events did not merely reflect the turbulent times in which Richardson lived, or even the effect of all this unrest on his commercial prospects – it also provided material in common around which father and son could write.[36]

These letters provide a glimpse into the varied commercial life of a British Shanghai merchant in the 1850s, even as they raise fresh questions about what was recorded, and what was omitted. After all, to be a merchant, to be a clerk, was to write, and yet much of that business correspondence, if it survived, has not yet been found. Instead, it is these private missives from Alt's and Richardson's company desks that serve to remind us that empire in the treaty ports did not merely take form through shipping, architecture, encounters and daily interactions, but in pen and ink, through the movements of innumerable slips of paper.

A final theme, then, concerns the centrality of power, politics and empire to our subjects' economic activities. Alt and Richardson were not merely witnesses to a turbulent period of change in the treaty ports, but were themselves part of the source of that instability and change. This is important for us to recognize, precisely because the two men so seldom recognized it themselves. Richardson complained of the turmoil wracking Shanghai's hinterland (and disrupting his supplies of silk and tea) during the Taiping Rebellion as if it were *deus ex machina*, the noises off to his own personal travails. In death, of course, that connection lay revealed: his murder led to the 1863 British naval bombardment of Kagoshima, a move similar to the aforementioned attacks on Chinese coastal cities during the Second Opium War. Even in life, however, there were numerous times in which his implication in these wider structures of power became much more explicit, whether personally taking up arms alongside the Shanghai Volunteers to attack Qing troops in 1854, for example, or assaulting his own Chinese servant (for which offence he was sternly rebuked by the British Consul).

In Nagasaki in the early 1860s, Alt found himself at the centre of burgeoning trades that emerged as Japan's internal landscape became more fractious. Aiming to gain stronger economic and political positions, domain and Tokugawa representatives came to the Kyushu port to purchase sail and steam ships for use in transporting goods and potentially armed contingents of men. (Steamships purchased at Nagasaki were in fact used to move men during the Summer War between the Chōshū domain and the shogunate in 1866.) In September 1863, Alt told his mother, with a sense of pride, of his 'unprecedented' buying trip: a foreigner dispatched to Shanghai by the Tokugawa shogunate to purchase a steamship for the regime.[37] During his time in Nagasaki which extended until late 1867, Alt was involved in numerous transactions for sail and steam ships acquired by the shogunate and domains in Kyushu and Shikoku.[38] As these business dealings reveal, as Westerners like Richardson and Alt invoked the principles of 'free trade', their very presence in East Asia at this time demands we explore their implication in, and their role in co-creating, the structures and imbalances of imperial power.

*

As an alternate way of exploring the so-called 'openings' of China and Japan, the chapters below allow readers to follow most prominently Alt and Richardson, but also several other Westerners (and even a merchant ship) as 'connectors', moving through the treaty-port enclaves and other parts of mid-nineteenth-century East and Southeast Asia and the wider world. Beyond giving details about daily lives, the chapters examine the commodity and bullion flows, as well as the maritime routes that moved people like Alt and Richardson around the globe. The chapters also explore the British and Qing imperial agendas and policies, as well as the motivations of Tokugawa and domain leaders which influenced the lives and activities of the profiled Westerners.

In the first chapter, Sano Mayuko places a spotlight on Yokohama, but with an eye to how diplomatic and commercial events there were tied to what transpired in China as well. She does so by examining the actions of Rutherford Alcock, a British diplomat, making him a connector akin to Alt and Richardson. Before becoming Britain's first consul-general to Japan, Alcock served in Fuzhou, Shanghai and Canton; in 1862, his robust response to news of Richardson's murder helped set in train the events that led to the bombardment of Kagoshima. Sano explores Alcock's career in Japan after 1859, focusing on his frustrations not only with his Japanese counterparts, but with British merchants as well. She notes that Alcock faced strong opposition from British traders in his attempt to assert British interests and thwart what he believed was an underhanded attempt by Tokugawa officials to establish the village of Yokohama as the site of the newly designated treaty port. Contending that Tokugawa officials were encouraging the establishment of Yokohama to allow them greater control over the new Western enclave, he instead sought to have the British and other foreign communities based at nearby Kanagawa, which he believed would afford a better commercial and strategic position. Sano details the successful lobbying of British merchants to remain in Yokohama, a campaign that ultimately shaped Alcock's life as a diplomat in China two decades later. The Treaty of Tianjin stipulated that its terms be renegotiated ten years after its signing, a task assigned to Alcock in 1868. Sano reveals Alcock's frustration after forging a revised treaty following extended negotiations with Qing officials. Upon learning of the treaty's new terms, China-based British merchants voiced strong opposition, helping to prevent its ratification by the British government, dealing another diplomatic blow to Alcock. Overall, Sano demonstrates the power of the British merchant communities in shaping diplomatic agreements in East Asia across two decades.

Alt's career helps to underscore the importance of Nagasaki as a venue in the initial formation of British-Japanese relations as the treaty port system was implemented in Japan in the early 1860s. In his chapter, Brian Burke-Gaffney profiles George S. Morrison, who served under Alcock as the British consul in Nagasaki in the years immediately following that city's designation as a treaty port in 1859. Like Alcock, Morrison, the son of a British missionary who had grown up in China, faced numerous challenges in developing relationships with Tokugawa officials, partly on account of his own obstinacy. Burke-Gaffney highlights the local processes of establishing British-Japanese diplomatic ties through the lens of issues of physical space, particularly surrounding the establishment of the British consulate in a Buddhist temple in Nagasaki. Burke-Gaffney also helps us to understand the tension and fear of physical attacks that gripped the Western community in Japan – a fear all-too palpable in the wake of Richardson's own killing in 1862 – as the movement to expel foreigners from the realm gained supporters.

The fallout from Richardson's killing is the focus of the book's third chapter. In it, Nakatake (Hori) Kanami engages with Richardson as a connector, by exploring how his violent death, in what came to be known as the Namamugi Incident (for the village where it occurred), led to the stationing of large numbers of British and French troops in Yokohama. Past scholarship has examined the military and geopolitical ramifications of these British and French military contingents. Nakatake (Hori) breaks new ground by focusing on how the stationing of the troops shaped life for foreigners and Japanese residing in the Yokohama treaty port. She also details ways in which the Anglo-French military presence influenced aspects of the military and institutional development of the Japanese nation-state following the Meiji Restoration.

In the fourth chapter, Fukuoka Mariko and Alexis Schwarzenbach follow the merchant thread running through this volume by taking up the story of the Swiss merchants, Hermann Siber and Caspar Brennwald. As their main themes, Fukuoka and Schwarzenbach explore the financial, commercial and personal networks necessary for these two connectors to establish a trading house in Japan in the 1860s. Consistent with other chapters, they draw upon personal letters and diaries to explain the paths of the two Swiss men to Yokohama who, like Alt and Richardson, arrived in East Asia while still relatively young (both were in their twenties). They offer a thorough account of how a Western firm began operating in Japan in the 1860s, detailing the profits Siber and Brennwald gained from selling ships and weapons to the Sendai domain (today's Miyagi Prefecture), then part of an alliance of northern domains challenging the nascent government established by the Satsuma-Chōshū alliance following a palace coup in January 1868 (an event largely seen as initiating the Meiji Restoration). Their chapter also explains the process whereby Siber and Brennwald transitioned to almost exclusively exporting silk, working closely with Japanese partners to develop a nascent silk manufacturing industry. Significantly the majority of the silk was exported to the United States, underscoring the broad, international market in which Siber and Brennwald and other Western merchants operated.

As Westerners established more permanent enclaves in East Asia during the mid-nineteenth century, burial for those who died from disease or violence like Richardson became a more pressing matter, as transporting home the bodies of the dead was impossible. In his chapter Bobby Tam tackles this issue, examining how issues of race and class intersected in death and burial in early colonial Hong Kong. Here, unlike at Shanghai or Yokohama, it took time for Western merchants to achieve prominence in local society and to view the colony as 'home': and thus a place they might consider for burial after death. In examining how Hong Kong's different merchant groups – Western, Chinese, Parsee, Jewish and Muslim – lobbied for burial privileges, set up cemeteries and defended burial practices, Tam's chapter asks us to consider the meanings of community, and of putting down roots, in the dynamic port cities of maritime East Asia.

Two other chapters use Alt as a connector to offer perspectives on the course of the British Empire's expansion in New Zealand and Australia. Annette Bainbridge unpacks the national symbolism of *Charlotte Jane*, a British merchant ship well-known today in New Zealand as one of the 'First Four Ships' to bring colonists to the Canterbury colony in 1850, and aboard which Alt served for several years prior to his arrival in Shanghai. Bainbridge follows *Charlotte Jane*'s voyages around the world following her launch from a British yard in 1848. She details the ship's participation in the global maritime trades of the nineteenth century, notably the flow of bullion from newly discovered Australian mines to Britain. Drawing on the letters Alt sent while a crew member of the ship from 1853 to 1858, Bainbridge explains the ways in which *Charlotte Jane* also became integrated into logistical networks of British military power, carrying troops to Bermuda and to Crimea to fight in the Crimean War. Bainbridge's chapter demonstrates that making a single ship a 'connector' can reveal fresh insights that challenge assumptions about New Zealand's national past, underscoring the colony's wider role in narratives of nineteenth-century British imperial expansion.

Ranald Noel-Paton also employs Alt as a connector, in this case to his father-in-law, George Windsor Earl, who held many roles in British colonial governments in Australia and Southeast Asia. Noel-Paton outlines the ambition that drove Earl to first travel to Western Australia and later champion an unsuccessful attempt to establish a British commercial entrepôt on Australia's northern coast. While tracing his simultaneous career as a scholar of Southeast Asian societies and languages, Noel-Paton also reveals the multi-faceted elements of Earl's subsequent stints as a law agent in Singapore, and his role in the nascent Australian gold mining industry. With the latter, he makes valuable intersections with the global contexts framing Bainbridge's chapter, as ships like *Charlotte*

Jane carried Australian gold (and other bullion) to London, part of a ten-fold increase in gold on the world market as mines and production also expanded in North America and southern Africa in the late nineteenth century.[39] Finally Noel-Paton illustrates how Earl was undoubtedly the most prolific Western chronicilier profiled in this volume; he kept copious records of his travels and experiences in Australia and Southeast Asia and later published them as books and as articles in prominent scholarly journals.[40]

Alt's marriage to Earl's daughter, Elisabeth, also shaped the scope of one of the private letter archives that partially inspired this volume; in moving from being a bachelor to a married man, William appears to have ceased writing as often to his mother. This example underscores the central role of family, both in the lived experiences of Alt and Richardson and others like them, and in how we, as historians, are able to study them. For us, as editors, the abrupt termination of this line of Alt's correspondence calls our attention to the overly male voice and perspective that may emerge in this book, given that the majority of the correspondences, diaries and other sources researched by our varied contributors were written by men. In the case of Alt and Richardson, for example, we both regret that the letters sent by their female family members are no longer extant, and thus could not be used to broaden the perspectives presented in this introduction.[41]

Moreover, because its authors rely primarily on Western sources, the book's conclusions obviously highlight the influence of Westerners in the course of nineteenth-century East Asia and Australasia. In this approach, we do not seek to present Westerners, or the British Empire of which many of the people discussed in this book were a part, along the lines of outdated narratives that portray Westerners primarily as representatives of a modern West, bringing enlightenment to 'backward' areas of Asia and Australasia.[42] Nor do we aspire to assert a primacy of the Western experience over that of Asians and indigenous Australasians in our analyses of events and trends in nineteenth-century Asia and the world. Instead, as its core, the book aims to reaffirm the value of historical study focused on individual lives, broadly cast. Human lives are complex, and past lives necessarily come to us in a manifestly incomplete form. For these reasons it is important that the study of lives be open to a variety of perspectives and approaches, and in this volume it has been our privilege to bring together knowledge from Asia, Australasia, North America and Europe, and from museum and heritage professionals, graduate students, family historians and the academy. Our subject is the life (and death) of Westerners, accessible to contemporary analysis because of the rich caches of personal documents preserved for posterity by the descendants of Alt, Richardson and others profiled in this volume. Thanks to the availability of such sources, which record experiences and observations in detail over many years, we hope that our combined studies can serve as a platform to consider anew broader aspects of Japanese, Chinese, Australasian and global history, particularly in relation to the British Empire.

1

Disturbed reciprocity: Rutherford Alcock's diplomacy and merchant communities in China and Japan

Sano Mayuko

Introduction

Rutherford Alcock (1809–97) was one of the more prominent Western diplomats in nineteenth-century East Asia. He was appointed as Britain's consul-general to Japan in 1858 – the year the post was created – and subsequently became Britain's minister to Japan (1859–65)[1] before being tapped for the same role in China (1865–71). Prior to assuming these high posts, he had been one of the first British consuls on the China coast, those officials charged with the administration of British affairs in the five treaty ports opened based on the 1842 Treaty of Nanjing: he had first been posted to Amoy in 1844, before being transferred to Fuzhou the following year.[2] From 1846 to 1855, he had served as consul at Shanghai, where he acted as a major architect of the foreign concession system before being appointed the consul at Canton.[3]

His career in East Asia spanned twenty-seven years, twenty-three of which were on the frontline representing British interests (the other four years in total being periods on leave).[4] Such an extensive career in one was rare at the time, when the climate in East Asia was especially severe and threatening to most Europeans, many of whom died or had to return home after serving for a short period of time because of sickness. Alcock was particularly proud of being an exception in this regard.[5] His career, therefore, unusually reflects a long-term evolution of British activities in East Asia. Alcock's stint in the field was still shorter than, for example, that of Harry Parkes (1828–85), who had lived in China during his childhood and who followed Alcock as Britain's chief diplomatic representative in Japan and China. Nonetheless, Alcock's career is especially interesting to follow, as his every step was on the leading edge of the expansion of the British presence in East Asia.

It is, of course, impossible to retrace all of Alcock's life in China and Japan in this chapter. I therefore must strictly limit my focus. In two distinct sections, I will zoom in on two windows in time, first on Alcock's initial days in Japan in 1859,[6] and a decade later – his final stint in China. I will explore how in both Japan and China, Alcock experienced heated confrontations with British merchants. His conduct on those occasions was based on a coherent thought process that would prove to be the chief distinction of his diplomacy. While drawing on previous studies, including my own, I will spotlight these confrontations and Alcock's reactions recorded in his official dispatches and other writings. Although the facts depicted from the two periods are not entirely new findings, I break new ground by looking at both scenes in a single scope across the life path of Alcock, the individual.

This chapter aims to illuminate these experiences of Alcock, by which to see how they affected his career, as well as British relations with East Asia. Through considering these questions, I aim to explore possibilities for diplomatic history of these empirical studies that closely follow not only the larger diplomatic policy, but also an individual intimately involved in making that policy.

◊

Before examining Alcock's experiences in Japan in 1859, it is worth looking at him, very briefly, about a decade earlier, when he served as the consul at Shanghai. In the course of his career in East Asia it was during his stint in Shanghai that Alcock became clearly aware of the presence of British merchants as an unignorable stakeholder in his official endeavours. His friction with British merchants is interesting because by definition, a 'consul' is supposed to take care of his/her fellow private citizens (largely merchants) and protect their interests in the area in which the consul is stationed. However, his former places of appointment – Amoy and Fuzhou – were literally new to Western trade and thus held no substantial community of merchants from Britain or any other Western countries. Therefore, in those posts, Alcock could concentrate on establishing his own presence, on behalf of his home government, vis-à-vis the local authorities.[7] In this sense, his duties were on a single track.

In Shanghai, his life drastically changed. The city was already a flourishing port, with a British community of about ninety people,[8] which sounds surprisingly small to us, but was fairly large in the context of the time. Upon the transfer

Figure 3 Felice Beato, Sir Rutherford Alcock K.C.B. Her Brittannic Majesty's Minister in Japan. The photograph was probably taken sometime during his service in Japan from 1859 to 1865.

Image: Tokyo Photographic Art Museum /DNPartcom

The photo is owned by the Tokyo Photographic Art Museum.

of duties from his predecessor, George Balfour, Alcock became involved in a number of disputes concerning commercial activities, while also taking care of British residents as well as temporary visitors including the crews of British ships. He found himself, in the first place, as the head of the British community,[9] which was completely different from the situation at his former posts. He struggled to adjust in this novel environment. Even in official documents, Alcock reveals his frustration of trying to respond fully to all demands from the British residents.[10]

These early experiences served as his on-the-job training, and through nine years of consulship at Shanghai, he became the founder of Shanghai's well-known foreign settlement system as well as the Maritime Customs Service of China (initially introduced in 1854). In 1851 Alcock became interested in supporting

Qing efforts to increase legal revenue from foreign trade by improving the custom system. Alcock viewed such efforts as a sound step forward within the Anglo-Chinese treaty framework.[11] I will not further delve into this phase of Alcock's life, but we should note that his support, which led to the Maritime Customs Service, was initially motivated by his frustration of seeing foreign merchants trying to evade customs duties. The British merchant community naturally disliked the new system, and many criticized Alcock for his role in implementing it. In response, Alcock declared he would gladly sacrifice his popularity among members of foreign community and not hesitate to take any criticism for operating in 'good faith' with China.[12]

The Anglo-Japanese Treaty of Amity and Commerce (1858) permitted a British diplomat to reside in Japan and represent Britain in the newly opened country. The British Foreign Office transferred Alcock, its most experienced official in East Asia, from China to assume the new post.[13]

I. 1859 Edo/Yokohama

1) Alcock's arrival in Japan and the 'Yokohama question'

Alcock arrived in Japan in time to be present on 1 July 1859, the day stipulated in the Anglo-Japanese Treaty for the opening of Kanagawa, Nagasaki and Hakodate to Western-style free trade. He left the China coast at the end of May aboard HMS *Sampson*, which first called at Nagasaki, the nearest port from China, to leave three of Alcock's colleagues to establish the consular service at that port (events explored in detail by Brian Burke-Gaffney in his chapter). He had a positive first impression of Japan based on his contacts with people in Nagasaki as well as the beautiful landscape of the city. Alcock thus appeared to have felt less dissatisfied about his new appointment 'at the farthest limits of our intercourse with the Eastern race, instead of nearer home [in Europe]'. (He had earlier intimated that the posting to Japan did not sufficiently reward his long service in China.)[14] On 26 June, HMS *Sampson* cast anchor in Edo Bay, off the coast of Shinagawa. Upon arriving in the shogun's capital, the Briton was cheered by the unexpectedly prompt and pleasant reaction of officials from the Tokugawa shogunate. Alcock was especially delighted that Tokugawa officials soon offered to take him around the city to observe places designated as possible sites for the British legation.[15]

Contrary to the conventional understanding of Japan's encounter with the West, the shogunate had been ready for Alcock's arrival. Following the conclusion of the initial treaties of amity with the United States (1854) and Russia (1855) and the abandonment of the so-called 'seclusion policy', Tokugawa officials had been challenged by rapidly changing events in foreign affairs. The flurry of interactions with foreign states had honed their diplomatic practices.[16] Moreover in 1858, they had also established a permanent institution in charge of foreign affairs (*gaikoku bugyō*) within the shogunate, instead of only temporary offices dealing with the visits of different foreign envoys.[17]

Accepting the Tokugawa offer, on 29 June, Alcock marked his initial step in Edo, becoming the first British representative (and the first from any Western country) to reside in the city. On the same day, he chose a large Buddhist temple, Tōzenji, for the British legation and his accommodation.[18] He was fascinated by the beauty of the place.[19]

However, soon after, he faced a new difficulty, which I call the 'Yokohama question'. While Yokohama, the port name, soon became famous, the Anglo-Japanese Treaty of Amity and Commerce (and US, Dutch, Russian and French versions, too) signed in the previous year clearly provided that the port of Kanagawa be opened to trade. Kanagawa was a busy post-town on the Tōkaidō, the most important trunk road of Japan at the time which connected Edo, the shogun's capital, and Kyoto, the emperor's capital. Moreover, as Kanagawa was very close to Edo (different from Nagasaki in the far west of the Japanese isles and Hakodate in the far north), it was supposed to be the core treaty port of Japan.

After signing the treaty, Tokugawa leaders began to worry about opening Kanagawa and accepting foreigners there; therefore, as a substitute, they quickly erected, before the designated date for opening the ports, a new town. Established on the site of a previously desolate village – Yokohama – not far from Kanagawa but opposite the bay from it, was conveniently isolated from existing Japanese business routes. The shogunate tried to direct the foreigners starting to arrive to trade to Yokohama instead of Kanagawa. Foreign representatives (Alcock and those from other nations who arrived subsequently[20]) were in the position to adhere to the treaty stipulations. They clearly objected to the arbitrary change of the port by Tokugawa officials. Nonetheless, merchants were attracted to Yokohama because the shogunate offered various advantages for residents and the site had the geographic potential to become a flourishing port. These merchants' attitudes eventually nullified the diplomats' protests to the shogunate.[21]

Traditionally, these circumstances have been attributed to the shogunate's poor understanding of legal instruments. Namely Tokugawa officials surmised that the change of the port's location was not a problem because Yokohama belonged to the broader vicinity of Kanagawa. They therefore could proceed as they desired.[22] However, my research has shown that concerned Tokugawa officials were well aware they were breaching the treaty (and also that Kanagawa was not a name covering as broad an area as it does today).[23] They knowingly chose to ignore the treaty in favour of their more urgent need to avoid allowing a foreign settlement to expand at Kanagawa. They therefore undertook enormous efforts to prepare Yokohama in advance of the foreigners' arrival. To mitigate potential complaints from foreigners, they built in Yokohama a customs house, piers, other indispensable elements for trade, and even invited Japanese merchants to trade there.

It is also important to note that Alcock, when he visited Yokohama to observe the port for the first time on 1 July, perceived immediately the intention of Japanese officials.[24] His report to the Foreign Office, drafted some days later, shows that he correctly divined the situation:

> [T]he Japanese Government should have so far committed themselves to a line of policy it seems impossible for the Representatives of foreign Powers to endorse. The large expenses incurred have no doubt had this object in view – of making its final adoption inevitable.... The real motive of the Japanese, I have no doubt, from what has reached me, added to my own means of observation, is, first, to conciliate a powerful party among the most influential 'Daimios' or feudal Princes, by removing the foreigners from the line of their route to the capital in their frequent progress, in great state, to and from the Court of the Tycoon; and, secondly, to carry out, under specious pretexts, a policy which long habit has taught them to consider most consistent with their own interest and dignity, however prejudicial or fatal, under both aspects, to foreign States.[25]

Thus, he began to firmly protest the actions of Tokugawa officials, which he did not see as emerging from ignorance. He knew their intent and decided to fight.

There was one more element from which he learned the shrewdness of his Tokugawa counterparts. Alcock relays this in his 1863 book. He describes how shogunal officials initially tried to persuade him to accept Yokohama by untruthfully saying that the US consul-general, Townsend Harris, had already done so. Harris had arrived in Japan three years earlier, establishing a consulate in the remote village of Shimoda (in today's Shizuoka Prefecture), a location stipulated in the US-Japan Treaty of Amity (1854). Harris had visited Edo a couple of times before he moved to reside permanently in the shogun's capital, a provision made in the US-Japan Treaty of Friendship and Commerce (1858) that he himself signed as plenipotentiary.

Even if what he was told by the shogunate had been true, Alcock would not have had any idea to yield to it. Coincidentally, Harris joined Alcock in Yokohama on 1 July, on his way from Shimoda to Edo. He confirmed to Alcock that he had never accepted the opening of Yokohama instead of Kanagawa.[26] The two men naturally decided that they should collaborate to battle with what they saw as Japan's wrongful act. We can imagine, however, that what struck Alcock more severely was the fact that the Tokugawa side, if not successfully, intended to manipulate each of the foreign representatives, assuming the possibility that they might not necessarily share all information.

2) Alcock's 'First Lessons'

It is notable that Alcock gave the title 'First Lessons in Japanese Diplomacy' to the chapter reflecting this 'Yokohama question' in his 1863 book *The Capital of the Tycoon: The Three Years' Residence in Japan*. This was literally the first problem in which Alcock became involved after arriving in Japan, which already resonates with the title. But what were the actual 'lessons' that he learned?

On the one hand, as I outlined above, it was no doubt about the shogunate, the government with which Alcock would have to deal. As a pioneer – the first resident representative sent to Japan which had been semi-closed to Western nations for centuries – he had been unable to possess any substantive knowledge about the actual character of Japan's government and its people. He could draw only on the very limited observations of envoys who had visited the country in previous years or dated accounts compiled by Dutch factory members, such as Engelbert Kaempfer in the seventeenth century.[27] His home government, possessing no additional useful information, offered only scant instructions to Britain's first representative to Japan:

> [T]he experience which your long residence in China has afforded you of the character of a people not altogether dissimilar from that among which you are about to dwell, will doubtless much assist you in the early period of your communication with Japan.[28]

This want of information, together with his equally long experience interacting with Chinese authorities, inspired him to learn about his new counterpart government. His first visit to Yokohama was obviously an important opportunity for observation, and his major impression of the shogunate at the time was well reflected in the quotation from his dispatch (13 July) in the previous section. While experiencing fits of anger about the immediate situation in Yokohama/

Kanagawa, Alcock discovered that the shogunate was made up of wise, experienced officials. This meant a tough counterpart to him, very different from what the British government had told him about the Japanese government in the same instructions cited above, '[y]ou must be prepared in the first instance to make due allowance for ignorance and timidity, and be content with gradual progress instead of insisting peremptorily on immediate compliance with suggestions or demands that you may see occasion to bring forward'.

Having the shogunate on one front, another element he had to recognize as an apparent obstacle was the British merchant community. The problem started on the day of his first visit to Yokohama; the merchants did not follow his instructions to observe the treaty and choose Kanagawa for the site of their residences.

Alcock did understand that Yokohama was attractively prepared for merchants. However, he persisted with respecting the treaty in order to 'protect those who might come after them [the merchants who were now flowing into Japan]', and for 'the permanent interests of trade in Japan',[29] which he believed possible only by founding a solid and sound relationship with Japan based on formally agreed conditions. He repeatedly deplored the fact that at such a critical moment of opening a new relationship with an unknown country, his own country's merchants did not support his efforts, even if it meant harm to some of their short-term business interests. He wrote to the Foreign Office, '[i]t is too provoking that it should be the ill-advised proceedings of our own people which create the greatest obstacles'.[30]

As mentioned earlier, Alcock had already experienced confrontations with merchants during his service in China. However, dealing with a foreign government, especially a completely unknown one like the Tokugawa shogunate, as the head representative of his country was a new experience for him. We can discern from his words a strong wish that his fellow citizens understand the current, special situation then unfolding at the beginning of building an entirely new relationship with Japan. Especially facing an apparent, calculated breach of an international agreement by Japan, he might have been particularly shocked if the merchants did not support their consul general. In this stage, they even seemed partial to the Japanese position. He described the situation that he and his diplomatic colleagues faced: '[we] were in fact, to all appearance, insisting upon a right in behalf of our merchants, which they themselves, the chief parties interested, repudiated as much as the Japanese Government!'[31]

This awareness was insightful, especially when combined with Alcock's above-mentioned observations of the shogunate. He had to admit that Tokugawa officials were playing their own game 'by setting the merchants and their Representatives at cross purposes and in unseemly antagonism'.[32] Therefore,

Alcock, upon his arrival in Japan, was not only compelled to mount operations on two fronts – towards the shogunate and his merchants – but, due to the shrewd conduct of Tokugawa officials, the two fronts emerged as a quasi-united front. For the meantime, we can conclude that this recognition about his own position vis-à-vis those he now interacted with was the core of his 'first lessons'.

Thus, his service in Japan began with certain hostile and disappointed feelings towards different parties. Alcock was uncompromising regarding his belief that his official mission would serve to 'protect those who might come after them'; he was firmly prepared, for that long-term purpose, to sacrifice the short-term interests of those who were now arriving in Japan. This means that put another way, he would always have to be disturbed by people with whom he directly encountered for his duties to later prove fruitful.[33]

Compared with the steady discontentment with the merchants, he would eventually demonstrate more understanding towards the Tokugawa regime that was experiencing unprecedented social changes. The leaders of the shogunate also faced extremely difficult situations in handling domestic and international politics. For Alcock, to build a solid foundation of Anglo-Japanese relations, it was important that his counterpart government keeps a firm foothold; this naturally led him to feel a certain amount of support for Tokugawa leaders. (When Alcock was in Japan, no foreign party had yet conceived of the overthrow of the shogunate as a political option.) This inclination particularly became clear during the summer of 1861, when, on the one hand, the British legation was attacked by a sect of anti-foreign samurai (known as the Tōzenji Affair, 5 July), but on the other hand, he had opportunities, partly thanks to this incident, of very intimate, closed meetings with high-level Tokugawa officials (14–15 August), which had not been possible earlier.[34]

At this time, the issue was whether the treaty powers might accept the Japanese petition to postpone the openings of additional treaty ports – Hyogo and Niigata – and the cities of Osaka and Edo scheduled to be implemented by 1863. The postponement would have been inadmissible if the parties involved closely adhered to the treaty provisions, like in the case of the Yokohama question. However, following the aforementioned had closed meetings where he learned about the acute political difficulties that the shogunate was experiencing, Alcock wrote the following letter, in private, to Edmund Hammond, Permanent Under-Secretary of State for Foreign Affairs, on whom Alcock much relied.

> The Government here, like a ship at sea, has got among shoals & breakers, & is straining every timber, in efforts to get into smoother & safer waters. In their distress, with a chance of going to pieces on one on the many rocks ahead, they

are throwing over some of their heavy freight, to lighten the vessel, & make it more sea worthy – willing if they can, to keep faith with the foreign shippers & save a part. If they <u>can;</u> but they have no idea of losing the ship in the attempt! – & if things get worse they will throw all overboard: even with the certainty of being held actionable afterwards for the whole value. And this is so natural, with individuals as with governments in like situations, that we can look upon the whole proceedings with something of unanimity, although our own property and interest are concerned. Indeed for aught one can see, it may be the worst course they could adopt. Freighters not being insured could lose everything <u>if the vessel went to pieces,</u> – whereas if she rights again, & gets out of her difficulties, at best a portion will be saved. Believing this to be the true state of the case, my advice therefore is, not to distract pilot & steersman at the helm with vain remonstrances or denunciations of wrath, if some of our property is sacrificed, but give them confidence to fight a good fight, & save what they can; telling them we will deal fairly, & hold them only responsible for bad faith & not for failure by the 'act of god & the Queen's enemies' – that is, by causes wholly beyond their power to control.[35]

The result of his support for this postponement is well known. Although the British government initially took a rigid stance concerning this issue, after various complications, the London Memorandum was agreed in 1862 between the British government and the diplomatic mission sent by the shogunate. It called for the postponement of the opening of additional ports and cities to 1 January 1868. It may be worth adding that this was the shogunate's first diplomatic mission to Europe, materialized almost entirely by Alcock's initiative and efforts.[36] The actual diplomatic processes surrounding the agreement are beyond the scope of this chapter. Suffice it say that while Alcock's attitude towards his counterparts in the Tokugawa government changed, that shift was consistent with his belief in 'the permanent interests' to be secured by the two countries' sound relationship based on 'good faith'. The same belief continued to be the source of his later confrontations with British merchants.

II. 1869 Beijing

1) Alcock Convention

I now will jump to Beijing ten years later, where Alcock was in the final stage of his career as a diplomat. He had been the British minister to China since 1865.

A brief explanation may be needed. In late 1864, Alcock had been recalled as the minister to Japan. His return to London followed a series of significant military events in Japan that year. Allied with France, the United States and the Netherlands, British naval units had shelled a port city of the Chōshū domain, which had been particularly menacing to foreign powers and actually endangered navigation on the Inland Sea, the water route essential for Western nations' commercial circulation between Japan and the treaty ports of China (the so-called Shimonoseki campaign). Alcock stressed that this was not a war against Japan but an act to 'deal a decisive blow'[37] to the most obstructive element in Japan's path to a complete opening to the outside world. The action was successful in that regard.

The British government reacted negatively to Alcock; before his detailed accounts on the campaign could reach London, he was instructed to leave Japan for home, ostensibly 'to explain the actual situation of affairs'.[38] He had no other choice but to accept his recall. He was quite bitter about the Foreign Office's decision, a fact which he did not hesitate to reveal in his dispatches.[39] Prior to his arrival in London in March 1865, however, the British government, having collected more information, changed its attitude,[40] and what waited Alcock there was an offer to send him to Beijing, to succeed the first minister to China, Frederic Bruce.[41] This was a promotion, as the minister in Beijing was regarded as Britain's highest diplomatic post in East Asia.

While being an extremely rare case to have already been promoted from the Consular Service to the Diplomatic Service in the first year of his office in Japan, Alcock now found himself at the top of the hierarchy of the British presence in East Asia. It is notable that at this juncture, in response to the present appointment, in a private letter he particularly conveyed his gratitude for his past promotion in 1859 to Lord John Russell, the secretary of state for foreign affairs. However to my knowledge, Alcock never openly mentioned his awareness of the rareness of his promotion, which would have been normally impossible due to the traditional class consciousness that firmly divided the personnel of the Foreign Office and the Diplomatic Service and that of the Consular Service at that time.[42] He wrote it as follows:

> I do not forget that to Your Lordship I owe my promotion to the Diplomatic service – the only addition made to an originally very inadequate salary, & lastly the honor Her Majesty has been pleased to confer. If you deem my services requisite or desirable therefore in the scene of my past labours, I should not consult my own feelings by placing myself at Your Lordship's disposal, only hoping to be spared actual loss.[43]

Just as an addendum, 'my own feelings' refers to his honest hesitation to go back to East Asia, evidently a 'hardship area', and the 'actual loss' means his expenditure to be incurred for the trips between Asia and Europe. After some more official procedures were completed, he was formally appointed to the new post on 7 April,[44] and assumed his duties in Beijing as from 1 December 1865.[45]

As the second British minister to China who would see the year 1868 within his term of office, he was supposed to prepare for the revision of the Treaty of Tianjin (1858), which had been concluded as a result of the Second Opium War. According to that treaty, China had to open additional ports for foreign trade (eventually eleven, an increase from the five stipulated by the 1842 Treaty of Nanjing), and allow foreign commercial vessels to navigate up the Yangzi River. The treaty provided that its commercial stipulations could be reconsidered at the end of ten years (Article 27). This task, to update the basic framework of the British (and Western) relationship with the Qing, was now entrusted to Alcock – at the age of fifty-six. We can imagine that he would perceive it as a rewarding winding up of his long duties in East Asia. Therefore, he obviously demonstrated a great zeal for the renegotiation process.

During the first year following his arrival in Beijing, Alcock apparently devoted himself to grasping not only the political situation in China but all administrative matters including those related to the personnel of the 'China establishment' as the entire British diplomatic/consular presence was referred to at the time.[46] Records indicate that he launched his own substantive work from early 1867; the most remarkable effort he made was a tour around the treaty ports for direct observation. The following is how he explained this tour to the Foreign Office:

> I am convinced it would be for the public interest if I made a tour of inspection to all the ports north of Shanghai, and as many further south as I might find possible without being too long absent from the capital.... Many years have been now elapsed since a British Minister has visited the consular ports, and to those north of Shanghai and in Formosa, so far as I can ascertain, no visit has been paid since the Treaty was signed, and these are questions continually arising in which some knowledge of the localities and persons would be of great advantage.[47]

He had actually done similar observations of the treaty ports during an early stage of his tenure in Japan. (He called on Nagasaki before he took up his residence in Edo; he travelled to Hakodate in the north in September/October 1859; Yokohama was close to Edo and easy to visit frequently, starting from 1 July as we noted above.) Now as head of the British presence in China, while the size of the country and the number of treaty ports under his supervision being much larger than in Japan, he desired to do the same. He departed Beijing in early May 1867 and carried out a two-month tour. At each port, he discussed with his subordinate consuls the state of affairs and also heard the voices of British merchants about current and future trade.[48] The purpose of his tour was not necessarily limited to preparations for treaty revision. Nonetheless all involved knew the revision was forthcoming, and thus those who were asked for their opinions naturally took it as preparatory hearings for that matter.

After returning to Beijing in July, Alcock received an increasing number of consular reports about local circumstances. Arriving in his office were also various requests from merchants for improved conditions for their activities that they wished to be included in the revised treaty, in many cases in the form of memorials in the name of chambers of commerce based in different ports.[49] This verifies that his visits facilitated communication with the minister. However, his relationship with British mercantile communities in China did not develop in a harmonious way. While merchants were acquisitive and their demands diverse – from the entire abolition of inland dues on commodities to the construction of railways – Alcock was not moved by them. He kept a stance to avoid imposing demands for any drastic reforms on the Chinese government.[50]

A dispatch from Alcock to the British Foreign Office in the spring of the following year interestingly summarizes the overall tendency of merchant appeals and Alcock's own thoughts on them. He reports of having recently instructed the consuls to convey his views to the British residents in the respective ports, in view of two objectives: first, 'to disabuse the minds of the memorialists of certain fallacies and misconceptions as to the practicability or the reasonableness of some of their suggestions'; second, and more importantly as he says, 'to repudiate any responsibility for the language employed [by the merchants] in speaking of the Chinese government and authorities generally, or the views insisted upon as to their rights under existing treaties'. Finally, he used the words 'very adverse' about the influence that the merchants were creating, to the success of his negotiations with the Chinese.[51]

Full-fledged diplomatic negotiations had already been underway since January 1868,[52] but following a series of protracted processes, it was only on 23 October 1869 that a legal instrument to revise the Treaty of Tianjin between China and Britain was finally signed. Now remembered as the 'Alcock Convention',[53] its major provisions included, notoriously for the merchants, an increase of the import duty on opium and the export duty on silk, and revisions of the payment system of transit dues in order to suppress the underhanded practices of tax dodging by merchants. The convention also allowed China to appoint consuls to reside in any port in British dominions including Hong Kong, equalizing the treatment of British consuls in China.[54] Apparently, Alcock's direct inspection of the treaty ports did not result in prioritizing the gain of British merchants involved in the China trade.

The fate of the Alcock Convention is well known; the Qing government of China soon ratified it, but the British government rejected it. The primary reason for the non-ratification was the severe criticism received from British mercantile communities in China and at home. Numerous proclamations protesting the convention were issued by chambers of commerce in different cities and associations representing different fields of industry.[55] The British government (mainly, the Foreign Office and the Board of Trade) was ready to support the results of its minister's efforts on the ground, according to Nathan A. Pelcovits due to its rather traditional 'policy of gradualism and limited objectives in China'.[56] Nonetheless in the end, British leaders could not ignore the voices of merchants. Non-ratification was decided on 25 July 1870 when Alcock had already returned to London.[57]

When travelling home to England (formally on leave), Alcock had a positive intention of following up the political and legal procedures required for the enforcement of the convention and witnessing its ratification, and then resuming his work in Beijing, based on the revised treaty. However, having seen the ratification rejected, he decided to retire from the diplomatic service (in 1871 officially) and never returned to China.[58]

2) Alcock's last lessons, or unlearned first lessons

Thus, Alcock's final work as a diplomat, in which he directly invested a great deal of energy over three years, and in a broader sense, his entire experience in East Asia, did not bear fruit because it was clearly disturbed by British merchants.

What did he want to accomplish at the time? To answer that question, we need to look first at the official dispatch by which Alcock reported the signing of the convention, with the convention text as an enclosure (this was eventually presented to both the Houses of the Parliament by the Foreign Office).[59] Besides stating that the entire instrument was, he believed, 'in general conformity' with the government instructions so far, as well as explaining the considerations vested on each article, he added his own views on some particular elements which he knew would invite major objections from merchants. He wrote that such was 'the price paid' for 'various advances in the path of progress and other concessions' from the China side, and necessary 'if there is to be any principal[sic] of reciprocity recognised in our relations with China'. He asserted, '[t]he legitimate trade can only gain by the measures proposed'.

A month earlier, when reaching the final stage of negotiations, he had sent out another dispatch to the Foreign Office. We can find that he had used similar wordings in it, such as, 'I propose to deal with [the remaining questions] in a spirit of reciprocity and concession as far as the different conditions of the two countries will admit, trusting the full approval of Her Majesty's Government.'[60] Furthermore, what did he say a month after the signing of the convention? The quotation below is the concluding part of his dispatch to the Foreign Office on 7 December 1869 from Ningbo, where he was visiting on his way back to the UK.

> The convention was the result of a negotiation based on principles of equitable consideration and reciprocity.... After all the only question worth discussion is how far the convention taken as a whole is calculated to advance the interests of commerce and improve our relations with the people and government of China. Believing that it was well calculated to do both, and that more could not be obtained by any means at my command, I had no hesitation in signing but the final decision rests with Her Majesty's Government, and my sole anxiety is to prevent misapprehension as to the actual condition under which the negotiations took place, and the objects which it was my aim to secure.[61]

At this time, he was already being heavily criticized by commercial communities, but he still had hope for ratification. He wrote this not in response to any query or instruction, and we can thus read it as an expression of his honest feelings. He writes with a mixture of confidence and anxiety, but the unmistakable key principles binding both aspects, common in the former two documents, are 'equitable consideration and reciprocity'. To aim at equity and reciprocity between Britain and China, was not, he understood, against the purpose of advancing the interests of British commerce, and he was not, of course, simply sacrificing the merchants for his idealistic thoughts. As he used the word 'calculated', he was seeking a path to maximize merchant interests by strategically placing them on the foundation of improved relations between the two countries. However, such a path was a long-term goal, which was obviously not compatible with what the merchant communities wanted immediately.

Ten years earlier at Yokohama, Alcock had been charged with overseeing the implementation of a new but already sealed legal instrument in order to secure a stable relationship with the Japanese government. In China, he had to be more creative to improve Britain's relationship with China by revising existing diplomatic instruments. As such, his roles were different but in both Japan and China, we can see his attitude was remarkably similar. Compared with the 'Yokohama question' to which he had to react almost instinctively upon arriving at his new Japanese post, in China, Alcock could have carefully prepared and mobilized all possible means at his disposal, including certain preliminary negotiations with the commercial communities, in order to attain his aim. However, he rather simply looked to advance his 'principles of equitable consideration and reciprocity'. Here, we have to conclude that he did not learn from his 'first lessons'; the lessons at that time had only ended in elucidating his position in Japan and seemingly not given him any tactics for better averting the obstructions he faced in China.

Rather than attempting to soothe potential criticism from merchants, Alcock created a difficult situation through his own actions. By visiting the ports and directly discussing matters with residents, he evoked unnecessary expectations that the minister's office would support the merchants' immediate desires. On the contrary, Alcock actually found their inappropriate use of legal prestige or deficiencies in the current system, detrimental to a long-term, sound relationship with the Chinese government. He was on the one hand too naïve to believe that after these processes, the merchants should understand the value of his 'reciprocity' principles and accept to sacrifice their short-term interests. On the other hand, he was also too cool, in a sense, to the British merchants in the treaty ports.

Besides these procedures undertaken by Alcock in the field, the British government's stance since the signing of the convention until the final moment of non-ratification was not usual either: the still unofficial and unratified text of the convention was published (in *The Times of London*, 11 June 1870) and exposed to the free criticism of those in concerned industries,[62] which soon invited a firm response, first from the Manchester Chamber of Commerce saying, '[i]t is feared that the convention with China may have a prejudicial influence on our trade with that country'. The chamber of commerce thus requested a suspension of the ratification process.[63] After this, the Foreign Office could not refuse more officially circulating the convention text, together with Alcock's explanations addressed to that Office, among the Chambers of Commerce throughout the UK.[64]

These facts made the government's handling of the matter towards the end of the course extremely difficult. Edmund Hammond, a long-time ally of Alcock who was ready to back him on this occasion as well, also regretted such disclosures of information. It was actually Hammond who thought of submitting the convention and Alcock's explanations to Parliament 'although contrary to the rule of not presenting unratified treaties', as he had already done the same to the chambers of commerce. It seems he was aiming to solve the problem all at once at Parliament, rather than tangling with each of the many chambers of commerce that were sending in proclamations objecting to the ratification.[65] His idea was carried out,[66] but it could not alter the course of what ended up as a non-ratification of the measure.

In this sense, the non-ratification as the final result must be attributed to the mismanagement of information, and this was a failure of diplomacy. Of course, from the perspective of Alcock and the Foreign Office, the merchants were too short-sighted and stubborn. However, it cannot be denied that Alcock himself created barriers. Towards the end of his career as he gained more confidence in his own belief in the principle of reciprocity, he may have become even less attentive to merchants' immediate desires. It is ironic to observe that the long-term objective of diplomacy that Alcock so earnestly tried to embody – bi-lateral relations respecting mutual equity and reciprocity – could end up in such an apparent antagonistic relationship between himself and his fellow citizens.

This frustration seems to have prompted Alcock to become more supportive of his diplomatic counterpart government (the Qing) than British merchants, to the extent that he worried about possible 'misapprehension as to the actual condition under which the negotiations took place, and the objects which it was my aim to secure' in the above-cited dispatch from Ningbo. In Japan, Alcock began by sounding out the stance and ability of the shogunate. He felt initially that the shogunate and his fellow merchants were potentially forming a united front against him. By contrast, he was calmer in China. While Alcock only gradually became sympathetic to the government of Japan, the same process was not necessary for him in China, the country where he had been trained on the job for fifteen years. Therefore, his consistent, remaining obstacle was the merchant community.

One additional condition that complicated Alcock's path should be mentioned before closing this section. That was India. Alcock's plan to increase the import duty in China on opium (together with the fact that the opium cultivation had been increasing within China during those years) would impact the economy of India, a key producer of that commodity and Britain's most important colony. Alcock was aware of the problem, and he thought of having 'personal communication with the Viceroy [of India] and his council, in order to make sure that they were in possession of all the information necessary to a full comprehension of the influences at work in China & the facts, bearing upon the present condition & future prospects of the Opium Trade'. He actually did so in Calcutta after he had singed the convention on his way back to London. He proudly reported successfully removing all doubts on the part of the colonial government of India.[67]

However, perhaps Alcock was still too confident in the treaty revision, and stayed in India too long – for nearly two months from late January to mid-March 1870 – discussing not only on convention matters but broader prospects of the region.[68] The Foreign Office in London was waiting for Alcock's arrival with an increasing sense of urgency, but he seemed to have underestimated the merchants' objections. It was not possible to counteract the situation after he arrived in London in late April.[69]

Conclusion

The Treaty of Tianjin itself remained in force until its revision in 1902 in the aftermath of the Boxer Rising, an extremely disadvantageous period for the Qing government. Concerning the unrealized Alcock Convention of 1869, Fei Wei has recently noted that the agreement was the first attempt to 'sign a contract… in peace and on relative equality since the Opium War'.[70] Historian Immanuel C. Y. Hsu indicates that '[t]he Tsungli Yamen was of course proud of this first equal agreement', and that 'while Chinese disappointment following the British rejection was limited to a small circle of officials without much public awareness', 'the rejection of the Alcock Convention reaffirmed Chinese suspicion of foreign trustworthiness'.[71] These comments clearly explain the potential historical value of the convention and what was lost due to its non-ratification. In light of the actual history experienced thereafter, it would not be a mistake to recognize that through the processes observed above, peoples in the world, not only the Chinese, missed an important opportunity of approaching a certain notion of equality between European and Asian nations as early as the late 1860s. From the opposite angle, it means that such an 'equal agreement', if 'relative[ly]', was very close to actualization at that time.

It may be possible to argue that Alcock was a typical example of '[o]fficials serving at isolated posts overseas… notably sensitive to local conditions of service, to the traditions and prejudices of their area'.[72] His support for the Japanese government and also his well-known inclination towards Japanese arts and crafts may be explained with this same analysis.[73] However, he was not always *kind* to Japan or China. We can discern from his words quoted above that he was at times too loyal to British interests; at least, his attitude did not seem to verify that 'the British official outlook in the East was influenced... by the "orientalizing" of British consular officers',[74] if such tendency was generally true. The nature of his thoughts is much closer to fairness, than orientalization, as he himself used as keywords 'good faith' in Japan, and 'reciprocity' in China. And, we see that these notions were intimately connected with, and rooted in his sense of guarding long-term, public interests, ultimately for the prosperity of Britain.

Yet Alcock was repeatedly blocked by the merchants' short-term interests. He continued to experience hard times because of this relationship, and in the end, he could not cap the last chapter of his diplomatic career with an expected historical success.

But the confrontation with the commercial sector itself was not unique to him. It is possible to say that the conflict between Alcock and British merchants was representative of broader diplomat-merchant dynamics in the region. Writing in the 1940s, Nathan Pelcovits spotlighted the series of harsh objections put forth by established British merchants in China – the 'Old China Hands' – to the Alcock Convention, as a culmination of long-existing antagonism between the commercial and public spheres over the control of Anglo-Chinese relations. In other words, this was a surge of lasting efforts of mercantile communities to influence the decision-making processes of diplomacy. Pelcovitz argues that, in fact, both parties never changed their respective attitudes, before and after this incident: the merchants always desired their government's firm approach towards China, to secure maximum concessions. He attributes this to their illusions about China as a dream land. By contrast, the government was more realistic and never judged that the Chinese market was important enough for Britain to invest a great deal of resources in it. For the public sector overall, there was no reason to pursue anything other than a conciliatory and gradualist policy towards China.[75]

Therefore, this was a matter of structure. In this rather dichotomous approach, Alcock's moves are presented simply as part of a realization of government policy. This forms a rational, convincing analysis, but I must say that it lacks one important element, that is, the attention to the personalities of individuals on the diplomatic frontline. Indeed, to some extent, Pelcovits looks at the politicians in London as individuals, but the very core diplomat in the field is treated as no more than an organ of central policy. We saw, however, that Alcock himself repeated his previous frictions with merchants, and in those struggles erupted with anger – of course based on his professional concerns, but apparently, rooted in his own personal and very human views. We also had to comprehend that he could have learned something from his first lessons in 1859 to avoid the final failure in 1869, but he did not. Is it not very natural to understand that diplomacy is inevitably influenced by the diplomats on the ground: their personal emotion, tastes, confidence, insecurities, thoughts and beliefs?

As responsible public servants, diplomats' competencies should involve the ability to control, when necessary, these human elements. However, after all, it is nothing other than the diplomats' actual deeds and actions, which can never be entirely detached from their individual lives, that embody the path of diplomacy. Even if Alcock's attitudes to merchants may be indicative of a general tendency of diplomacy in East Asia at the time, his actual train of thoughts and each action he took cannot be explained without attention to Alcock, the man. I agree with the recent conclusions of Markus Mössalang and Torsten Riotte, who in charting a new approach to the diplomatic history stress that it is 'the diplomats themselves, their individual agency as well as their attitudes and experiences'[76] that should be centrally taken into account.

Moreover, what seems to be overlooked by Pelcovits and other historians is the sense of distance between London and Alcock's location. If we consider the distance, which usually required four months or longer for an exchange of reports and instructions between London and Beijing, or Edo, we should naturally assume that Alcock enjoyed broad discretionary power, and was not simply articulating policy made in London. This physical distance also explains the ignorance of local conditions on the side of the home government that a diplomat had to face, in many cases in bitter isolation. Alcock and other members of Britain's Far Eastern Diplomatic and Consular services had to work under these particular conditions before the age of the telegraph. As P. D. Coates describes, these were 'most abnormal conditions' imposed on a 'small group of British officials whose working lives were spent in alien surroundings far from home'.[77] It adds particular significance to, and further urges us to understand, as other authors do in this volume, the necessity of looking at individual human beings on the scene.

Overall as explored above, this chapter has provided an example of research that emphasizes the importance of experiences and personal feelings of a diplomat. As such it is especially important to look at Alcock's career on a long-term basis covering his time in Japan and that in China. This *wholistic* approach reveals the personality of Alcock which would have not otherwise been obvious. If historians of China analyse only his days in China and historians of Japan look exclusively at his time in Japan, they can only capture fragmentally his personality.

However, as I have explained in this chapter Alcock made similar statements in Japan and China, which demonstrated some unchanging characteristics of his thoughts. His distinctive belief in reciprocity, in order to establish long-term, sound relationships, is evident across his time in China and Japan. Nonetheless he obviously gained more confidence as time went by and his beliefs became more defined. I wish to emphasize that the early evolution of British diplomacy in East Asia was inseparable from this personal development of Alcock.

Furthermore, I believe it valuable to view Alcock as a person who lived his professional life within a continuous process of Anglo-Chinese diplomacy and Anglo-Japanese diplomacy. By taking such a pan-East Asian view, Japanese and Chinese diplomacy cease to be two different, predetermined fields, and re-emerge as a combined one covering a broader region where people – such as the arriving British and other Westerners – moved back and forth. As other historians have shown in this volume, by employing a line of natural chronology of human lives it is possible to re-evaluate even well-known incidents. Finally, in this chapter I did not have space to explain why Alcock found 'reciprocity' so valuable and prioritized 'good faith' over other strategic options when negotiating with his East Asian counterparts. However, further research that more thoroughly examines his life, including not only his time in East Asia but also his education, medical career and military engagements in foreign lands, will help open avenues to more fully explain the fascinating life of Rutherford Alcock.

2

George S. Morrison and Japan's first British consulate at Nagasaki

Brian Burke-Gaffney

Building on the discussions presented by Sano Mayuko in Chapter 1, this chapter also focuses on British diplomats in Japan in the mid-nineteenth century. Consistent with the larger thematic approach of this volume, it traces an individual life – that of George S. Morrison – during the 1850s and 1860s. In exploring Morrison's relations with other Westerners and with local officialdoms, the chapter touches on numerous lives and locations of significance to the subjects of other chapters in this volume. In a similar vein to Annette Bainbridge and her exploration of *Charlotte Jane*, it also examines the importance of place – in this case the actual consular buildings and the city of Nagasaki itself – in the experiences of Westerners and the inauguration of British-Japanese diplomacy in mid-nineteenth-century East Asia.

The modern history of contact between Britain and Japan begins with the visit of four Royal Navy warships to the port of Nagasaki in September 1854. Admiral James Stirling submitted a letter to the Tokugawa shogunate and, on 14 October 1854, sat down with Nagasaki Magistrate Mizuno Chikugo-no-kami to sign the Japan-Britain Treaty of Amity and lay the foundation for a new era of international cooperation.[1] The 13 January 1855 issue of the *Illustrated London News* carried a detailed description of Stirling's visit, along with a number of lithographs that gave British readers a rare glimpse into a country mostly hidden to date from the outside world.

Nagasaki had served since the seventeenth century as Japan's only official window to the world and only place in the country where foreigners were allowed to reside. The Dutch and Chinese had enjoyed exclusive trading privileges, inhabiting the artificial island of Dejima (Deshima) in Nagasaki Harbour and a walled-in quarter in the nearby Jūzenji district, respectively. For more than two centuries they coexisted peacefully with their Japanese neighbours, sharing the profits of trade and contributing to the development of a diverse regional culture.

Like the American and Russian pacts concluded a few months earlier, the Japan-Britain Treaty of Amity was purely diplomatic: Japan agreed to allow British ships to visit a few designated ports in times of emergency but made no concessions regarding commercial or residential rights. A period of rumination and procrastination continued until Sir James Bruce, 8th Earl of Elgin and 12th Earl of Kincardine, arrived in Japan in the summer of 1858 to sign the Anglo-Japanese Treaty of Amity and Commerce, one of the epoch-making Ansei Five-Power Treaties (named for the Ansei Period which ran from 1855 to 1860).

Effective 1 July the following year, the Ansei Five-Power Treaties called on the Tokugawa shogunate to open several ports including Nagasaki as sites for foreign settlements and to grant rights of free trade and extraterritoriality to British, American, French, Russian and Dutch nationals taking up residence in the treaty ports. The five countries, on the other hand, would establish consulates in the treaty ports as conduits for communication with Japanese authorities and offices for matters related to their citizens.[2]

Scottish merchant-adventurer Kenneth R. Mackenzie arrived in Nagasaki a few months before the official opening of the port, commissioned to open a local branch of Jardine, Matheson & Co. and establish contacts with Japanese merchants and officials.[3] Like all the other early foreign visitors, he chose Nagasaki as a matter of course, not only because it was the nearest port to Shanghai, but also because it was still the only place in Japan with an infrastructure geared to trade and a population accustomed to dealing with foreigners.

Mackenzie found the port abuzz with activity. In addition to residents of the Deshima (Dejima) Dutch Factory and Chinese Quarter, a team of Dutch engineers was supervising an iron foundry and engine works on the other side of the harbour. Russian naval personnel had established a depot nearby, and the crews of a few foreign ships were coming ashore and mingling with the local populace. For the Japanese hosts, the sudden inundation brought unexpected benefits but challenged the system of trade and cultural coexistence entrenched in Nagasaki for more than two hundred years. An American traveller visiting Nagasaki in June 1859 wrote to his family as follows:

> There has been such a rush of traders to Japan that almost everything that can be bought has been carried off. Nearly 100 ships have already been to Nagasaki. There were twenty-five in port when we arrived, including war steamers. Such an influx of trade as this upon a people unused and unprepared has of course cleaned them out and prices rise rapidly.[4]

The Tokugawa shogunate had chosen the village of Tomachi Ōura, formerly part of the Ōmura Domain, as a tentative site for the Nagasaki Foreign Settlement. Bordering the Nagasaki *tenryō* (imperial territory, i.e. the area in and around Nagasaki placed under direct shogunal jurisdiction) to the south, the village included a coastal area with a few fishermen's huts huddling near the harbour and hillsides cut into ledges for the cultivation of fruits and vegetables. The latter rose away from a creek penetrating the brim of flat land at the water's edge. Mackenzie arranged to rent a farmhouse on the hillside south of the creek, near a Buddhist temple called Myōgyōji.

On 4 June 1859, HMS *Sampson* sailed into the long inlet of Nagasaki carrying Rutherford Alcock, a former army surgeon appointed consul-general to Japan and leader of the first British delegation to Edo. The other passengers included Abel A. J. Gower, a former assistant under Alcock in the Canton (Guangzhou) Consulate, and Captain Howard Vyse and C. Pemberton Hodgson, consuls-designate for Kanagawa (Yokohama) and Hakodate, respectively. George S. Morrison, the consul-designate for Nagasaki and second in command, had been delayed and unable to join the group. The men were the first members of the Japan Consular Service, a body organized by the British Foreign Office on the same model as the diplomatic service established earlier in China.

Soon after reaching Nagasaki, Alcock arranged to rent buildings at Myōgyōji as a temporary residence for the British consular staff, probably with the assistance of Mackenzie whose rented farmhouse was located only a few steps away. The use of a Buddhist temple as a foreign accommodation had a precedent in Goshinji, the temple on the opposite side of Nagasaki Harbour offered as a refuge for the Russian navy the previous year.[5]

Founded in 1658 as a branch of the Ōtani School of Shin Buddhism, Myōgyōji consisted of a large *hondō* (main hall) and a number of smaller buildings perched on the hillside overlooking Ōura Creek and the village of Tomachi Ōura. Although little more than a country temple serving the local farming and fishing community, Myōgyōji's location in the centre of the proposed foreign settlement pulled it willy-nilly into a new era of contact with foreigners.[6]

While still aboard the HMS *Sampson* in Nagasaki Harbour, Alcock informed C. Pemberton Hodgson in writing of his appointment to the position of acting consul in Nagasaki:

> Finding on my arrival here that British trade to a large extent was already established and that many British firms had opened houses of business and taken up their residence at Nagasaki, I have deemed it desirable to establish a consulate at this port without delay. Mr Morrison, the consul appointed to this

port, cannot be expected to arrive before the middle or end of July – prior to which the provisions of Lord Elgin signed in August last will come into effect, opening the three ports on this coast to British trade under the regulations of trade thereby annexed, probably leading to a large and rapid development of the commerce. At Hokodadi [sic] on the contrary I have no information that there is any trade under the British flag or a single British resident there. Under these circumstances I have no hesitation in appointing you provisionally – and in accordance with your wishes – to take charge of the consulate at Nagasaki.[7]

Educated at Eton and Cambridge, Hodgson had travelled the world, published books about his adventures in Australia and served as British consul at Caen, France. He had been appointed along with Morrison to the Japan Consular Service in a royal declaration dated 21 February 1859.[8]

Hodgson made an adventurous first excursion into the streets of Nagasaki while the British warship lay at anchor, only to run into a crowd of gawkers and flee back to the safety of the ship. The principal object of curiosity was apparently Mrs Hodgson and her daughter, the first Caucasian women to set foot in Japan since the controversial stopover of Titia, the wife of Dutch Factor Jan Cock Blomhoff, at Dejima in 1817. Hodgson later reported that a Japanese artist ran along beside her, sketching away, and produced an illustration that was later converted into a woodblock print and mass-produced on a *sake* (rice wine) label but looked 'as much like the original as a butterfly to a salamander'.[9]

Mrs Hodgson meanwhile wrote to her mother in England, recounting in colourful detail the startling visit ashore. She also provides the following description of Myōgyōji, site of Japan's first British Consulate:

> Its situation is far from beautiful, being on the edge of a low cape, far from the town (which rejoiced me, as I shall see less of the people), surrounded by handsome pines, and having a limited view of the bay. We had in all seven rooms, about eight feet high, and the largest (which is small) is to be office and dining room; but a very gloomy one, I fear. My own room, which is to be 'à ma volonté,' either of one or two pieces, as I move the sliding partitions, was light and gay, with an agreeable aspect to the north and the bay. This is to be my bedroom, and every afternoon the drawing-room, for we have the society of two charming young men, who are attached to the Consulate, and are to live with us.
>
> On the whole my impression was that I would like the place. The priest and his wife were very civil, and tried all in their power to assist us, and as long as the 'Sampson' was in sight, I felt I should not be an exile here. There is to be a room for my maid and [daughter] Eva, and one room apiece for Dr Myburgh and Mr Annesley, and then a second office, and a large room, capacious but not clean, which is to be larder, kitchen, and dormitory for the servants.

While the diplomatists were discussing graver matters, I, with the officers of the 'Sampson,' and some marines kindly lent us, and my own servants, were hastily arranging our rustic furniture in this 'maisonette Japonaise;' and with such success, that on Monday the 13th, nine days after our arrival, we were able to sleep on shore. On that same day the British flag in Japan was hoisted by my husband, with three cheers from our loyal community.[10]

Mrs Hodgson's report indicates that the inauguration of the consulate coincided with Rutherford Alcock's letter of appointment dated 13 June and therefore that the consul-general was still in Nagasaki at the time. Most descriptions of the 1859 voyage of HMS *Sampson* mention briefly that the ship stopped in Nagasaki but gloss over the fact that the first consulate was established there. The omission reflects a tendency among historians to neglect Nagasaki's role in early British-Japanese relations in favour of discussions related to Yokohama and Kobe. The fact is, however, that the modern history of diplomatic relations between Britain and Japan began at Myōgyōji, not Tōzenji, the temple in the shogunal capital of Edo where the first British Legation was established after Alcock's arrival there on 26 June.

The 'two charming young men' mentioned by Mrs Hodgson were Francis G. Myburgh and Adolphus A. Annesley, recruited in London to serve as assistant and interpreter at the Nagasaki consulate. Myburgh was a medical doctor, while Annesley was a former midshipman in the Royal Navy whose father had served as British consul at Amsterdam. Both men had been welcomed into the Japan Consular Service because of their fluency in Dutch, the *lingua franca* of Japanese-European exchange in Nagasaki for more than two centuries and still the principal means of communication with local officials.

Despite the assistance of interpreters, Hodgson may have had trouble even writing documents and eating meals in a dignified manner. The first dispatch from the Nagasaki British Consulate – that is, the first dispatch from a British diplomatic station in Japan – was a rather urgent request, dated only two days after the opening of the consulate, for permission to purchase 'a few chairs, two tables, and a large cupboard in which to deposit the consular papers and books'.[11]

On 7 July, Hodgson penned a report on the state of affairs in Nagasaki and sent it directly to the Foreign Office in London. With regard to the progress made to date, he states that:

> I have selected a site for the consulate and a burial ground for foreigners, have obtained the use of a prison, established the right to hire [Japanese] servants, obtained a depot for H.M. Naval Service, fixed upon the Port Regulations and opposed the prohibition of fishing and shooting unless as a means of obtaining a

> livelihood. I also refused to take under British protection the swarms of Chinese who claimed it, unless such Chinese were registered at the consulate as in the service of British subjects... I propose in a few days sending your Lordship a list of all articles capable of being exported, or which, if encouraged, might be exported.[12]

The 'site for the consulate' was of course Myōgyōji, and the prison to which Hodgson alludes was part of the Japanese detainment facility in Sakura-machi, an arrangement necessitated by the lack of a lockup in the old wooden temple and the increase in delinquent behaviour among British sailors.

In connection with the latter, Hodgson hired a constable to maintain law and order and to arrest wrongdoers, a consular position that would retain its importance until the abrogation of extraterritoriality in 1899. The consul and assistants were enlisted in London on the basis of academic credentials, linguistic ability and diplomatic experience, but the constable was usually a discharged soldier or policeman from the municipal force in one of the Chinese ports engaged on the spot in Japan and paid a workingman's salary. The first constable in Nagasaki was Edward T. Kettle, enlisted from the police force in Shanghai, followed from the summer of 1860 by Matthew Green, a native of Cheshire, England, and former sailor who would go on to contribute to the development of the foreign settlement.[13]

Despite the opening of Yokohama and Hakodate, Nagasaki continued to serve as the gateway to Japan for most of the foreign ships sailing from China and the principal business and communication venue. Hakodate was proving impracticable because of its great distance from the centres of power, and Yokohama was still a fledgling port with little experience in foreign trade. Ernest Satow, another British diplomat in Japan at the time, describes conditions during the early months after the opening of the treaty ports and comments on the difference between Nagasaki and Yokohama:

> At Nagasaki most of the territorial nobles of Western Japan had establishments whither they sent for sale the rice and other produce received in payment of tribute from the peasants, and their retainers came into frequent contact with foreigners, whose houses they visited for the purchase of arms, gunpowder and steamers. Some sort of friendly feeling thus sprang up, which was increased by the American missionaries who gave instruction in English to younger members of this class, and imparted to them liberal ideas which had no small influence on the subsequent course of events. At Yokohama, however, the foreign merchants had chiefly to do with a class of adventurers, destitute of capital and ignorant of commerce. Broken contracts and fraud were by no means uncommon.[14]

Morrison arrived in Nagasaki on August 6 – two months late – and took over from Hodgson. The latter proceeded to Hakodate to open a consulate in that port, but illness forced him into retirement only two years later. He died in France in 1865 after publishing his groundbreaking work on the first British consulates in Japan.[15]

Born in Macao in 1830, George Staunton Morrison was the son of Robert Morrison, the first Protestant missionary to China and celebrated translator of the Bible into Chinese. His parents undoubtedly named him after the English traveller and scholar Sir George Staunton, Robert Morrison's forerunner in Chinese studies. The younger Morrison underwent schooling in England and entered the public service in 1848, going on to serve in various posts in China. In 1856 he was appointed First Assistant and Keeper of the Records in the Superintendency and, the following year, Secretary to the Hong Kong Government.

Not all had gone well for him in China. Morrison had fallen ill along with several other British residents after eating bread poisoned by a malevolent Chinese baker, and, on another occasion, he had almost been killed by shots fired from a rebel junk anchored in the harbour. He returned to Britain on leave in 1858, only a few months before his appointment as Senior Consul in Japan, a position of responsibility that would entail acting as chargé de affairs in the event of the death or absence of Rutherford Alcock.[16]

Morrison was still suffering from poor health in early 1859 when, writing to the Foreign Office from the Oriental Hotel in London, he declined to follow the itinerary proposed by the Foreign Office and instead asked for permission to board a vessel sailing directly from Liverpool to Shanghai later in the year.[17] Also, unlike his predecessor Hodgson, he travelled alone, unable to enjoy what likely would have been the therapeutic effects of familial companionship.

Upon arrival in Nagasaki, Morrison reeled in shock to see the state of his new workplace. In contrast to Mrs Hodgson and her husband, who had written in a rather light-hearted tone about their life and work in Nagasaki, the new consul threw his arms up in horror and astonishment, groaning in his first letter from Nagasaki that:

> The disagreement of my position exceeds all belief or power of description. We are domiciled in the outhouses and sheds of a temple which were resigned to snakes and centipedes before being appropriated for Her Majesty's consulate. The floor is of planking raised two or three feet from the ground – the ceiling of planking two or three feet above our heads. The sides of the house are of paper windows sliding in grooves, and to admit light and air they are taken out. Hence

you are exposed on every side to the entrance of any thief who takes a fancy to your property, and some of the sheds occupied by foreigners have already been gutted. You make take a slight precaution by closing the plank shutters, and at the same time place yourself in complete darkness without air... This and mosquitoes swarm about your face like you were a piece of butcher's meat. Everything you possess, that the thieves leave, is destroyed by rust and mold... But I have said enough to show that our condition is <u>miserable</u> (the only word that proximally describes it).[18]

Despite several years of experience in China, Morrison seemed incapable of enduring the unpleasant if temporary conditions in Nagasaki. He continued the tirade in another letter to the Foreign Office:

The air is at all times laden with the foul odours of a thousand cesspools, while the water procurable is little better than slow poison... Whatever the motives of those who last year invented and published the fabulous accounts of this country and its people, they have done an irrevocable injustice to those whose misfortune it is to pass a proportion of their time here dependent upon their means of economizing sufficient to enable an escape from their unenviable position.[19]

The disgruntled consul nevertheless picked up the reins from Hodgson and resumed discussions with the Nagasaki Magistrate regarding the establishment of the foreign settlement. The consulate staff celebrated their first Christmas and New Year in Japan and congratulated themselves on the progress made in diplomatic relations, but the spirit of the holiday was dashed a few days later when a mob of Chinese residents attacked the constable, Edward T. Kettle, and sent a shockwave through the tiny British community.

Kettle arrested a Chinese ruffian for throwing a stone at him. But when he tried to march the man off to a Japanese police box at the edge of the (still proposed) foreign settlement, a horde of the man's compatriots poured out of the Chinese Quarter waving clubs and demanding his release. Other British residents arrived in time to fire guns and scare off the crowd. Kettle escaped to a boat and fled to Myōgyōji, where he informed Morrison of the skirmish. Fearing further attacks, Morrison hurried to HMS *Roebuck*, a British warship visiting Nagasaki at the time, and asked the commander to land an armed party. That was done, but the mob had already dispersed, and Morrison's subsequent supplications to the Nagasaki Magistrate failed to elicit any firm promise to arrest the perpetrators or to take preventive measures. Without commenting on the cause of the conflict or guessing the reasons for the grievances of the Chinese community, the consul ends his report as follows:

The Roebuck will probably be in the neighbourhood only for a few days, and but little of that time in port, while it is hopeless to look to the Japanese for assistance in an emergency. Few in number and scattered, [British residents] must still depend entirely upon ourselves until circumstances permit of the continued presence of a ship of war, the want of which is every day made more apparent.[20]

The anxiety persisted as Morrison continued his negotiations with Nagasaki officials. Two issues were of particular importance. The first was the identification of viable merchandise and mutual agreement concerning the rules of trade, including the rate of exchange between the Mexican silver dollar and Japanese *ichibu* silver coin. The second was the reclamation of land from the harbour, allotment of properties and other preparations for the establishment and operation of the foreign settlement. Since the Nagasaki Magistrate's Office served merely as a reception desk for the Tokugawa shogunate, the negotiations were repeatedly stalled, sometimes for weeks on end, by the long waits for decisions from Edo.

With regard to trade, Morrison grumbled in a report to Rutherford Alcock about the various obstacles encountered by British merchants trying to drive a wedge into the commercial interaction monopolized for more than two centuries by the Dutch and Chinese. Many Japanese merchants continued to snub the Mexican silver dollar and to pass transactions through government channels, causing intolerable delays. It was difficult to hold Japanese merchants to their promises, he said, or to appeal for official intervention when contracts were breached. Morrison pointed out that Chinese merchants had no official treaty with Japan but continued to enjoy unfair privileges based on longstanding cultural and historical ties. To make things worse, the lack of suitable storage facilities in the temporary buildings acquired in the Japanese town left merchandise vulnerable to theft and fire. Still, the British Consul ended his report on an unusually magnanimous and optimistic note:

All these obstacles to trade are such as were to be naturally anticipated; it would indeed be remarkable if they did not exist, in a country so jealous and exclusive as Japan, opened for the first time to an order of things diametrically opposed to the policy and habits of the nation; they cannot be overthrown in an instant but must be left to the operation of time and persevering endeavours gradually to overcome.[21]

Morrison informed Alcock that the trade in 1859 was confined largely to exports and that most of the British ships arriving in Nagasaki carried only ballast. He also submitted a summarized table that sheds a valuable light on the status of exports from Nagasaki to Shanghai during the first half of the year.[22] The table presents thirty-four export commodities including, in order of value: seaweed ($307,805), ginseng ($128,611), raw silk ($109,926), isinglass ($38,775), silk piece goods ($36,000), vegetable wax ($34,190), coal ($25,000), vegetable oil ($23,930), sea cucumber ($18,860) and dried fish ($18,680). Copper, a mainstay of Dutch exports during the Edo Period, barely made the list at $125. Coal was still being collected by primitive methods but would gain great importance a decade later when Thomas B. Glover imported mining equipment from Britain and established Japan's first modern coal mine on the island of Takashima near Nagasaki.[23] Tea, meanwhile, although not even cited by Morrison, would shoot to the top of the export roster in two or three years when William J. Alt and other merchants established tea-firing plants in the rear quarter of the foreign settlement.[24]

Morrison pressed the Nagasaki Magistrate for cooperation in meeting treaty obligations regarding the physical and legal establishment of the foreign settlement and the smooth initiation of socio-commercial functions. The latter arranged for teams of labourers to carry gravel, build stone embankments, and install all the necessary roads, bridges, gutters and foundation walls in the new commercial district around the mouth of Ōura Creek. As to the method of renting land in the foreign settlement, Morrison suggested a down payment for each lot plus a small stipend payable yearly to the Tokugawa shogunate as a guarantee against buildings and warehouses erected by the renter. However, the Nagasaki Magistrate overruled the proposal, insisting that each renter should pay a fixed annual fee regardless of buildings. In May 1860, Morrison agreed tentatively (pending final instructions from the British Legation) that foreigners would pay an annual rental fee of $37, $28 and $12 per 100 *tsubo* (about 330 square metres) for lots on the waterfront, rear quarter and hillside, respectively.[25] The leases would be considered perpetual; that is, the renter would hold a permanent title deed and enjoy full rights of ownership to buildings but would not actually possess the land upon which the buildings stood. A renter could transfer a lease to another foreign resident with consular approval. If a renter relinquished his/her claim to a lot, ownership would revert to the Japanese government without refund. The perpetual lease was an arrangement unique to the foreign settlements that would remain in place until being unilaterally abolished by the Japanese government during the Second World War.

The same month, Morrison compiled a list of twenty-three regulations to be followed by British subjects – and by extension other foreigners – regarding entry and anchorage in Nagasaki Harbour, the conduct of seamen on shore leave and manner of dealing with violations of local laws, as well as prohibitions on the discharge of firearms, excursions beyond the limits of the *tenryō* and 'riding quickly through the streets of the town'. The list also stated that:

> No British Subject may establish either a boarding house, eating house, or other public house of entertainment without the sanction of the Consul and under such conditions as he may require. Any person harbouring a seaman who is a deserter or who cannot produce his discharge, with written sanction from the Consul to reside on shore, will be liable to the penalty attending breach of these Regulations [not exceeding five hundred dollars, or three months' imprisonment.[26]

Approved by the British Legation in June and published for the information of the public the following year, the regulations established foundations for life and business in the foreign settlements of Japan.

Morrison escaped from the discomforts of Nagasaki in June 1860, leaving the consular duties to Francis G. Myburgh for a few weeks. The latter kept a short diary that sheds light on the activities of the consulate a year after its inauguration. It also reveals that the consul spent a considerable amount of time in the consular court dealing with theft and other petty crimes, quarrels over business transactions, and the rowdy conduct of British sailors in the town.[27] In an entry dated 12 June, he mentions a complaint from Japanese authorities about an attack on a woman by a British sailor in a Nagasaki teahouse. Two days later, he reports that:

> I had sent for the woman who was stabbed by the sailor in the Tea-house to take her deposition. She came as far as the Custom House, when she was obliged to be taken back, owing to the painful condition of the wound. Her son, named Tahe, stated that her name was Sono, and her age 57 years. That on Sunday last the 10th instant, the Defendant, Ammat Alie, was with four other sailors in the Tea-House called Hikitaia, and while upstairs made such noise that the Plaintiff, who is mistress of the house, went up to ascertain the cause of it, when the Defendant drew his knife and cut her in the left forearm, and also damaged the screens in the room. Ordered them to appear at this Consulate on Tuesday, the 19th instant, at 11 o'clock.

Hikitaia (correct spelling Hikitaya) is the former name of Kagetsu, a posh Japanese restaurant that remains in operation to this day with its buildings and gardens intact. A slash on a wooden pillar in one of the second-floor rooms has been popularly attributed to Sakamoto Ryōma, a Tosa samurai who spent time in Nagasaki in the 1860s, but it is more likely a remnant of the disturbance caused by British sailors in June 1860.

Myburgh learned from an interpreter that the woman had not recuperated enough to make the trip to Myōgyōji. Finally on 28 June, he dismissed the case because of the woman's failure to appear at the consulate, bringing the affair to a rather surprising conclusion. Whether or not the British provided further assistance to the woman or compensation for the damages to the building is unknown.

Back in Nagasaki in September 1860, Morrison followed up his list of regulations concerning the conduct of foreigners with a set of rules pertaining to the rental of lots in the Nagasaki Foreign Settlement.[28] A month later, he joined with John G. Walsh, Joseph H. Evans and Kenneth R. Mackenzie – representing the United States, Portugal and France, respectively – in compiling the first list of lot renters. Morrison was the only career diplomat in the foursome: Walsh was proprietor of the American trading firm Walsh & Co., and Evans and Mackenzie were agents for the China-based Dent & Co. and Jardine, Matheson & Co., respectively. All of the men except Walsh were British. The list of renters is provided in the form of a table, with separate columns for frontage and rearage.[29] The owners of business establishments were given priority in renting the waterfront lots, while public houses and hotels were banished to the rear quarter.

The Netherlands, Russia and China were not represented in the discussions. The Dutch continued to maintain their grip on the island of Dejima and to insist on its treatment as a legal entity separate from the foreign settlement. Russia, meanwhile, was yet to engage in commercial relations, and the Qing government had still not signed a treaty with Japan. In a letter to Alcock the same month, Morrison reports that '[The Russians] have now three gunboats here, and I believe that it is intended always to have at least one, which shows that though without any trading interests in Japan they consider it of importance to have a show of force ever present.' He goes on to mention the Chinese and reports that, despite their lack of any formal treaty, the Chinese residents of Nagasaki were enjoying the same rights as other foreigners and in fact were 'taking advantage of the facilities which foreign powers had obtained to monopolize the trade and to override us with their numbers'.[30] Continues Morrison:

> It may not be too out of place in the general description of Nagasaki to mention that the Japanese take every opportunity of acquiring foreign knowledge. A Dutch physician Dr Pompe van Meerdervoort has a school of about forty pupils, and the Dutch gentleman Mr de Vogel has a class learning English, and I have seen very fair photographs taken unassisted by a pupil of Mr Rossier. Many

Japanese are making good progress in Russian, which they seem to consider easier to learn than English. There are however several very tolerably proficient in our language.

The main purpose of the letter was to describe the progress made in the construction of the foreign settlement and to explain the content of several photographs of Nagasaki enclosed therewith. Taken by Swiss photographer Pierre Rossier (who had been dispatched to China and Japan by the London-based company Negretti & Zambra),[31] the thirteen photographs – amalgamated in several panoramic scenes – captured the appearance of Nagasaki Harbour, Dejima, the Minamiyamate and Higashiyamate hillsides and the area at the mouth of Ōura Creek where flat land for the foreign settlement was still being reclaimed from the harbour. The first of their kind taken in Japan, the photographs provide an invaluable record of Nagasaki the year after the opening of the port. Morrison ends the letter with a post facto request for money to offset the considerable cost:

> It only remains for me to conclude this letter by requesting authority to charge in my accounts the cost of having these photographs executed, namely seventy dollars. I confess the amount was more than I had expected it would be, but considering that Mr Rossier's time is specially devoted to other purposes, and that he was occupied with them for several days, it does not on consideration appear unreasonably high. Under any circumstances, as he is not a tradesman here for the sale of photographs I was not in a position to bargain with him on the subject, nor could I have felt it becoming so to do.

In another report submitted in early 1861, Morrison provided information on the state of trade and expressed his opinion that steady advances were being made in mollifying Japanese reluctance and opening up new markets.[32] With regard to imports and exports, he pointed out that the cotton and woollen cloth sold by British merchants was winning favour and increased demand in Japan, while several ships had been dispatched directly from Nagasaki to England carrying cargoes of tea, silk, wax, camphor and gallnuts. Tea in particular, he wrote, 'is likely to be the staple of export from Nagasaki: The anticipations of its quality and suitability for export were not at all exaggerated, and the Japanese are learning to prepare and pack it… it has been estimated that not less than 2,000,000 pounds have been sent to England alone.'

In his next dispatch, dated 13 April 1861, Morrison informed Alcock about his negotiations with the Nagasaki Magistrate concerning the expansion of the boundaries of the foreign settlement to include hillside residential lots.[33] The area originally granted by the Tokugawa shogunate had not included the hillsides that would later develop into elegant neighbourhoods scattered with Western-style houses. The lots had a prototype in British hill stations in India and the terraced heights in Canton and Hong Kong where expatriates enjoyed not only scenic vistas and cool breezes but also an escape from the clash of cultures in the cities below.

The Magistrate bent to Morrison's request for space on the hillside above the Ōura commercial district (later called Higashiyamate) but remained adamantly opposed to any concession regarding the stretch of hillside overlooking Nagasaki Harbour to the south of Myōgyōji (Minamiyamate). Morrison informed Alcock that he had submitted his personal request during an interview with the Magistrate, pointing out that space was needed for the health and comfort of residents and that the existing settlement was too cramped to accommodate the rapidly growing foreign population. It was the first time for Morrison to sit at the same table with the Magistrate, rather than on opposite sides of the room as in the past. When the latter gave the stock answer that he would have to consult the shogunate in Edo, Morrison pressed for an immediate decision, cleverly suggesting that the rental of Minamiyamate lots could be adopted as a *temporary* measure. Permission granted, the foreign consuls invited the residents of their respective countries to submit applications for lots on the hillside by the end of the summer.

On 21 April the same year, Morrison convened a meeting of land renters to select a Municipal Council to supervise the administrative affairs of the foreign settlement. Alt, John Major and Franklin Field were elected to seats on the council and submitted an initial report three weeks later. At Morrison's behest, the foreign merchants also came together in June to form the first Chamber of Commerce. Alt was appointed along with Glover and Robert Arnold to 'act in conjunction with the Consuls and Japanese authorities for the suppression of illegal traffic and to bring to their notice any breaches of the trade regulations or abuses of treaty privileges that may come under our observation' and to 'compile and publish a statement of trade and otherwise assist in making the resources of the country more generally known'.[34]

One of the other early inhabitants of the Nagasaki Foreign Settlement was a Briton named Albert W. Hansard who established a printing shop at No.31 Ōura and launched Japan's first English-language newspaper, *The Nagasaki Shipping List and Advertiser* in June 1861. In a letter to Alcock, Morrison relayed Hansard's request for the appointment of the newspaper as an official organ of the British government and added his personal recommendation to that effect.[35] The first issue of the four-page newspaper carried the following message at the top of its front page: 'OFFICIAL NOTIFICATION – It is hereby notified that from and after this date, and until further orders, the "Nagasaki Shipping List and Advertiser," is to be considered the Official Organ of all Notifications proceeding from Her Britannic Majesty's Legation, Consulate General, and Consulates in Japan.' This shows that Nagasaki was not only the cradle of foreign-language journalism in Japan but also the early mouthpiece of British diplomacy in the country.

On 1 June 1861, Morrison left Nagasaki with Alcock on the same overland journey to Edo made regularly in past decades by the Dutch *opperhoofd*, passing along the old Nagasaki Road to northern Kyushu, through the Seto Inland Sea to Osaka, then down the fabled Tōkaidō Highway to the capital. Among the entourage, which assembled at Dejima and departed in a long procession through the streets of Nagasaki, was Dutch Consul-General Jan Karel de Wit, British Legation assistant Abel A. J. Gower, *London Illustrated News* artist Charles Wirgman and dozens of Japanese officials, interpreters and labourers. The month-long journey proved a great success, the travellers encountering friendliness and hospitality all along the way and enjoying sites of scenic and historic interest previously concealed from foreign eyes.

What waited for Morrison and his companions in Edo, however, was not a cordial welcome but a close brush with death. On the night of 5 July, a group of angry samurai advocating the forcible expulsion of foreigners from Japan (part of what historians have dubbed the expulsion or *jōi* movement) stormed the British Legation at Tōzenji bent on assassinating Alcock and his staff. Lawrence Oliphant, first secretary of the legation, came out of his room into a dark corridor armed with only a hunting whip and ran into a few of the sword-wielding intruders, one of whom almost cut off his arm. Morrison, awakened by the noise, fired his revolver at the assailants and managed to defuse the immediate danger but also suffered a cut on his head during the scuffle. The intruders entered several rooms but were unable to find Alcock. Pursued by the Japanese guards who arrived belatedly on the scene, they either fled or committed ritual suicide.[36]

The incident at Tōzenji rubbed salt into the wound of Morrison's discontent in Japan. The hapless consul returned to his duties in Nagasaki but applied for permission to return to England to recuperate. Over the following months, it fell on Francis G. Myburgh and later Charles Winchester, as acting consuls, to continue negotiations with the Nagasaki Magistrate and to oversee business and social developments in the foreign settlement.

Morrison may have thought when he returned to Nagasaki in April 1863 that a year and a half would have afforded ample time for improvements to living conditions in the consulate at Myōgyōji and relations between the foreign and Japanese communities. But he was disappointed on both counts.

In his first dispatch to the British Legation after returning to Nagasaki, Morrison complained that 'the only persons in Nagasaki improvided [sic] with comfortable habitations are the officers of Her Majesty's Consulate, and I beg your sanction to procure for their proper accommodation on the best terms I can until such time as I am authorized to build a suitable consulate'.[37] Finally, in June, he made arrangements to move the consulate temporarily to Green's Hotel, a large Western-style building on the hillside lot directly below Myōgyōji. Matthew Green, the owner of the hotel and a former constable at the consulate, agreed to rent the building to the British government for a period of two years at $1,800 per annum.[38]

Although empowered to procure new consular premises, Morrison had few options when it came to the *jōi* (expel the foreigner) movement persisting among a small but determined samurai element throughout the country. Rumours circulated that Shimazu retainers and their sympathizers might at any moment launch an attack on the Nagasaki Foreign Settlement. Anxiety rose to such a level that Morrison called an emergency meeting on 13 May 1863 to decide whether or not to abandon the settlement. The majority of foreign residents, including Glover and Alt, opted to stay and to brace themselves for a collision, stowing their valuables on ships anchored in Nagasaki Harbour, gathering for mutual protection in a building on the Ōura waterfront every evening and sleeping with revolvers under their bedcovers.

The uneasiness mounted over the following weeks, hampering trade and fanning the fire of Morrison's fears. In a letter dated 12 July, the British consul wrote to his superiors, relaying information from Glover – whom he described as 'fluent in the Japanese language and is on terms of intimacy and friendship with many Japanese of rank, amongst whom he is much esteemed' – that insurgents from Shimabara were planning an attempt on his life. He had declined Glover's offer, he said, to keep watch over the consulate, resigning himself to passing 'my nights in vigilance instead of sleep'. Morrison ended the letter with the following plea:

> The history of the last few years in Japan sufficiently proves that Japanese assassins never fail to attain their end sooner or later, and I ask Her Majesty's government to consider this condition of things and decide whether it is the right position in which public functionaries should be exposed. I ask them to consider in my own case (if it not be too late) my long tropical service, extending over fifteen years, the many risks and dangers I have encountered, and finally

my present exposure to the (moral) certainty of assassination by concealed and treacherous enemies, and to remove me to another sphere of service, where the last condition at least, may be less imminently impending.[39]

The attack by angry samurai would never come to pass, but Morrison submitted a signed statement from a British physician declaring himself constitutionally unfit for the job of consul and recommending that he vacate his post and take up residence in Europe.[40] On 28 July 1863, Edward St. John Neale, who was serving as chargé de affairs during Alcock's absence, granted Morrison permission to retire, on a pension, from the Japan Consular Service.

Morrison returned safely to England and married Emma Louisa Bushby at All Souls Church, London on 5 February 1867.[41] He subsequently settled into a life of retirement, watching from afar as Japan abolished the order of old, overcame the last remnants of civil strife, and embarked on a career of modernization and international cooperation. The 1881 UK Census shows the forty-nine-year-old former consul residing with his wife and eleven-year-old son George A. Morrison in Brighton, Sussex.[42] He died at Nice, France on 20 August 1893 at the age of sixty-three and was buried in the Cimetière Communal de Ste. Marguerite.

Despite his many complaints about life in Nagasaki and hardships in the course of service, Morrison served as the first official British representative in western Japan, as a trailblazer in diplomatic negotiations, and as the architect of institutions and policies in the Nagasaki Foreign Settlement that served as precedents for those adopted throughout the country.

Today, a small sign outside Myōgyōji identifies the temple as the first British Consulate in Japan and the site of the earliest negotiations between Britain and Japan after the opening of Japanese ports in 1859. Morrison, however, is not mentioned.[43]

3

Making safe the settlement: The British troops at Yokohama and their influence on foreign and Japanese society

Nakatake (Hori) Kanami

For Charles Lenox Richardson, the infamous incident at Namamugi in 1862 brought his own East Asian career to a sudden end. For Westerners, however, it marked the beginning of a new era. In response to the events at Namamugi, and in the context of fears of escalating violence against the foreign community, British and French troops were stationed at Yokohama for the first time, and instructed to prepare for the defence of the Foreign Settlement. The history and the lives of these troops have long been of interest to Japanese scholars.[1]

In the Yokohama Foreign Settlement that the troops were now asked to defend, the British composed the majority of the Western residents. Successive British Ministers Rutherford Alcock and Harry Parkes led diplomatic negotiations between Japan and the Western powers for many years during this tumultuous time. Focusing on the British troops stationed in the foreign settlement from 1863, this chapter explores some of the primary and secondary literature that has been produced around their lives in Yokohama. It considers the origins of their deployment, their influence within the foreign settlement and the arguments that have been made about their putative influence over wider Japanese society. The presence of these foreign troops could be considered a form of humiliation for Japan, but did the Japanese government argue for their withdrawal consistently? For their part, did foreign governments' stances about the presence of these troops change across the period? What pressures did their deployment place upon the Japanese government, and what influence did the troops have upon both the foreign and Japanese society? While existing studies offer only superficial answers to these questions, this chapter seeks to draw on a range of documents to re-examine both the deployment of British and French troops to Yokohama, and the consequences of their presence.

Throughout this chapter, I follow the usage of the time in employing the phrase 'foreign residents' to refer to Western residents. Nonetheless, it is important to recognize that from the beginning of the Yokohama Foreign Settlement there were many Chinese working there, often as assistants to Western merchants; by the beginning of the Meiji period (1868–1912), their actual number was larger than that of the British.

The troops come to Yokohama

The question of sending British troops to Yokohama to protect the foreign settlement was brought into focus by Richardson's murder in September 1862. In the hours following the attack, among the foreign residents of Yokohama, calls for various forms of an armed response could be heard. In the absence of Rutherford Alcock, who was on leave in England at the time, Britain's Acting Minister Colonel John Neale faced down demands for immediate punitive action, which most of the merchants in Yokohama favoured. But throughout the months that followed, and running alongside diplomatic attempts to resolve the crisis, the fear of a general attack upon the foreign community at Yokohama persisted. In April 1863, after Britain's formal demands for an apology and compensation arrived at Yokohama, these fears became ever more widespread. For example, N. P. Kingdon, an agent of Dent & Co. in Yokohama wrote to his mother:

> Our minister [Neale] behaved in a very weak and undignified manner with regard to the whole affair and the Community assisted by the French men of war in harbor at the time were nearly taking the matter in their own hands, by marching on the village where the murder was committed at once and attacking the Daimio who had put up there for the night.... In the meantime the British residents were informed of the terms of the ultimatum and advised to make immediate preparations for leaving the Settlement.... During all these days the Settlement was alarmed at the reports of night attacks or wholesale massacres, etc. and our minister himself was alarmed and was taking all the available guards to protect his own person we of course caught the same panic fever and applied for protection and prayed that some men might be sent on shore to guard us from any sudden attack or incendiarism and to guard our embarkation should the attacking force be greater than our means of defense. This was listened to by

the Admiral [Augustus Kuper] in a very cold manner and resulted in his sending on shore 20 men! from a force of 1500! afloat.[2]

In this context, in the summer of 1863 Neale wrote to the Foreign Secretary in London requesting that troops be sent to Yokohama for the defence of British lives and livelihoods. Together with the British Admiral Kuper, the French Admiral Constant Jaurès and France's Minister in Japan, Gustave Duchesne de Bellecourt, Neale also began to negotiate with the shogunate for the right to station their own armed forces in the settlement to protect the lives and properties of its foreign residents. The British and French representatives had agreed to cooperate to defend the settlement at the time of the Namamugi incident, and Neale's agreement along these lines with Duchesne de Bellecourt had enabled him to remove the entire Royal Navy squadron from Yokohama to Kagoshima to conduct military operations there in August 1863. The need for a coordinated response was further underlined by the murder of the French lieutenant, J. J. H. Camus, near Yokohama that October. But there were also tensions in this relationship, and during the negotiations with the shogunate, Duchesne de Bellecourt and Jaurès tried to forestall their co-operators and rivals by calling in French troops first, getting ahead of Britain.[3] In a confidential letter to the US Minister R. H. Pruyn, Duchesne de Bellecourt wrote that he and Jaurès sought to act as conciliators between the government of Japan and the British representatives on this question.[4]

Figure 4 Royal Marines Light Infantry, Parade Ground, Huts, Yokohama, 1864–5. From an album of H. J. L. Norcock, an officer of the Royal Marines Light Infantry, courtesy of the National Museum of the Royal Navy.

For the British, the dispatch of troops to Yokohama also presented a problem of imperial resources. Neale's initial request for troops came to Major-General W. G. Brown, the officer commanding British forces at Shanghai, where Neale had heard some 2,000 troops were on the point of being sent back to England. The situation in Japan, he told Brown, had 'reached a critical and alarming point', and that while British merchants still had the support of Admiral Kuper's squadron, that was 'insufficient to protect the principal foreign settlement in Japan against attack'. He requested as many troops as might be spared from Shanghai, perhaps 1,000; France would look to land 300 in the first instance, and a further 800 from Saigon.[5] Brown, however, refused to let the troops go to Japan. He frankly told Neale that he could not spare a sufficient number of troops to defend Yokohama from a serious attack, and that sending a smaller force would only place it 'in a false and dangerous position'.[6] Indeed, doing so might imperil the safety of Shanghai, and a foreign commercial community he clearly considered to be of greater importance. Both Neale and Kuper kept up the demand for troops throughout the summer, sending appeals to London as well, and the relationship with Brown became somewhat strained. These difficulties remind us of the interconnections between different Western communities around mid-nineteenth-century East Asia, as well as the place of sites such as the Yokohama Foreign Settlement within the wider networks of British and indeed French imperialism.

As the discussion went on, the rationale for having the troops at Yokohama also changed. Neale noted that even when the threat of attack seemed less imminent, their presence could be of use in the indemnity negotiations with the Japanese, 'as want of good faith is a characteristic feature in the conduct of the Government'. By August, the British War Office relented to pressure from the Foreign Office, and Major-General Brown was sent a message by telegraph, through Russia, to send to Japan any men he could spare. Indeed, the Secretary of State for War later suggested that while Brown had been right to refuse Neale's initial request for a large force, he ought to have responded more positively to Neale's later calls for more limited support.[7] In January 1864, HMS *Vulcan* anchored at Yokohama with two companies of the 20th Regiment aboard, and the men moved into the temporary barracks which had been built for them in the centre of the foreign settlement. Four months later, the Japanese built a larger barracks for the British troops on a hill near the Settlement, called 'the Bluff'. James Smyth, who arrived at Yokohama on 22 January as the lieutenant of a detachment of the 20th Regiment, wrote to his father:

> The *Conqueror* arrived here about 10 days ago with 500 marines on board greatly to our relief, and to the disgust of the Japanese. We expect the remainder of our

regiment up in about a fortnight time. The marines are under canvas on a hill over the Settlement. The Japanese are building wooden huts for our regiment, up near the marine camp. The Japanese at first refused to give any barrack for our men. But when they saw the marines arrive, & that we were in earnest, they set about building at once, & in a short time, whole fields of half ripe corn were cut and wooden huts sprung up in every direction, under the hands of 2 or 300 custom house *yaconins* (officials) and coolies. It seems incredible them doing this.[8]

The troops were landed, Neale reassured the Foreign Secretary, 'with no prospect of aggression or hostile undertakings, but as a precautionary measure calculated most effectually to allay constantly recurring panics, threatened attacks of wandering bandits or incendiarism disorganising the trading operations of, and alarming the Foreign Communities, of whom one half are British Subjects'.[9]

On the Japanese side, the stationing of troops was authorized by letters from Sakai Tadamasu, a *wakadoshiyori* (a low-ranking Tokugawa official), to Admirals Kuper and Jaurès. In his letters, Sakai supported the decision of the *Kanagawa bugyō* (the governor who controlled the Yokohama trading area, including the Settlement) to permit British and French troops to be stationed to protect the Settlement on a short term basis. In doing so, the Tokugawa leadership was careful to prevent this undertaking from becoming an official convention or agreement.[10]

Table 1 provides an overview of the different British and French Regiments stationed at Yokohama between 1863 and 1875, as well as indicating their home 'station' during their deployment. Table 2 shows the troops' strengths and movements across this period. The number of foreign troops at Yokohama peaked in August 1864, when Britain, France, Holland and the United States together sent a military expedition to Shimonoseki of about 4,000 naval officers and men, with seventeen warships. Some 2,000 British and 300 regular troops accompanied this naval expedition, for a combined foreign military presence in Japan of 6,300 men – that is to say, several times larger than the foreign merchant population of Yokohama.

Foreign troops and the life of the foreign settlement

Outside of incidents such as the combined Western attacks on Chōshū domain batteries in the Shimonoseki Straits in 1864, the primary function of the foreign troops at Yokohama was to protect the lives and property of the city's foreign

Table 1 'British and French Regiments stationed at Yokohama between 1863 and 1875'

	Army/Navy	Former station	Regiment	1863	1864	1865	1866	1867	1868	1869	1870	1871	1872	1873	1874	1875
Br.	Army	Shanghai	① 67th Regiment (South Hampshire Regiment)		7	12										
			② Royal Artillery		7			----								
			③ Royal Engineers		7			----								
			④ 29th Bombay Native Infantry (Beloochees)		8	12										
		Hong Kong	⑤ 2nd Battalion 20th Regiment (Lancashire Regiment)	1			5									
			⑥ 2nd Battalion 11th Regiment (Devonshire Regiment)				9 4									
			⑦ 2nd Battalion 9th Regiment (Norfolk Regiment)				3		4							
		S.Afr.	⑧ 1st Battalion 10th Regiment (Lincolnshire Regiment)						4			8				
	Navy	England	⑨ Battalion of Royal Marines Light Infantry		5	8						8				3
Fr.	Army	Shanghai	⑩ 3ᵉ Bataillon d' Infanterie Légère d' Afrique	6	6											
	Navy	[Shanghai]	⑪ Infanterie de la Marine	6	6			----								3
			⑫ Fusiliers de la Marine													

Note 1: Number at the ends of solid line means the month.

Note 2: Dashed line means that the time of withdrawal is unknown.

Note 3: ⑪Infanterie de la Marine, French Navy is considered tentatively to have stationed from 1863 through 1875, because there is no documents which indicate its withdrawal between 1864 and 1868.

Table 2 'Troop strengths and movements'

	Regiment	Year & month of (Forces of arrival in Yokohama → and withdrawal)	Accompanying family
①	67th Regiment (South Hampshire Regiment)	1864.07 (6 officers and 167 rank & file; 1864.08 ([] men) → 1864.12 (8 officers and 248 noncommissioned officer & men)	
②	Royal Artillery	1864.07 (1 officer and 60 rank & file) → ([1867 ?])	
③	Royal Engineers	1864.07 (4 rank & file) → ([1867 ?])	
④	29th Bombay Native Infantry (Beloochees)	1864.08 ([] men) → 1864.12 (2 [English] officers, 4 native officers and 151 NCO & men)	
⑤	2nd Battalion 20th Regiment (Lancashire Regiment)	1864.01 (2 batteries);1864.05 (23 officers, 530 NCO & men);1864.07 ([800 men]);1865.09 (24 men) → 1866.04 (1 major, 2 capt, 6 lieut. and 289 NCO & men);1866.05 (1 col., 1 lieut. col., 3 capt, 3 lieut. and 388 NCO & men)	1865.09 (59 women & about 100 children) → 1866.04 (9 women & 15 children);1866.05 (21 women & 21 children)
⑥	2nd Battalion 11th Regiment (Devonshire Regiment)	1865.09 (151 men) → 1866.04 (2 capt, 2 lieut. and 143 NCO & men)	[1865.09] → 1866.04 (3 women & 8 children)
⑦	2nd Battalion 9th Regiment (Norfolk Regiment)	1866.03 (Left wing);1866.05 (19 officers and 340 rank & file) → 1868.04 ([All] men)	1866.05 (8 women & 4 children) → 1868.04 ([All])
⑧	1st Battalion 10th Regiment (Lincolnshire Regiment)	1868.04 (1 col., 27 officers and 652 NCO & men) → 1871.08 (All 934 [or 1,022] persons)	1868.04 (64 women & 103 children) → [1871.08 (All)]
⑨	Battalion of Royal Marines Light Infantry	1864.05 (23 officers and 530 NCO & men) → 1865.08 ([All]) 1871.08 (All 309 persons) → 1975.03 (All)	
⑩	3e Bataillon d'Infanterie Légère d'Afrique	1863.06 (1 battery);1863.07 (2 batteries) → 1864.06 ([All])	
⑪	Infanterie de la Marine	1863.06 ([] men) → 1975.03 (All)	
⑫	Fusiliers de la Marine	1864.06 (50 men) → [1867] ([All])	

Note: [] means that the specific figures are unknown.

residents. In this, their mission was a success, even though their numbers were reduced sharply following the conclusion of the Shimonoseki campaign. In this period, Yokohama became a military sanitarium for the larger reserve of British troops stationed at Hong Kong, taking up an important role in the wider networks of British power in the region. Many British soldiers, and their families, were seriously sick and blamed their illness on the Chinese climate, which was considered too wet, and thus left them prone to diseases such as cholera.[11] This was a serious problem for the officials of the War Office. For example, the 2nd Battalion 11th Regiment, Devonshire Regiment and the rest of the 20th Regiment arrived at Yokohama in September 1865, followed by the 2nd Battalion 9th Regiment, Norfolk Regiment and their wives and children in March 1866. Many of them had been sick in Hong Kong. The *Japan Times' Daily Advertiser*, a newspaper published in Yokohama, reported the arrival of the 11th Regiment in 1865 as follows:

> H.M.S. *Adventure* with 151 men of H.M.'s 11th Regt. and 24 men, 59 women and about 100 children of the 20th arrived yesterday afternoon.... We are sorry to hear that there has been a great deal of sickness on board and that two deaths occurred. The fine climate of Japan will soon re-invigorate the invalids.[12]

Two months later, the *Japan Times* reported on a rumour that the troops were to be transferred again, to Yokohama's disadvantage:

> A rumour is prevalent that a recommendation has gone home, advising the War Office to send down the 20th Regiment to Hongkong and send up the 9th or 11th here in its place.... we have advocated and shall advocate again the establishment here of an extensive sanitarium for India and China, but we emphatically protest against sending such a Regiment as the 2nd 20th to be decimated next summer in Hongkong, while the defense of Yokohama is committed to the care of wasted invalids.[13]

Despite such complaints, these exchanges were carried out. Yet several of the officers stationed at Yokohama refused to return to Hong Kong, and instead requested to be discharged from military service to live in Yokohama with their families. For example, Frederick Davies, a member of the military band of the 20th Regiment, wrote in his memoir:

> In March, 1866, the left wing of the 2nd Battalion 9th Regiment, arrived from Hong-Kong to relieve us, and all the time we remained in Japan together there was a coolness existing between the two Regiments, for our men did not at all like the idea of them turning us out of that fine place, to return to the graveyard as China is appropriately termed. A great many of our men bought their discharge,

and settled down in Yokohama, preferring to take their chance of ever seeing their native country again, than go back to China, just as the fever season was coming on.[14]

The 2nd Battalion 9th Regiment arrived at Yokohama in March 1866. A century later, its regimental history described their situation in those days as follows:

> In 1864 the 2nd Battalion was at Gibraltar, under orders for China. Like the West Indies, Hong Kong is one of the more sought after stations in the 20th century; not so in the 19th. During the Battalion's year in Hong Kong, disease (which accounted for far more soldiers in the 19th century than enemy bullets) struck at the 2/9th with its usual savagery – two officers, 53 other ranks, six women and 32 children died; one officer, 150 other ranks, 26 women and 30 children were invalided home in varying stages of physical debility. To be invalided home in the 20th century, a soldier has to be in a comparatively advanced state of illness; in the 19th it can be assumed that he was at death's door, if not half-way through it.
>
> The health of the British Army was not normally a matter of grave concern to anyone, but the sickness rate of the 2/9th must have attracted some attention, for in March 1866 the Battalion sailed from Hong Kong for the healthier climate of Yokohama in Japan.[15]

Henry James Vincent, a Sergeant-Major of the 20th Regiment, was one of the discharged officers. When he died in 1907, at the age of seventy-seven, his obituary described how he had resigned from the service when the 20th Regiment left Japan in 1866, declining the commission which awaited him in Hong Kong. Instead, he joined the staff of the British Consulate at Yokohama as Superintendent of the Gaol. He held this post in the Foreign Settlement until his retirement on a pension in 1886. His obituary added that 'none followed with a keener interest the exploits of the Japanese Army than did the late Mr Vincent, for he had seen it develop from infancy'.[16]

His wife, Eliza, probably arrived in Yokohama from Hong Kong on 17 September 1865 with her children, along with many other wives and children of men in the Regiment.[17] While living in Yokohama, Henry and Eliza brought up their two sons and three daughters. According to the directory,[18] in 1872, Eliza opened a milliner's and draper's shop in the Settlement, which became Vincent, Bird & Co.; her children later supported her until c.1904. The Vincent family seems to have left Yokohama around 1911; Eliza died in Victoria, British Columbia, in 1922.[19]

Another discharged officer who has been identified is J. R. Anglin, an Irishman who went on to secure a job in the *Japan Gazette*, one of the leading newspapers in Yokohama. He later became its proprietor, having previously worked at the office of the *Japan Times* with his colleagues.[20] A number of other British troops would go on to begin new lives at Yokohama after being discharged.

The arrival of the 1st Battalion 10th Regiment, Lincolnshire Regiment from South Africa in April 1868 came at a time of high political drama in Japan, but nonetheless the troops played no direct part in events. During the Boshin War between the new Meiji Government and supporters of the deposed shogunate, all Western diplomats declared neutrality, and while individual representatives and officials may have harboured their own sympathies in private, the foreign troops continued to stay and protect the Settlement. The changing of the Japanese regime occurred peacefully in Yokohama.

Commerce, 'colour' and conflict: Foreign troops in the settlement community

The great increase in the number of troops stationed at Yokohama created significant commercial opportunities for the local society. Maurice Russel, a British food importer who first came to Yokohama in 1873, recorded this in his memoir in 1909:

> On my arrival in 1873 I found business in a flourishing condition, and money was spent very freely. The merchant in the retail business was not at that time primarily dependent for his trade upon the foreign merchants and residents as is the case to-day. Foreign men-of-war made Yokohama their port of call more frequently than at present – and of course the work of supplying the ships meant a considerable item in the income of the provision dealer who could meet the requirements of the commissariat department. In addition to this there was the provisioning of the foreign regiments which in those days were stationed on the Bluff in the neighbourhood of what is now known as Camp Hill.[21]

In 1873, the Royal Marines Light Infantry consisted of about 300 men. In 1866 we can see an example of the commercial transactions of this time in a notice for tenders by the Commissariat Office for about 1,000 men:

> Tenders... will be received... from persons willing to contract for the undermentioned supplies and services for Her Majesty's troops stationed in Yokohama during the year commencing from the 1st April next, viz.
>
> For the supply of fresh beef; the supply of miscellaneous articles, such as Japanese flour, tea, sugar, forage, fuel and light, etc.; the supply of spirits, ale, etc. for Hospital use; the supply of all other miscellaneous articles required

for Hospital use, such as fresh beef and mutton, flour, fruit and vegetables, groceries, fuel and light, etc.; and for washing and repairing Hospital [and] Barrack bedding etc.[22]

It is clear that the foreign merchants constantly needed the help of the local Japanese merchants to supply these articles and services. Figure 4, which comes from an album in the library of H. J. L. Norcock, an officer of the Royal Marines Light Infantry stationed in Yokohama from 1864 to 1865, shows the British barracks with ten Japanese men and women who are recognized. They seem to be servants.

As part of their daily life in Yokohama, the troops also started to enjoy their leisure activities – sports and theatrical and musical performances – including horse racing, cricket, bowling, shooting, regattas and football. These were leisure activities, but I suppose they were also good measures for training. For indoor amusements they organized Garrison amateur theatrical companies and performed in the Settlement's local theatres. Their military bands played at horse races, theatrical performances and balls. These activities were very much welcomed by the foreign residents.

An article in the *Japan Weekly Mail*, issued just after their evacuation on 2 March 1875, reported that:

> The departure of the Marines has been the great event of the week, and the depression in commercial affairs which is so marked seems increased by the unusual quiet of the settlement. Our landscape has lost 'its dash of red,' and is now colorless enough. The troops will be much missed by the Japanese in and near Yokohama, to whom they were source of considerable revenue, and society loses an agreeable ingredient which, in a dull place like this, it can ill spare.[23]

Nonetheless, the departing troops were clearly not to be missed by all. Some soldiers succeeded in making trouble for the other foreign residents through their riotous behaviour. The following is a record of one incident witnessed by Caspar Brennwald, the Swiss merchant profiled in Chapter 4 of this volume, and recorded in his diary on 26 November 1866. On that day a 'great fire' broke out, which damaged a large part of the Foreign Settlement:

> The behavior of the British soldiers in the garrison, the 9th Regiment, was appalling, the city was actually in a state of pillage by the soldiers. They forced their way into houses everywhere, drank like pigs and plundered whatever they could lay their hands on. We were also robbed but happily I came upon them as they attempted to blow open our chest of money and rob us.[24]

Ernest Satow, a young British interpreter student of the British Legation and a future British Minister in Japan, also witnessed these events, and left similar impressions in his diary:

> [S]oldiers came down from the camp to work at the fire engines. There was no discipline among the men, and no organization existed for dealing with the disaster.... Some of the redcoats behaved disgracefully. They had managed to get hold of liquor, and stood by drinking and jeering, while we civilians did the work they had been brought there to perform.[25]

Brothers in arms? The foreign troops and the Yokohama Volunteer Corps

Despite their established presence in Yokohama in the late 1860s and early 1870s, the foreign troops were not the only Westerners with a responsibility for Settlement defence. On 24 September 1862, soon after word of the Namamugi Incident had reached the Foreign Settlement, its residents, led by the British merchants, established the Yokohama Volunteer Rifle Corps. The *Japan Herald* reported upon their enthusiasm for this undertaking, and an American attempt at independent action, as follows:

> At a meeting held on the 24th ultimo convened for the purpose of concerting measures for the organization of a Volunteer Corps, at which it was resolved 'that any of the Foreign Community willing to join should form themselves into a Rifle Corps for the defense of our lives and properties.' It having then transpired that a Meeting of the American residents had been called by the American Consul at his office on the same subject, it was resolved to adjourn till the result of that meeting should be known.... The chairman read a letter from the American Consul communicating a resolution passed at a Meeting of American citizens, to the effect that they did not consider separate organization desirable.
>
> Mr Gower having come provided with a copy of the rules of the Shanghai Volunteer Corps... and when not objected to or amended, should be adopted as the rules of the Yokohama Volunteers.[26]

While the Corps was established not only for the British but also all foreign residents, the leaders of the Volunteer Corps were leading British merchants of companies such as Jardine, Matheson & Co. and Dent & Co. Woodthorpe Clarke, one of the victims of the Namamugi Incident, also became one of its officers.

Because no foreign soldiers were stationed in Japan at the time, except the Legation guards, all members of the corps were civilians. It was difficult for them to maintain the necessary training, drilling and handling arms. Furthermore, they had to bear the expenses involved following the regulations. There is a document that described their mobilization on one occasion in January 1863:

> It was to the effect that a special band of *ronin* (lordless samurai) had been discovered in the neighbourhood of Yokohama, who had bound themselves with an oath that they would not rest satisfied until they had slain all the foreign diplomatic chiefs. True or false it sufficed to put everyone on the *qui vive*, and the Volunteer corps… turned out and took their share in the duty of patrolling the streets. At that time there seemed to be every probability that they would be called upon before many weeks, perhaps days, were over, to prove themselves worthy brothers of the Shanghai Volunteers, who had faced the Taiping rebels in 1861.[27]

Shanghai had been a treaty port since 1842 and there were frequent exchanges between Shanghai and Yokohama's foreign societies. Many foreign residents in Yokohama came through Shanghai and had connections there – including Charles Lenox Richardson, who died in the Namamugi Incident, and who was for some years a merchant in Shanghai before he came to Yokohama. It is important to pay attention to the close relations of these two cities in East Asia.

It is not clear how long the Volunteer Corps continued its activities, but it did survive the arrival of regular soldiers to Yokohama. At the beginning of 1864, a Yokohama Mounted Volunteers Corps was established at the suggestion of Major Mears of the 2nd Battalion 20th Regiment, who had arrived in Yokohama in command of a detachment that January.[28] This new corps seems to have been a successor to the initial Rifle Corps, though it did not train seriously before 1866. This may have been due to the presence of an unusually large number of soldiers in the intervening years, with the 20th Regiment, other British forces, the Royal Marines Light Infantry and French troops all standing ready in the event of a great crisis in Japan at the time. In 1866 the Volunteer Corps was fully supported by the Regiment, and was invited to participate in drill exercise with both foreign and Japanese troops at Yokohama:

> On Saturday afternoon the 6th inst. [January 1866] the first Drill meeting of the Yokohama Mounted Volunteers took place on the Garrison parade ground. Drill commenced at 3 p.m. in the presence of a large number of officers and soldiers of the Garrison and many civilian residents not belonging to the corps.… Men and horses acquitted themselves very creditably indeed and the corps was complimented by Colonel Browne commandant of the Garrison at the close of the drill.[29]

The following notices in the English-language press give further indications of the Corps' activities:

> Yokohama Mounted Volunteer Corps – Until further notice the members of this Corps will meet for drill on the following days. – Mounted parade at the Bluff every Tuesday at 4 p.m. Dismounted Drill for sword exercise at No.5 every Thursday at 5 p.m.
>
> For the Committee, H. S. J. Browne
> Yokohama, 6 March 1866.[30]

> The troops in garrison, English and French sailors, and the Mounted Volunteers are to have a grand field-day together shortly on ground on the other side of the *Tokaido* (the main highway from Yedo to Kyoto). The Japanese government have asked permission for a thousand of their troops to brigade with our people, and we believe that this has been granted: about 2,500 men altogether will be in the field and we anticipate a very interesting spectacle. The volunteer cavalry will do outpost or vedette duty, we presume, and doubtless on such an occasion all will turn out. We recommend every one who has not yet obtained his uniform, to get it at once.[31]

After the 20th Regiment left Japan for Hong Kong in May 1866, there were few articles about the Corps' activities in the local newspapers. The Yokohama Mounted Volunteers Corps seems to have become inactive, perhaps after losing army support.

What attitude did other nationalities take to the Volunteer Corps led by the British? While it made a contribution to Settlement defence, it could clearly also be a source of friction among Westerners. A good example is provided by that of the first Prussian diplomat to Japan, Max A. S. von Brandt, who stayed in Japan, mostly in Yokohama from 1862 to 1874. In his memoir, published in 1901,[32] he made a number of interesting observations (the following is my summary from its Japanese translation):

> Admiral Kuper, who came to Yokohama from Hong Kong in March 1863, deployed a scout and a sentry at the entrance to guard the Settlement. Then he requested the Volunteer corps to join them without referring to foreign diplomats. He thought that this action threatened the neutrality of the Settlement and in the case that a military clash had occurred between Britain and Japan, the Settlement became the only safe area for the other nationalities including the Prussians. When Kuper sent a guard to a Prussian merchant's house, Brandt finally made an objection to him and rejected it. The Prussian residents participating in the corps seemed not to understand that their actions would

cause trouble and seemed to enjoy acting as soldiers because they had too much free time caused by the slow pace of business in the port. Brandt persuaded them not to participate.[33]

Brandt also wrote that he, a young diplomat of an emerging nation, had experienced the unpleasantness shown by the arrogant attitudes of British diplomats. He made every effort to perform his duty as a diplomat until his transfer to China as a minister in 1874. The following describes some of Brandt's key decisions and actions in 1868, the year of the Meiji Restoration:

> In 1868, when the Boshin War broke out, the representatives of foreign countries in Japan declared neutrality. Brandt, on the other hand, took actions such as permitting the people from his country to use the treaty port of Niigata, occupied and managed by the *Ōuetsu Reppan Dōmei* (the Alliance of Northern Domains) acting as though he was in opposition to the British Minister, Harry Parkes, who supported the restored government. Recent discovery of new historical materials reveals that Brandt intended to negotiate secretly with the northern alliance domains of Aizu and Shōnai.[34]

Brandt's memoir reminds us of the importance of studying the British and French troops in Yokohama from a broader international perspective, and to explore how these troops were considered by other, less represented, nationalities.

The British and French troops also served as police for the foreign community. In 1865 the foreign residents set up a self-governing organization, the Municipal Council, with three sub committees: a Finance Committee, a Sanitary and Road Committee and a Police Committee. Each of the British and French troops supplied a few soldiers to the Police Committee. The following extract from the Report of the Police Committee explains the arrangement:

> It is understood that the Commander of H.B.M.'s troops stationed here, will allow the present constabulary force at the British Consulate to be kept up, and a like force will be established at the French Consulate. The respective Consuls of the nationalities just named, have kindly offered to give their constable instructions to patrol the streets, and to arrest offenders against the ordinances of the Council, and generally to preserve order in the settlement.
>
> Your Committee then proposes to appoint a superintendent and three sergeants, who, together with the Consular Constables, will compose a sufficient force for present purposes.
>
> The estimated expense of the organization is about $470 a month.... The present scheme will remain effective only so long as men from the foreign regiments are available, and the Council must be prepared at any time for their withdrawal.[35]

Just two years later, the Municipal Council failed because of its shortage of funds and lack of official authority. Members had to surrender the council's function to the Japanese local government. The soldiers who had been assigned to the now defunct Police Committee were re-hired as policemen and continued to serve until their departure from Japan in 1875. The following newspaper article reveals aspects of the policing of the foreign society in Yokohama after 1875:

> Our Municipal director[36] invites applications from persons desirous of serving the community in the capacity of constables, in lieu of the French and English Marines now engaged in the duty.... The motto of the force for the future would seem to be 'cheap and nasty',... It is to be regretted that the necessity arises for parting with the men now engaged in the task, who have conducted themselves in a very exemplary manner, and exercised the delicate and sometimes difficult duties they have been called upon to perform in a manner which has left little or nothing to be desired. We fear it will be found impossible to replace these men with others of an equally good sample, at the figure offered.[37]

In this regard, the troops had carried out an important mission as policemen in the Yokohama Foreign Settlement during the *bakumatsu* and Meiji Restoration periods.

The foreign troops and Japanese society

Shortly after the evacuation of the troops in 1875, an article in the *Japan Weekly Mail* declared that the troops 'will be much missed by the Japanese in and near Yokohama, to whom they were a source of considerable revenue'.[38] It seems likely that the foreign merchants who contracted with the troops stationed at Yokohama subcontracted the provision of certain services from local Japanese merchants. The foreign merchants contracted to arrange deliveries of fresh beef, Japanese flour, tea, sugar, fruit and vegetables, as well as washing and repairing bedding for the barracks and the hospital. In this sense, and in particular at times of greater military deployment, the presence of the foreign troops was a significant source of revenue to the local Japanese community.

An example of this is provided by the apparent success story of a Japanese laundry-owner named Wakizawa Kinjirō. He came to Yokohama from the Shinshū area, present-day Nagano Prefecture, and started his laundry business in 1865. He learned the Western style of washing from his elder brother, who had already opened a laundry in Yokohama. Wakizawa's best customer was the 20th Regiment. It is not clear whether he contracted with them directly, or worked through foreign merchants. Either way, he achieved great success and later became a councillor in a local assembly.³⁹

At the same time, the foreign troops occasionally made trouble for Yokohama's Japanese residents. It is difficult to find articles reporting these troubles in the English-language local press. But evidence of disturbances can nonetheless be found, and we might assume it to have been more widespread than was reported. One example of such a disturbance appeared in Shanghai's *North China Herald* in the summer of 1864:

> By advices from Yokohama dated the 30th ultimo, we learned that a soldier of the 20th Regiment has been sentenced to six months imprisonment for assaulting a native farmer. We congratulated the authorities on the promptness with which they punished the outrage.⁴⁰

Further examples can be found in the 1870s, this time from one of the first Japanese newspapers in Yokohama. In 1872 the *Mainichi Shimbun*, Japan's first daily, reported on:

> An attempted case by three British soldiers [which] happened near the Yokohama Settlement. They attempted to assault the wife of a Japanese rice keeper and to rob money while he was absent. He came home just in time and neighbors gathered to see what happened. As one of the soldiers was carrying a rifle, he resigned himself to their violence against him, and they escaped. The victim visited the offices of the British Consul to explain what had happened. It was heard that the Consul replied to him that he would make inquiries and deal with this case properly.⁴¹

Several similar cases were reported in the *Mainichi*. In 1873, it informed readers of another occasion on which, with no provocation, a Japanese officer working in the Yokohama Custom House was violated on the street by a soldier of the Royal Marines stationed at the Bluff. As he could speak English, the Japanese man visited the commander at the Barracks, giving him details of the assault, and asked him to punish the criminal. The commander took him to their parade ground and asked him to point out the man involved. He did so, and his commander punished him. The newspaper concluded the tale by remarking upon the importance of learning English for the young Japanese generation.⁴² Such is the fragmentary evidence on the relationship between the foreign troops and the local Japanese population; enough, perhaps, to conclude that the troops' influence on Japanese living in Yokohama was commercially and socially significant.

An important question about the broader significance of the foreign troops stationed at Yokohama in this critical period of Japanese history concerns their putative influence on the modernization of the Japanese army. The shogunate certainly requested that British troops train men in their nascent army, and the two forces often drilled together. In those days, a great worldwide evolution of firearms was unfolding. The British Army and Royal Marines were equipped with the latest guns: first muzzle-loading and later, breech-loading rifles. It would thus have been useful for shogunal forces, and later those of the Meiji government, as well as representatives of domains who wanted to introduce new rifles into their own forces, to directly observe the training of the British troops. However, according to Suzuki Jun, who studied the condition and development of Western-style military systems and technologies within various *han* (feudal domains) during the early years of the Meiji period, British troops had limited influence.[43] Tokugawa officials ultimately decided to emulate the French army system and invited French officers to serve as instructors. They arrived from France in 1867.

Suzuki pointed out the important impact of the French army system on the modernization of the Japanese army. A new army trained on this system needed volunteers, both samurai and commoners, consisting of physically strong men. The creation of a Japanese national army thus consequently helped to dissolve the feudal system and bring about an evolution of Japanese society.

The coordinated withdrawal of the British and French troops

At the beginning of 1875 British and French diplomats unexpectedly proposed to jointly withdraw their troops the following March. As Kishi Motokazu has written, it is still not definitively known why they reached this decision, but a closer examination of some of the relevant primary documents is revealing.

Hora Tomio, pioneer a historian of this subject, drew upon a range of published and unpublished Japanese sources, but did not make use of foreign diplomatic documents. In analysing the reasons for the withdrawal of the foreign troops, he concluded that Britain and France did so because they had surmised that retaining their forces was a serious affront to Japanese sovereignty, and a source of humiliation. British and French diplomats recognized that, with the Meiji Restoration, the new government was building a new Japan and gaining a solid footing as a nation governed by an absolutist Emperor system.[44] I think Hora's view is one-sided, which emerged from his limited use of diplomatic sources.

Kishi Motokazu has examined British diplomatic documents dealing with the negotiations, which started in May 1869 at the request of the British Minister in Japan, Harry Parkes.[45] Parkes met Sanjō Sanetomi, a leading noble in the Meiji government, and implied that he wanted to hand over his duties to protect the foreign residents to the Japanese government. However, Sanjō voiced objections to this withdrawal.[46] From June 1869, Iwakura Tomomi,[47] another leading noble and a high-ranking diplomatic official, took charge of the meetings with Parkes (and with F. O. Adams, *Charge d'affaires* in Parkes's absence). At this time, the Meiji government passively accepted that the presence of the foreign troops was necessary, considering the instability of the political and social situation in Japan. They recognized officially that the presence of foreign troops infringed upon Japanese sovereignty, but unofficially remained opposed to their premature withdrawal. In adopting this position, Meiji leaders recognized that during a period marked by their ongoing efforts to implement centralization and impose Meiji government authority over all of Japan, the foreign troops performed a useful, stabilizing function. Parkes, too, thought that the most realistic way forward was not a complete withdrawal, but rather a reduction of the numbers of troops stationed in Yokohama. The Meiji government's consent in practice permitted a continuation of the foreign troop presence.

Nonetheless in 1871 a significant change and reduction in the number of troops nonetheless occurred. The 10th Regiment, about 1,000 men in total, was withdrawn and replaced by about 300 men of the Royal Marines Light Infantry. This change was not the result of discussions between British representatives and their Japanese counterparts, but instead flowed from a change of circumstances on the British side. Prime Minister William Gladstone's Cabinet adopted a fiscal restraint policy, and a British army commander in China also requested the transfer of part of the troops stationed in Yokohama to China, because of the politically unstable situation there after the Tianjin Massacre in 1870.[48] Therefore at both the beginning and the end of the story of the Yokohama foreign troops, the importance of the wider imperial and Chinese contexts is clear. Drawing on French diplomatic correspondence, Richard Sims has also briefly explained the background of the withdrawal mainly from the perspective of the European political situation, the rivalry between France and Britain, the poverty of their military budgets, and the pressures of the Franco-Prussian War.[49]

Kokaze Hidemasa has put forward a different explanation, stressing the ways in which US actions threatened British leadership among the Western nations in Japan.[50] In 1873 a Postal Convention between Japan and the United States was concluded. When this came into effect in 1875, the American postal offices in

Yokohama and other Foreign Settlements were closed. But the British and French continued to keep their offices open. In the *bakumatsu* era there was no modern postal system in Japan, so the foreigners built their own offices. Kokaze has pointed to the place of this Convention in the politics of repealing the unequal treaties; it offered proof that Japan had become a 'civilized' country. In January 1875, the US Minister in Japan also offered to repay the huge reparations Japan had paid after the Shimonoseki Campaign of 1864. (The money was indeed returned in 1883.) Kokaze suspected that these activities forced the British to adopt an appeasement policy towards Japan, and that the withdrawal of troops was one instance.

Kokaze's hypothesis offers intriguing avenues for future research. To explore this question further, it is necessary to consider the end of the foreign troop presence in Yokohama from a more global perspective, or within the framework of international relations. Future researchers may need to consult further the documents not only of the countries directly concerned – Japan, Britain and France – but also those of other countries, such as the United States and Germany.

Conclusion

The Namamugi Incident, whose victims were British, led to the stationing of British and French troops in Yokohama for twelve years. Their mission was to protect the lives and properties of foreign residents, most of whom were British merchants. And for the British diplomats it was also important to keep open newly established trade links with Japan.

At its peak, the number of troops totalled about 2,300 men, consisting of 2,000 British and 300 French. There were about 500 foreign residents in Yokohama when the Shimonoseki Campaign occurred in September 1864. In 1865, the purpose of their deployment changed. For the British Station in China, Yokohama became an attractive military sanitarium for troops and their families, seeking respite from the perceived harsher climate of Hong Kong.

Within the Yokohama Foreign Settlement community, the military provided opportunities for both commercial and cultural activities, though some soldiers made trouble for the residents. To the local Japanese society, they provided significant commercial opportunities but were also the source of numerous incidents.

As I have shown in this chapter, the Tokugawa and Meiji regimes both viewed the presence of Anglo-French troops as a national humiliation but accepted the

Western military presence on practical grounds. Why British and French leaders chose to withdraw their troops in 1875 remains unclear, and requires further research.

Acknowledgements

I wish to express my gratitude to Ms Mizuyo Oyama and Mr Michael Wace for their help translating my original essay into English. I also thank Dr Robert Hellyer and Dr Robert Fletcher, our editors, for their helpful advice.

4

Between trade and diplomacy

The commercial activities of the Swiss silk merchants Siber and Brennwald in late Edo and early Meiji Japan

Fukuoka Mariko and Alexis Schwarzenbach

Introduction

This chapter focuses on the origins of the Swiss raw silk trading house, Siber & Brennwald, established in Yokohama in 1866.[1] Founded in the last years of the Tokugawa reign, the company became one of the most important raw silk exporters in Meiji Japan. Data documenting the overall volumes of raw silk exported from Yokohama between 1867–8 and 1884–5 shows that Siber & Brennwald ranked first among twenty foreign firms, exporting 19,863 bales of raw silk during the ten silk seasons covered by the survey.[2] In 1903, the successor firm of Siber & Brennwald, Siber, Wolff & Co., was awarded a certificate of commendation from the Dainippon [Greater Japan] Silk Foundation. It praised the contribution of the company to the development of the Japanese raw silk industry, highlighting its efforts to improve the quality of Japanese raw silk by helping to introduce modern European silk reeling systems as well as its longstanding efforts to pioneer the highly important US market.[3] For most of the twentieth century, the company was called SiberHegner. In 2002 it became a component part of DKSH Holding Ltd., to this day one of the largest Swiss trading houses with strong ties to Asia.[4]

The nineteenth-century success of a Swiss trading house in Japan comes as a surprise.[5] Given the importance of raw silk as Japan's top export commodity until well into the twentieth century, we might expect British and US trading houses to have dominated this market.[6] They had more experience dealing with Asian commodities and a naval presence in East Asia, while landlocked Switzerland had no navy and acquired a small commercial fleet only in the course of the Second World War.[7] The fact that the newly founded Siber & Brennwald became a well-established player and a leading exporter of Japanese raw silk thus needs to be explained.[8]

Siber & Brennwald was founded by two merchants from the Swiss Canton of Zürich, Caspar Brennwald (1838–99) and Hermann Siber (1842–1918). Brennwald was the secretary of the first Swiss trading mission to Japan in 1864, and served as the Swiss Consul General in Japan from 1866 to 1881.[9] He kept a diary from 1862 to 1878, recording his trading and diplomatic activities extending from his first visit to his later life in Japan, as well as his business trips to Europe and the United States. Since 2008 a Yokohama Archives of History based team, which includes Fukuoka Mariko, has been engaged in translating Brennwald's diaries into Japanese, after DKSH Holding's Japan branch presented the archive with a typescript copy.[10] Both the handwritten originals and the transcript are today held at the Swiss headquarters of DKSH in Zürich.[11] This chapter also draws on an extensive series of letters by Brennwald's business partner, Hermann Siber. Between 1862 and 1871, Siber regularly wrote to his elder brother and business partner, Gustav Siber-Gysi (1827–72). Over 300 letters survive, some in the Swiss headquarters of DKSH in Zürich, and the larger part in the city's Zentralbibliothek.[12] In the course of a research project on the history of the Zürich silk industry led by Alexis Schwarzenbach the letters were transcribed.[13]

Despite the wealth of information provided by these sources, they also have limitations. First, both sources cover only the 1860s and 1870s: the Brennwald diary was kept until 1878, three years before the author left Japan to return to Europe, while Siber's letters end in December 1871, shortly before he returned to Zürich after the death of his brother.[14] This means that the firm's history from the 1880s to the turn of the century must be left unanalysed, while the founding period can be examined in detail. The lack of material covering the later Meiji period is frustrating, since the firm remained a significant force in overseas trade, pioneering the vast US market for Japanese silk. Nonetheless, the earlier period allows us to explore how Siber & Brennwald, in competition with larger Western firms, secured a foothold in Japan's export trade.

Secondly, our sources also lack specific evidence on the company's financial performance. Apart from sporadic information about successful and unsuccessful deals and a single balance sheet drawn up by Siber, there are no serial records such as annual balance sheets to throw light on the profitability of the company.[15] If this excludes the possibility of quantitative analysis of the company, a transnational and cultural history approach based on a close reading of these sources does allow for valuable insights into the inner workings of a commodity trading house in the second half of the nineteenth century.[16]

The Founders

Caspar Brennwald was born in 1838 in Männedorf on the shore of Lake Zürich. His father was a master baker and appears to have died by the time Brennwald began his commercial career.[17] He first worked for the cotton trading house, Hunziker & Company in Aarau, a small provincial capital between Zürich and Basel. In that capacity, he travelled widely throughout Europe dealing in cotton.[18] While working for Hunziker, he appears to have fallen in love with his employer's daughter. As nothing came of the union, however, Brennwald did not become a partner in Hunziker's business.[19] A clear indication that Brennwald was looking for a new career was revealed in October 1862 when at the age of twenty-four, he was appointed by the Swiss federal government as the secretary of the first Swiss trading mission to Japan.[20] The Swiss trading mission was headed by the Neuchatel lawyer and politician Aimé Humbert-Droz.[21] Together with four Swiss merchants, Brennwald and Humbert-Droz departed Marseilles in

Figure 5 Hermann Siber, as a young man (undated).

Source: DKSH Japan K.K., Tokyo.

Figure 6 Caspar Brennwald as a young man (undated).

Source: DKSH Holding Ltd., Zürich.

December 1862, travelling via Egypt, India, Singapore and China to reach Japan. The delegation arrived in Yokohama in April 1863.[22] The aim of the mission was to establish diplomatic relations with Japan and a trade deal allowing Swiss citizens to do business there along the lines of similar treaties Japan had already signed with other Western powers.[23] However, as the Japanese government was reluctant to conclude further trade deals and even wanted to annul existing ones in order to assuage public opposition to the growing foreign presence, the Swiss mission was left frustrated and stranded in Yokohama for almost a year.[24]

Brennwald made use of this unexpected delay to compile a series of reports on the Japanese economy, later published by the Swiss government to foster trade. While one report dealt with imports to Japan, two others focused on the main possible export commodities, silk and tea.[25] The importance of the silk market was underlined by a special report on silkworm rearing in Japan, for which Brennwald did substantial research among European traders in Yokohama.[26] Once negotiations with the Japanese government finally got underway in early 1864, the Swiss delegation accomplished its mission by establishing diplomatic relations and securing a trade deal with Japan in February 1864.[27] Although Humbert-Droz immediately returned home, Brennwald stayed five more months in Yokohama before departing for Switzerland in July 1864.[28] Upon arriving home several months later, he began a job search, receiving offers from several Swiss trading houses. Nonetheless, he yearned to establish himself as a trader in Yokohama, ideally with a partner who could complement his own knowledge in cotton with an expertise in silk.[29] That person was Hermann Siber.

Siber was born in 1842 in the northern Italian city of Bergamo. There, his Swiss father, together with a business partner, had established a silk trading house, Zuppinger, Siber & Co.[30] In addition to dealing in raw silk, the company operated a major silk throwing factory with no less than 35,000 spindles.[31] Located in the heart of the Italian silk rearing district, Zuppinger, Siber & Co. was also closely connected to the large Swiss silk weaving industry of the Canton of Zürich,[32] where the company also had an office and sold large quantities of raw and thrown silk to local textile manufacturers.[33] Yet the outbreak of pébrine silkworm disease in the 1850s seriously damaged European silk production. In order to fill the gap created by this crisis, European traders began to import large quantities of East Asian silks, mainly from China and after 1859 also from Japan. In the 1860s, London emerged as one of the major European trading points for East Asian silks.[34]

In October 1862, Hermann Siber, after completing his school and university studies in Zürich, went to London, aged twenty, to work for the trading and banking house, Fred. Huth & Co.[35] One of the main reasons for Siber's stay in London was to familiarize himself with East Asian silks. Employed in the silk department of Fred. Huth & Co., he was constantly 'hanging around the warehouses' inspecting bales of raw silk from overseas.[36] As silk is a natural product and thus not standardized, it was essential to inspect it in a good light. Thus as Siber explained to his brother, when London's heavily polluted air plunged the city into darkness, inspecting silk became impossible.[37] He later reported that 4,000 new bales of raw silk had arrived, all of which he wanted to inspect individually.[38]

Siber stayed in London for two years, building valuable expertise about East Asian raw silk varieties ranging from Chinese tsatlees and kahings to Japanese maibashis (Maebashi), ōshios (Ōshū) and other, unspecified varieties. At the beginning, he sometimes overestimated the quality of a given lot: more than once, he faced criticism and had to justify why he sent particular silk shipments to Bergamo.[39] Over time, however, the home office issued fewer complaints and Siber hatched a new plan: to establish himself as an independent trader and go to Asia. In letters to his brother, he discussed going to either China or Japan, but made no decision before his stay in London ended in December 1864.[40]

On 24 July 1865, Caspar Brennwald noted in his diary: 'Hermann Sieber [sic] spent the whole afternoon with me; during our conversations I proposed to do something together in Japan, to which he is not uninclined, but he wishes to talk it over with his brother.'[41] In the following days, the two met several times. Brennwald also had discussions with Siber's older brother, Gustav.[42] Brennwald's diary noted: 'This morning I had a conversation with Mr. Siber concerning an association with his brother Hermann for Japan. The project makes a lot of sense to him if we can find a rich London house readily supporting us with money.'[43] This highlights the importance of international capital to trading houses. In the following weeks, Brennwald and Siber contacted their extensive commercial networks in Zürich and London. In Switzerland, they approached several manufacturers who were prepared to send them goods for sale in Japan, and they were able to get an important bank guarantee. Brennwald's diary notes a meeting with Caspar Huber, director of the Kreditanstalt, today's Credit Suisse, which offered them a credit for 100,000 to 150,000 francs.[44] In London, they also established connections with local manufacturers to consign goods, and found another important creditor for their project, Meynerzhagen, director of Fred. Huth & Co. He offered them not only credit but also allowed them to refer to his respectable London banking house in a circular announcing the beginning of their joint enterprise.[45]

Gustav Siber soon arrived in London too and a contract between Hermann Siber and Caspar Brennwald was drawn up.[46] Although the contract does not survive, the correspondence between Hermann Siber and his brother shows that the two partners were made equal beneficiaries of the company, despite not investing the same amount of money.[47] While Siber invested 200,000 francs mostly taken out of the family firm in Bergamo, Brennwald was able to invest 50,000 francs which added up to a total of their own capital of £10,000.[48] Brennwald received part of that sum (20,000 francs) as payment for his participation in the Swiss diplomatic mission to Japan, with the rest probably derived from his inheritance.[49] Siber's and Brennwald's own capital was matched with a blank credit from Fred. Huth for £15,000.[50] Together with the Swiss bank credit and the fact that Zuppinger, Siber & Co. had issued a guarantee 'for each kind of eventuality', the new company could thus start on a sound financial basis.[51]

Once the name of the company, Siber & Brennwald, had been decided upon by drawing lots in order to determine which surname was to be mentioned first,[52] the two business partners printed 100 copies of their first circular:

> We beg to inform you that we intend to establish ourselves in the beginning of next year at the port of Yokohama, in Japan, under the firm of SIBER & BRENNWALD, as General Commission Merchants. A thorough knowledge of the chief Import and Export articles of that country, and an adequate capital, will, we hope, enable us to do justice to any business entrusted to our care, and we shall use our best endeavours to give satisfaction to those friends who favour us with their confidence. Messrs. Fred. Huth & Co., of London, have permitted us to refer to them, and will be kind enough to give you any further information which you may require.[53]

The circular went to all major London banks with links to Japan, and on their way home to Switzerland, Siber and Brennwald stopped in Paris to introduce themselves to the main French banks with Asian business ties.[54]

As the two partners set up their business, Brennwald used his contacts in the Swiss government to assure that he would become Switzerland's consul general in Japan.[55] On 15 February 1866, the day after Brennwald's nomination was officially confirmed, the two partners set out for Japan, arriving just over two months later. Brennwald faced unanticipated difficulties in assuming his diplomatic post. During his absence from Japan, a Prussian citizen, Rudolf Lindau, had taken charge of Swiss diplomatic affairs. Lindau not only refused to step down, but retained a title deed the shogunate had issued to him for the construction of a Swiss consular building. A long and tedious litigation ensued before this document was annulled and re-issued by the shogunate.[56] While the litigation was ongoing, Siber & Brennwald bought another property, Lot 90A of Yokohama's foreign settlement, which was to remain the company's base until the 1923 Kantō earthquake destroyed large parts of the city.[57]

Yokohama was a mere fishing village when in 1859, the shogunate decided to make it a major port for Japan's interaction with foreign traders.[58] Possessing a deep sea harbour and within a day's reach by boat of the Tokugawa capital at Edo, Yokohama had been strategically chosen by the shogunate as a main thoroughfare for new interactions with the outside world.[59] Constructed along a straight waterfront, the city's centre held docks, the custom house and other government buildings. The foreign settlement lay to the southwest, with the Japanese city to the northwest. In her chapter in this book, Sano Mayuko explores Rutherford Alcock's ultimately unsuccessful attempt to prevent the shogunate from making Yokohama, and not his choice of nearby Kanagawa, the main foreign settlement.

Early trading in Yokohama

Silk had brought Siber and Brennwald to Yokohama, and their diaries and letters show they immediately began preparations to buy raw silk for export to Europe. On 1 May 1866, two weeks after their arrival in Japan, Brennwald noted that the mail from England of 12 March had brought 'a great many letters of credit from Lyon and London for silk purchases'.[60] The intense preparation of their commercial venture in Europe was thus paying off. Nonetheless, due to high demand, Siber found it difficult to obtain the commodities he desired at the prices set by their customers.[61] Half a year after their arrival in Japan, Brennwald noted: 'Today Siber buys silk for the first time.'[62] In October 1866, Siber's letters mention the company's first shipment of thirteen bales of raw silk, presumably for a French customer in Lyon.[63] Further shipments followed, including sixty bales exported to Europe in December 1866.[64]

In addition to raw silk, exporting silkworm eggs was a major business. This was directly linked to the pébrine crisis damaging raw silk production in French and Italian silk-rearing districts. As Japanese silkworms were not particularly affected by the disease, European traders and governments began buying large quantities of silkworm eggs mounted on cardboard. Both Brennwald and Siber had anticipated the importance of this line of business.[65] Thanks to Brennwald's contacts in the Swiss government, the partners were able to buy silkworm eggs not only for private entrepreneurs but also for the governments of the Swiss cantons of Ticino and Grisons, Switzerland's main silk rearing regions.[66] Siber & Brennwald had entered the trade at exactly the right moment, as the market for silkworm eggs began to boom in 1864, reaching a peak at the end of the decade.[67] In May 1867, the Canton of Ticino ordered silkworm eggs for no less than 100,000 francs[68] and in August 1868, Siber proudly told his brother that in silkworm eggs they were making 'a solid business & for ourselves a good name because our cartons are exquisitely beautiful & most Italians want to buy some'.[69]

Siber and Brennwald quickly realized that Japanese language skills were important in order to conclude successful purchases of raw silk and silkworm eggs. In China, European merchants often depended upon *compradores*, bilingual intermediaries, to facilitate transactions. In Japan, in addition to using *compradores* from China, Japanese intermediaries, *banto* or *kodzukai*, played an important role.[70] They expected their European employers to acquire some working knowledge of the local language.[71] This was probably why Siber began learning Japanese after arriving in Yokohama.[72] To his brother he explained: 'In view of the fact that I shall probably have to stay in this country for many more years, [...] it is my aim to learn the language as well as possible.'[73] A month after his arrival, Siber described his daily routine. 'Each morning at 7, I go for a little walk into the Japanese city where I try to make the acquaintance of the silk merchants, thereafter I return to our charmingly located bungalow [...] for a cup of tea and a sandwich.'[74] In addition to learning Japanese, Siber also scrutinized Japanese raw silk production methods. Returning from a four-day excursion on horseback to the Yokohama hinterland, he told his brother that in Japan mulberry trees were kept much shorter than in Italy, noting his surprise at 'the enormous care dedicated to [silkworm] rearing, a point in which Italy is certainly far behind Japan'.[75]

Given the firm's initial difficulties in buying raw silk, Siber & Brennwald also started exporting tea, the country's second most important commodity.[76] In July 1866, Siber told his brother that Siber & Brennwald planned to ship no less than £2,000 worth of tea to the United States.[77] Siber's letters and Brennwald's diary also mention coal, Japan's third most important export commodity, but more with regard to imports than to exports.[78] In addition, Siber & Brennwald sometimes exported silk waste used for the production of schappe silk and unspecified curios.[79]

Another important export business hinted at in one letter by Siber, but for which there is no evidence that the company became active, is the transport of Japanese citizens overseas.[80] Given the difficulty of entering the silk trade and in view of the California Gold Rush which led to large-scale immigration of Chinese labourers into the United States, Siber wrote to his brother four months after his arrival, on the prospects of 'the human trade, for as the Japanese are now free to leave their country if they want to, it may be possible to engage in a profitable coolie business to the American west coast [...], similar to the one which is formidably done from China.'[81] Thus during the firm's initial trial-and-error phase, Siber & Brennwald dabbled in exporting tea, coal and perhaps even transporting people, but none became regular activities of the firm.

Imports: Textiles, foodstuffs, steamers and arms

While still in Europe, Siber and Brennwald had made connections with many manufacturers to solicit imports of goods into Japan. In Switzerland, they contacted producers of various kinds of textiles, among them mouchoirs, printed indienne cottons, Turkey reds as well as taffachellas, multicoloured striped cotton textiles.[82] In Britain they networked with tobacco dealers, Manchester cotton manufacturers and Bradford wool merchants, taking some of their commercial samples with them to Yokohama.[83]

Textiles became an especially important product imported by Siber & Brennwald. Cloth frequently appears in the Brennwald diaries, though seldom with references to details beyond colour.[84] In the only surviving balance sheet, cloth contracts amount to 127,000 francs or 20 per cent of the company's business.[85] Many cloth contracts were destined for military use as the shogunate began to use European-style uniforms.[86] However, in a letter to his brother, Siber also hinted at more widespread changes in fashion among Japanese elites. In November 1866 Siber asked:

> Could you not arrange for consignations in black cloth for us? I believe that this is going to be a very important article because acting like a European has become very fashionable ever since the new tycoon 'Motsbashi' has come to power [i.e. the last Tokugawa shogun Yoshinobu[87]]. Apparently he himself walks around in European clothes in Osaka and all his officers are already wearing black European clothes. [88]

Siber & Brennwald also imported a wide range of other products, and from the letters to his brother it appears that especially Siber was keen on taking up any opportunities that arose to counterbalance the company's exports. Imports included foodstuffs such as flour, sugar or rice, the latter at times imported from Hong Kong or Saigon, but also cotton, iron, saltpetre, medicines and shoes.[89] As these ventures often proved unprofitable, Siber had to justify them to his brother, repeatedly telling him that certain risks had to be taken.[90] In April 1867, he reported: 'I was extremely busy with the sale of sugar and rice as [we] had chartered an entire ship. Unfortunately we are losing money on this deal because all of a sudden and without any plausible reason <u>white</u> rice fell 30 per cent, while the price of black rice has gone up.'[91]

After 1869, Siber & Brennwald embarked on a new line of imports which they hoped would prove very profitable: the sale of steamers. During the Boshin War (1868–9), Siber & Brennwald made considerable profits chartering steamers on behalf of certain domains, while many other Western firms in Yokohama earned even more profit by selling ships. (As mentioned in the Introduction, William Alt also profited from selling sail and steamships in Nagasaki.) In February 1869, Siber & Brennwald sold its first steamer, *Snap*, to the 'prince of Bizen' (the lord of the Okayama domain), for a 4,000 dollar profit.[92] The firm later bought the *Wilhelmina Emma*, selling it to the Kokura domain in December 1870 after difficult negotiations (because the vessel turned out to be very slow, and could only be disposed of at a loss).[93] Nevertheless, Siber continued to entertain high hopes for the steamer trade, since he presumed that political instability in Japan made a resumption of war likely.[94] He was forced to abandon this line of business after the Meiji government eliminated the domains as potential future buyers with an 1871 declaration that abolished all feudal domains and established instead prefectures headed by governors who answered to the new central government in Tokyo.[95]

Weapons and other military supplies were another profitable line of business in late Edo and early Meiji Japan. In Brennwald's diary from September 1866 to August 1867 we find frequent references to negotiations about rifles, cannons, gunpowder and military clothing. Many of these discussions, which involved officials of the shogunate or lords, were held at Shōsenji, the temple which housed the Swiss consulate general in Edo. (It is useful to note that temples remained sites for European consulates. As Brian Burke-Gaffney outlines in his chapter, this practice began in Nagasaki.) For such deals, a German trader, Edward Schnell, often served as Brennwald's mediator and translator.[96] Military deals with Tokugawa officials were mostly made following Swiss-Japanese diplomatic discussions. For example, high officials of the shogunate visited the Swiss consulate general in the autumn of 1866 with the aim, among others, to ask Brennwald about Swiss weapons and to order samples of Swiss or other foreign rifles.[97] Samples of Swiss breechloading rifles, ordered by Brennwald, arrived in Japan in spring of the following year.[98] Alas, after detailed negotiations and some test-firings, the head of the shogunate's army declined to complete the purchase, stating that his men were insufficiently trained in the use of those weapons.[99]

From Japanese sources we know that the high-ranking shogunal officials who oversaw the possible Swiss-Japanese weapon deal included the governor for foreign affairs, Kikuchi Iyo no kami, and the governor for infantry, Koide Harimano kami. In October 1866, they had received instructions from their superiors to 'ask the Swiss consul to submit two or three samples of breechloading Minié rifles newly invented in Switzerland'.[100] At that time, Tokugawa Yoshinobu had just assumed the position of shogun, and had instituted a drastic reorganization and modernization that included developing a shogunal army and navy. Breech loaders, including 'Vetterli' and 'Martini', which Brennwald ordered in Switzerland upon Japanese request, were the latest and strongest type of rifles, which remained rare in Japan until the early Meiji period.[101] Again, however, this deal did not come about. Siber blamed the French Minister, Léon Roches, and 'the crafty Jesuit Abbé Mermet', who 'got wind of the matter, and in order not to lose such a fat business [...] threatened Tokugawa ministers using all possible pretexts, so that the people got worried and had to withdraw, although they had been so willing to make a contract with Brennwald precisely to get independent from the French'.[102] Roches had been actively assisting the shogunate in its military modernization efforts since 1864.[103]

Although not winning a big government contract, Siber & Brennwald found success in smaller transactions: 2,500 Enfield rifle-muskets sold at 11 dollars apiece ordered from Hong Kong and Singapore for an unknown buyer (11 September 1866); 2,000 barrels of gunpowder for 25 dollars a barrel (21 September 1866) and another 1,000 barrels (30 May to 10 June 1867) both for the shogunate; American carbines with 200 cartridges for the above-mentioned governor Kikuchi Iyo no kami (9 November 1866); 300 hunting rifles of 20 dollars apiece for an unknown buyer (31 March 1867). Officials of various domains also dealt with Brennwald to purchase weapons or gunpowder (see Table 1). Interestingly, with the exception of Satsuma, they were domains traditionally allied with the Tokugawa house. Thus, these connections probably resulted from previous negotiations with Tokugawa officials.

In general, possible buyers of weapons and other military supplies were officials of the shogunate or various lords who maintained residences in Edo. In this regard, Brennwald, as Swiss consul general, as well as his diplomatic colleagues representing other Western nations, had the advantage of residing in the capital and of having frequent opportunities to talk with representatives of lords and the shogunate. This commercial advantage seems to have aroused the envy of ordinary Western traders, who could only reside in Yokohama until Edo was opened for foreign settlement in 1869 (the city was renamed Tokyo

Table 3 Table of Brennwald's negotiations over Weapons in 1866–7

	Domain	Negotiations	Diary Entry
1	a domain in Bitchū	visited Brennwald in Yokohama and discussed plan to order a set of Swiss cannons	25 September 1866
2	Satsuma domain	visited Brennwald in Edo by mediation of E. Schnell to see samples of breech loaders and gunpowder	28 April 1866
3	Yūki domain of Shimousa	visited Brennwald in Edo to see samples of 'new weapons' including Henry rifles and promised to order over 1,000 rifles	10–11 May 1867
4	Owari domain	visited Brennwald in Edo to see samples of weapons and told him they could recommend the purchase of weapons to several daimyos	10 May 1867

Source: Diaries of Casper Brennwald [DCB].

that year). For example, in November 1866 Brennwald noted that a fellow countryman residing in Yokohama, probably James Charles Favre-Brandt, had criticized him for making commercial contracts in Edo, and that Favre planned to draw up a petition against him.[104]

Trade and upheaval during the Meiji Restoration

During the Boshin War, Siber & Brennwald found a lucrative outlet for the weapons trade through emerging connections with a northern domain, Sendai, which also contributed substantially to the growth of the firm's silk trade. When the war broke out, Brennwald was in Europe, and Siber was serving as the acting Swiss consul general. Drawing on this official status, Siber developed ties with Sendai, then part of the *Ōuetsu Reppan Dōmei*, an alliance of the domains of Mutsu (including Sendai), Dewa and Echigo, all of which opposed the newly formed Meiji government. During the war, Sendai officials exported silk and silkworm eggs to purchase weapons, clothing (most probably for military uniforms), and other military supplies from Siber

& Brennwald and a Dutch firm, Textor & Co.[105] Sendai silk belonged to the Ōshū (Oshio) type which, along with Maebashi silk, gained renown on the contemporary London market.

We find references for this development in Siber's letters beginning in April 1868, when he writes that '[for the coming silk season] I have already taken steps with the people who provide us with Sendai silk, which should give us a good result'.[106] 'I'm indispensable for the business here at the moment, [...] namely I hope I'm now more and more getting into a new line of business & am also already getting off the ground with these Sendai people for silk & it will probably go the same way with silkworm eggs, too.'[107] In July 1868, he added that 'the Sendai affairs go well & I could have obtained 30 more bales of silk if the steamer of the prince, which transported them, had not suffered bad sea damage, unfortunately. 30 bales were soaking wet, which is a considerable loss for the people.'[108] This shows how Sendai officials themselves, represented ultimately by their prince (*daimyo*), brought silk and silkworm eggs to Yokohama by steamships probably chartered by Siber & Brennwald. Yet Siber & Brennwald also sometimes dispatched steamers to Sendai, one of which returned with 'ca. 10,000 most beautiful cartons of Oshio Janagawa, which the *banto* purchased on our account & 13,000 cartons Sendai on the account of the prince for purchase'.[109]

In letters to his brother, Siber did not describe what he was trading in exchange for silk and silkworm eggs, but Japanese sources reveal that it was weapons and other military supplies. Table 2 lists articles that the Sendai domain imported from the Swiss company and its Dutch competitor, Textor & Co., during the Boshin War. According to Hayakawa Yōko, these articles were imported to an island near the city of Sendai, the capital of the domain.[110]

This trade was highly illegal. In February 1868, Western diplomats in Japan had jointly declared their nations' neutrality towards both sides in the Boshin War.[112] It was thus forbidden for subjects and citizens of treaty nations, let alone for the acting Swiss consul general, to provide either side with weapons and military supplies. Moreover the port of the Sendai domain had never been officially opened to foreign trade according to the treaty regulations in force at that time. Indeed, in September 1868 Siber told his brother that 'the local government arrested the steamer of Textor & C. here in this port [Yokohama], namely the "Vulcan," which the house sent to the Bay of Sendai with weapons and which brought back rice and silk & the load was confiscated as having come from a non-treaty port'.[113] Siber seems to have been fairly confident in the safety of his own, similar trading activities:

Table 4 Imports of the Sendai domain from Siber & Brennwald and Textor & Co. (August to November 1868)

Article	Number	Amount (dollar)
Shōjū (Muskets)	40	1,025
Renpatsu jū (Repeating rifles)	17	765
Teppō motomonan (gun motomonan?)	1.500	24,750
	13	195
Bajō hō (cannons on horse?)	1.375	23,375
Raifuru (Rifles)	112	4,480
Shasupō jū (Chassepot)	2	3,000
Dai jū (Cannons)	280	4,760
Futasu Bantō (two bantō's?)	20	660
Motogome jū (Breech loaders)	1.000	3,000
Jū Fuzoku hin (Gun accessories)	2.010.000	3,550
Raikan (Percussion caps)	20.719	6,215,70
Kayaku (gunpowder)		
Tōzan (a kind of cotton cloth)	400 rolls	600
Saten (Satin)	200 rolls	900
Rasha (Thick woolen cloth)	100 rolls	500
Kuro rasha (Black thick woolen cloth)	140 rolls	1,840
	200 rolls	3,000
Mōsen (Felt)	150 rolls	1,650
Shiro kanakin (Calico)	50 rolls	600
Hada juban, Matahiki (Undergarments)	404 rolls	6,517,40
	221 rolls	2,673,06
	140 rolls	1,800
	300 rolls	1,050
	8 boxes	920
Kaijō Ukeai kin (alloys received on the sea?)		243
Sum		102,666,82

Source: Hayakawa, 'Boshin sensō ki no Ni'igata kō no kinō ni kansuru ichi kōsatsu', 18.[111]

I hear now that the people are protesting against me, because allegedly I have applied my influence in order to obtain a permission from the [Japanese] Custom House; in reality the Sendai officers have been able to obtain the permission for me themselves, which the government gave to them (and not to me) [...] – Walter [of Siber & Brennwald] is still up there in Sendai with a ship, but I'm doing the things in a cleverer way [than Textor and Co.], of this you can be sure.[114]

Despite the efforts of its leaders to obtain more weapons, the alliance of Sendai and other domains was eventually defeated by Meiji government forces. At the end of the Boshin War, Sendai owed 47,188 dollars to Siber & Brennwald. Sendai leaders, whose territory was substantially curtailed after the war, also saw their debt steadily mount because of the high interest rate charged by Siber & Brennwald (1 per cent per month). The domain had only partially repaid its debts when in April 1870, Siber & Brennwald asked for redress in court.[115] Following strict instructions issued by the Foreign Ministry, Sendai paid another 10,000 dollars by April 1871. In the end, Sendai's remaining debt of 19,586 dollars was assumed by the Finance Ministry of the Meiji government.[116]

Siber, silk mills and the development of the Japanese silk industry

Through the silk trade, Siber built connections with two important Japanese business circles: the Maebashi domain, one of the most important silk-producing districts in Japan, and the silk-trading branch of the Kyoto-based trading and banking house, Ono-gumi Ito ten, represented by the merchant, Furukawa Ichibé, the *banto* of Ono-gumi's Tokyo branch. Both sets of connections led to the establishment of the earliest silk mills, or filatures, on the European model in Japan, the Maebashi Silk Mill run by the domain, established in 1870, and the Tsukiji Silk Mill run by Ono-gumi, established in 1871.

Siber's letters combined with Japanese sources provide valuable information on this transfer of technology. In June 1870 Siber reported to his brother about his efforts to involve himself in the establishment of the first machine silk-reeling filature in the Maebashi domain, by introducing an experienced Swiss silk spinner, Caspar Müller, to the domain's representatives. This attempt was closely connected to Siber's rivalry with the British Legation and British merchants in Japan:

> By the way, he [Francis Adams, Secretary to the British Legation] is staying again in the silk region at the moment & tries to strengthen the English influence there & if possible, to bring the silk industry under English supervision and control, by promoting an Englishman as the filature's supervisor & offering to the people [of the Maebashi domain] the silk-reeling machines which were used in the filature of Jardine Matheson in Shanghai. I have worked against this for a long time already, by recommending Casp. Müller, the brother of G. Müller who is engaged in Gütschow [a German trading house in Yokohama], who is an accomplished silk spinner with a 15-year-long experience in filature practice, as a supervisor for their filature to the government of the prince of Maebashi. Better a Swiss than an Englishman, who, if they can attain such a position, would try to monopolize all for themselves, according to the principle & model & instruction of their minister Sir Harry Parkes.[117]

Adams undertook a research trip into the silk districts around Maebashi in 1869 and later compiled three reports on Japanese silk districts and sericulture.[118] These caught the eye of E. Wittal, who led the Yokohama branch of Jardine Matheson. Wittal later asked the British minister, Sir Harry Parkes, to assist him in obtaining permission from the Meiji government to establish a filature in Japan, and discussed the matter with representatives of Jardine Matheson's Shanghai branch and Hong Kong headquarters. They developed a plan to transport the silk-reeling machines of Jardine Matheson's filature from Shanghai, and began ultimately unsuccessful negotiations with the Maebashi domain. Maebashi officials apparently rejected a proposal that would see Jardine Matheson maintain joint management of the filature.[119]

Thereafter, a high-ranking Maebashi official, Hayami Kenso, visited Siber & Brennwald in Yokohama in April 1870, with the aim to consult Siber on 'silk reeling in Europe, the market rate of exported silk to London, and the way to improve the quality of local silk'.[120] Siber's advice on the last point was to employ an instructor for silk reeling, upon which Hayami asked for further instructions on the necessary procedures.[121] At Siber's recommendation, in June 1870 Maebashi awarded Caspar Müller a four-month contract at a wage of 1,200 dollars.[122] 'After endless efforts and work', Siber told his brother in July 1870, 'I succeeded in realizing the employment of C. Müller as supervisor of the filature for the province of Maebashi and in obtaining a permission from the [Meiji] government for that. It was really not an easy matter & I was often in despair for its ultimate success.'[123] Siber went on to explain that this success benefitted not only Müller but was also 'a personal satisfaction for me, because by this I can celebrate a great triumph over Parkes, who will get extremely annoyed anyway, that my proposal was finally accepted instead of his'.[124]

Upon the request of Maebashi officials, in July Siber set out for the domain accompanied by Caspar Müller, a Japanese translator, and a retinue assigned by the Maebashi domain.[125] After several days in Maebashi city, Siber's group was invited to visit a famous hot spring in the area.[126] An agreement was struck during that sojourn, and Müller subsequently began to supervise the establishment of the first filature in Maebashi, which comprised three silk-reeling machines made on the European model.[127] Until October, Müller instructed Hayami and others as they learned, by trial and error, the new silk-reeling process. In his diary, Hayami wrote of being so engrossed in learning 'the practice of European silk reeling' that he would sometimes not return home in the evening.[128] In October, the filature moved to Ōwatari, a suburb of Maebashi, where the domain installed twelve silk reeling machines (with twelve reelers).[129] In the middle of that month, Hayami was forced not to renew Müller's contract, a situation caused by the Maebashi domain's refusal to continue to pay Müller's expensive salary. Hayami recalled that xenophobic sentiments within the domain led to criticism of the employment of a foreigner.[130] Müller thus returned to Yokohama in November.[131]

The Swiss silk expert soon found new employment with Furukawa Ichibé, the head of the silk-trading branch of the Ono-gumi in Tokyo. Headquartered in Kyoto, the Ono-gumi, or Ono-group, was one of the biggest trading and banking firms in Japan at that time.[132] As was the case with Hayami, the plan to hire Müller came about during Furukawa's consultation with Siber. Since early 1870, Furukawa had been trading silk and silkworm eggs with Siber on a scale that made other Yokohama merchants envious.[133] Siber described Furukawa as:

> One of the biggest & richest Japanese merchants, absolutely the biggest trader of Oshio silk. He does not want to sell his silk here, since the market price here seems too low to him & he could be convinced to consign his stock to us, hoping to get a better price in Europe. If this silk has the good luck to be sold at a better price than here & we can thus satisfy our friend [Furukawa], then we can be sure to do big business with him almost every year... since my friend buys 2,000 to 3,000 bales of raw silk in Oshiu every season, mostly for Yokohama, also partly for the weavers in Kyoto.[134]

According to Furukawa's memoir, he developed close relations with Siber and the manager of Siber & Brennwald whom he called 'Ōtoru'.[135] Siber and Furukawa consulted each other over commercial and other issues in Japan and overseas, and once travelled to Kyoto together.[136]

Inspired by his exchange with Siber, Furukawa developed a plan to establish a silk mill in Tokyo. Upon his Swiss friend's recommendation, Furukawa decided to employ Müller and to establish the filature in Tsukiji,[137] a district along Tokyo Bay, where a new foreign settlement for Tokyo had been established in 1869. The Tsukiji Silk Mill of Ono-gumi opened in Autumn 1871 and was on a much larger scale than its Maebashi predecessor, equipped with thirty silk reeling machines attended by sixty reelers.[138] It reflected the capital strength of the powerful Ono-gumi, as well as the ambition of its *banto* Furukawa. Siber noted the scale of Furukawa's ambition, and thought it 'could possibly even be very lucrative'.[139] He further explained to his brother: 'This new emerging industry deserves to be paid maximum attention, since it will make it possible to order fixed yarn counts here in Japan & namely I think we would be ready for that as early as the next season.'[140] In the short term, these high hopes were not fulfilled. The Tsukiji Silk Mill had to close in 1873 when it became clear the Tokyo area would not become a silk centre. The Ono-gumi transplanted the filatures, along with workers and machines, to Japan's main sericulture districts, Shinshu and Oshio. There, however, the technology transfer assisted by Hermann Siber began to have a significant impact on the development of Japanese machine silk reeling.[141] This contribution of the Swiss trading house is what the Certificate of Commendation of the Dainippon Silk Foundation, mentioned in the introduction to this chapter, was referring to in 1903.[142]

Conclusion

By the mid-1870s Siber & Brennwald was becoming one of the most important exporters of Japanese raw silk. After a rather cumbersome beginning, and once the craze for silkworm eggs abated due to the elimination of pébrine in Europe in the early 1870s,[143] the amount of silk traded by the company increased to reach hundreds of bales each season.[144] This success needs to be explained, for nothing predestined a newcomer from Switzerland to capture such an important share of the East Asian commodity market.

The most important prerequisites for this success were the sound and diversified financial, commercial and technological networks that the two founders had in place in Europe before setting out to Japan in 1865. In addition to their private fortunes they had secured financial backing in Switzerland, Italy and Britain, namely two major banks, Fred. Huth & Co. in London and Kreditanstalt in Zürich, and an important European silk trader, Zuppinger, Siber & Co. in Bergamo. In addition, they had successfully curried favour not only with potential European buyers of Japanese raw silk, but also with European manufacturers eager to export goods to Japan. Thirdly, because of Hermann Siber's stay in London, one of the founders was already familiar with assessing the quality of East Asian silks and comparing them to raw materials produced in Europe. In the emerging global commodity market of a natural product for which international quality standards had not yet been established, this was another competitive advantage of Siber & Brennwald. Finally, through Hermann Siber and the silk throwing enterprise of Zuppinger, Siber & Co. in Bergamo, the company had excellent connections to experts familiar with the latest technological developments in silk reeling – a process which had first been mechanized in Piedmont at the end of the eighteenth century and which was, throughout the nineteenth century, constantly being improved, especially in Northern Italy.[145]

Once they had arrived in Japan, Siber and Brennwald were able to benefit from their double role as traders and diplomats. As their country's sole diplomatic representatives in Japan before the posting of a first Swiss career diplomat in 1893,[146] they could reside both in their trading house in Yokohama and in their consulate general in Edo/Tokyo, while normal foreign merchants were bound to Yokohama. Their residence in the capital gave them privileged access to Japanese government officials and feudal lords before and after the Meiji Restoration. Especially in the first years, before the silk trade really began to take off, this facilitated lucrative imports of weaponry and other military supplies. In addition, the position of Switzerland's consul general allowed them the right to travel in the inland of Japan, a privilege traders without diplomatic status did not enjoy under the unequal treaty system.

It was Siber, in particular, who took advantage of this right and explored the promising silk producing regions when he was acting consul general during his partner's absence in the early Meiji period. Although this gave Siber & Brennwald an advantage over their Swiss competitors, it must be pointed out that major trading houses from other Western states secured themselves similar advantages, most notably Jardine Matheson who cooperated closely with the British Legation in Japan. We have seen that when the two firms competed for access to the Maebashi silk district the Swiss David and not the British Goliath succeeded. This was probably due to Herman Siber's more cooperative approach. In the eyes of the Japanese, Siber & Brennwald provided them with an opportunity to access state-of-the-art European silk-reeling technology in exchange for opportunities of trade, while behind Jardine Matheson's offer loomed London's intimidating military and financial power.

The role of trade and diplomacy is frequently discussed in the two main sources analysed in this chapter. Yet while Caspar Brennwald's diaries highlight the importance of his diplomatic contacts for generating business opportunities, his partner's letters draw a considerably different picture. From the very beginning, Hermann Siber took a critical view of Brennwald's consular activities, and repeatedly complained to his brother that his partner devoted most of his time to diplomacy. One reason for this was the fact that Switzerland did not remunerate its consular representatives and thus conflicts, such as that over the title deed with Rudolf Lindau, proved costly. Two months after their arrival in Yokohama, Siber asked his brother: 'How should I deal with the very important additional costs caused by the consulate which only regard Brennwald?'[147]

Yet Siber did not only complain about costs; he also expressed frustration with his partner's lack of business acumen. In November 1866, Siber called

Brennwald 'frightfully timid' in business matters, and in early 1867 he wrote to his brother that 'Brennwald lacks the necessary steam, otherwise we certainly would have completed several more deals'.[148] Shortly thereafter Siber discussed sending Brennwald to Europe to handle commissions because 'here he's anyhow not doing anything in the company'.[149] In August 1867, Brennwald left for Europe 'hopefully to induce rather sound & lucrative business for us'.[150] As we have seen above, during Brennwald's two-year absence Siber took over Switzerland's diplomatic representation in Japan. The experience did not improve his impressions of diplomacy. On a particularly hectic day, Hermann Siber told his brother: 'Apart from inspecting silk, selling goods & haggling with the Japanese all day long, I have the not so pleasant & even less profitable burden of the consular affairs upon me.'[151] Shortly before Brennwald's return, he complained that consular duties tied him down in Yokohama:

> But how can one leave if one has a business to attend to and has to act as consul general, has to deal with all sorts of legal cases and stories, is Chairman of the Board of Consuls & furthermore at times also has to take over the business of the other consuls, [...] I'm so much looking forward to laying down all these posts and honours, which are certainly quite honourable but bring in bloody little profit.[152]

To what extent the two partner's diplomatic status on the one hand and their business skills on the other were responsible for the success of Siber & Brennwald can, of course, never be fully established. More interesting, however, is another dimension of their commercial enterprise, namely its legal basis, the contract they set up in London in 1865. About this we learn a great deal from Siber's letters once Brennwald had returned to Yokohama in December 1869. Immediately Hermann Siber resumed his complaints about the perceived shortcomings of his business partner, but despite this, the company's profits continued to be evenly split between the two. This is the context in which Siber called Brennwald an 'egotist in the full sense of the word & without respect for what he owes to others, only out for his own material advantage'.[153] It is testament to the strength of their contract that despite this and countless other livid complaints all Siber could do was being angry. As their partnership had been established in London it was probably based on English Common Law, on the legal principle of *lex loci contractus*, and as it was limited in time, there was no way Siber could alter its terms.[154] Yet as soon as the original came to a close in 1877, Siber refused to renew it. In 1878, he took on a new partner, Arnold Wolff, a Swiss silk expert who had worked for the company in Yokohama since 1869, Brennwald himself returning to Europe three years later.[155]

The fact that the company was now called Siber, Brennwald & Co. and kept this name until Brennwald's death in 1899 suggests that some sort of business relationship between Siber and Brennwald continued. Apparently Brennwald kept working for the trading house in charge of its London office from 1881.[156] As Arnold Wolff was now also a partner and given the doubts Siber had about Brennwald's business skills, it is likely, however, that for Brennwald the terms of the association between 1878 and 1899 were less favourable than in the first decade. Despite Hermann Siber's critical views of diplomacy, however, also in its second phase the company combined trade and diplomacy – before Switzerland posted its first professional diplomat to Japan in 1893, the Swiss consul in Yokohama was always a partner of Siber, Brennwald & Co. – first Arnold Wolff and later on Arnold Dumelin.[157]

5

Afterlife of the wealthy: The burial of mercantile communities in nineteenth-century colonial Hong Kong

Bobby Tam

When the British colonized the island of Hong Kong in 1841, death bedevilled them from the outset. Hundreds of soldiers fell from diseases within months and graveyards were swiftly set up for them. Though a spacious cemetery was set up for the British colonial community few years later, the merchant class of the colony hardly expected to die and be buried in the colony. The cemetery was a sad acre reserved for soldiers fallen from disease, infants who had lived only for a few months, impoverished transients (like sailors), or other colonists who had unexpectedly perished well before their prime. Outside this colonial burial space, Chinese graves or occasionally exposed bodies were scattered across the hillsides. European colonists thus constantly found themselves surrounded by the dead. In their minds, sharing the same fate of dying and being buried in the colony was the last thing they would have wished for.[1]

A few decades later, by the end of the century, Ho-Tung, an influential Eurasian comprador and businessman, who was reputed as the wealthiest man in the colony, demanded that the government create a private cemetery for prominent Eurasian families. Inside this private cemetery, prominent Eurasian businessmen could freely design large tombstones for themselves and their families based on their beliefs in Chinese geomancy. The Colonial Cemetery, once filled with fallen soldiers and victims of untimely deaths, had now become a beautiful garden cemetery. Fountains, flowers and trees were neatly interspersed with decorative tombstones and monuments. The cemetery became a comfortable and intimate site where European families could reflect and recuperate. Spending one's final days and being buried in the colony no longer seemed such a horrifying notion to the merchant class.

Figure 7 Cemetery, Happy Valley, Hong Kong. Photograph from a negative by John Thomson (1837–1921), *c.* 1868.

Source: Wellcome Collection.

The perception of Hong Kong as a place to die and be buried in certainly changed throughout the second half of the nineteenth century. In the first two or three decades of colonial Hong Kong, neither British nor Chinese merchants would imagine themselves spending their final days in this colony. Most merchants who had the financial means would spend their retiring years in their homeland in Europe or China. Hong Kong, unlike other recently opened treaty ports along the Chinese coast like Shanghai or Ningbo, was a formal colony with a stronger British military presence. Contrary to popular belief, the young colony was not particularly friendly to merchants, and the colonial state put most of its efforts into catering to the needs of the military first. By the end of the century, however, merchant opinion had become reconciled to the idea of being buried, or burying their loved ones, in the colony. In fact, as merchants and businessmen became increasingly wealthy and invested in Hong Kong, they tried to emulate each other in the realm of funerals and burials. This was particularly obvious for Chinese and Eurasian businessmen, as they sought to emulate European colonists and to counter some of the previous unequal treatments towards them, through demonstrating their increasing political influence and higher social status. Despite their small populations, merchants of other ethnic origin, such as Jews and Parsees, also played a considerable role in the story, and carved out their own spaces of death quite early on.

By studying the dynamics between mercantile communities and the colonial state in matters of death and burial, this chapter explores the relationship between wealth, race, social influence and the fate of the dead. In nineteenth-century Britain, death offered the growing middle class a chance to demonstrate their social status, wealth and individuality, by marking out a spacious plot and an elaborate tombstone for their families or themselves. In nineteenth-century Hong Kong, where racial boundaries could be found in every aspect of life, how did wealth and race play out for the merchant class at the point of death? In death, were racial boundaries, which undergirded colonial power itself, able to be transcended through economic influence?

The demonstration of wealth and status through funerary rites and burials often raised debate in nineteenth-century British society, where the subject divided opinion. On the one hand, ostentatious displays of grief became a norm among the middle and upper classes. On the other hand, this practice was never unanimous and elicited strong criticism for being overly extravagant and lacking emotional authenticity.[2] To what extent was this debate applicable to the mercantile communities in nineteenth-century Hong Kong? When wealthy Chinese pushed for their ideal death practices and burial spaces, their behaviour could be frowned upon by the colonial population as extravagant and materialistic, lacking emotional authenticity. Such criticism reflects the interplay of wealth and race in this context: having the economic power to carry out certain practices did not imply that those practices would be respected by the dominant part of society.

Part 1 Early years: Prioritization of the military and merchants' reluctance to die in Hong Kong

In the earliest years of colonization, British merchants were generally unsure about the prospect of turning this small island into a prosperous trading port. The seemingly barren landscape and 'deadly' subtropical climate did not appeal to the British. Nevertheless, certain British mercantile firms invested considerably in the colony early on. One was Jardine Matheson & Co., the largest trading firm in Canton.³ The company set up godowns, quarters and offices in East Point (today's Causeway Bay).⁴ The military also quickly set up barracks and naval stores all across the island in the earliest years.⁵ As hundreds of soldiers fell from disease, graveyards were swiftly set up in the colony. A Protestant graveyard and a Catholic graveyard were created for fallen soldiers in 1841 and 1842 respectively.⁶ Various military graveyards were also set up near the barracks.

These graveyards were, however, in a poor condition; as noted by British travellers, coffins were exposed and sometimes even bones lay scattered on the ground.⁷ Such graveyards were also quickly filled up after only a few summers of high mortality from epidemics. In summer 1843, an epidemic devastated the colonists with an unprecedentedly high rate of mortality.⁸ This prompted the colonial government to recognize the necessity for a larger and better-organized cemetery. The Wong Nei Chung Valley, later named Happy Valley, was selected for this purpose. The valley itself was severely hit during the epidemic. Being one of the very few natural flatlands on the island, the valley was originally intended to be the business centre of the colony.⁹ As Jardine Matheson had invested heavily in nearby East Point, the company, with the permission of the government, also had large-scale plans to invest in the valley.¹⁰ The severe impact of the epidemic, however, made the colonists abandon the plan of transforming this area into a business centre, and it remained one of Chinese paddy fields and streams. Chinese graves were scattered across the valley before the creation of Western cemeteries.¹¹ After taking over the paddy fields, the colonists began to use this piece of flat land for recreation and burial.

A Western cemetery was formally established there in 1845. In the early years, it was usually referred to as the 'Protestant Cemetery', but was later referred to as the 'Colonial Cemetery' by the late nineteenth century, and is now known as the 'Hong Kong Cemetery'. The Catholic Cemetery was created next to the Protestant Cemetery in 1848, and maintained by the Catholic community autonomously, although the colonial state ultimately had indirect authority in regulating the area.¹² In comparison, the 'Protestant Cemetery' was not in fact specifically reserved for the Protestant community, but instead acted more like a state cemetery, directly administered by the colonial government. It just happened that the religion of most British colonials by default was Protestantism, or more accurately speaking, Anglicanism. As a state cemetery, it was theoretically not exclusive in religious and racial terms, yet in reality, Chinese, both the living and the dead, were virtually barred from access to it throughout the nineteenth century.¹³

The colonial state dominated the management of the Protestant Cemetery, from deciding the burial fees to its day-to-day maintenance. It is worth keeping in mind that official and public cemeteries were not really a common phenomenon in mid-nineteenth-century Britain, where private cemetery companies had predominated since the early nineteenth century. These profit-making cemeteries gradually took over overcrowded burials in churchyards at city centres.[14] In Hong Kong, however, the colonial state theoretically bore the development and maintenance costs of the Protestant Cemetery, though this did not mean that European civilians in the colony could be buried there for free.

The burial fees policy of the cemetery heavily favoured employees of the colonial state, including soldiers, sailors, military officers, policemen and their family members. The colonial state originally intended to charge everyone a $15 basic ground fee for burial.[15] After a petition by a lieutenant for his deceased friend in 1849, the colonial government agreed to waive this ground fee for all colonial state and military personnel and their family members.[16] They virtually bore no cost in burial except a minimal digging fee. On the other hand, civilians of the colonial community not working for the state or the military needed to bear the full cost of burial. This arrangement ensured a proper burial for every soldier and colonial state employee, and gave the cemetery a non-commercial flavour.

This funding formula favouring official personnel over civilians did draw criticism. One person wrote to the local newspaper *Friend of China* to complain, sarcastically criticizing the fees for civilian burial as a 'Death Tax' to 'deter people from dying without just cause'.[17] European civilians in the colony were dissatisfied at what they saw as unreasonable charges for burial as a means of maintaining the cemetery.

For the most successful among the European merchant class, these burial fees, and an accompanying monument, remained easily affordable. Yet very few elite merchants chose to be buried in the colony. Thanks to Patricia Lim's meticulous field research in the cemetery, we have a much better understanding of the occupations of the deceased who were buried there during the early years.[18] If we take the narrow definition of a merchant, someone who owned or ran a mercantile firm, only a very small number of European merchants were buried here. Lim recorded that only fourteen men, who were merchants or bankers, and one related woman and one related child, were buried in the cemetery between 1845 and 1860.[19] Among these burials, only one, the infant child, was associated with Jardine Matheson, as the child of a merchant working for the firm. Many of the other burials belonged to either non-British Europeans or visiting merchants from other treaty ports.[20] It is likely that their deaths happened suddenly during their business travel in Hong Kong.

Table 5 Schedule of fees for interments in the cemetery in 1854

For all Graves, a Ground Fee	$15.00
Grave digging extra	$1.32
Total for all Graves,	$16.32
EXCEPTIONS	
Pauper funerals, expense of grave digging only	$1.32
Children under 9 years, Ground Fee, And the Grave digging extra…	$5.00
Officers, non-commissioned Officers and Privates in the British Army, Officers, Warrant Officers and Sailors in the British Navy, Police Constables and their families, are exempt from Ground Fee and pay only Two Rupees for digging grave,	$0.88 (Two Rupees)
All monuments of which the base exceeds 25 Superficial feet,	$ 50
Monuments occupying less than this space,	$ 25
Upright head stones, and flat Stones not occupying more space than the Grave, free	

Source: Extracted from *Hong Kong Government Gazette (1854)*, No. 64, p. 217.

It would take at least three months to travel between Hong Kong and Britain in the mid-nineteenth century and it was certainly not easy to transport bodies or coffins from Hong Kong back to Europe.[21] While it is a rather common practice for deceased Chinese migrants to be sent back to their ancestral home for burial due to their strong attachment to their homeland (even from faraway places, such as California), the extent of deceased Europeans being transported back to Europe for burial was considerably smaller.[22] Travelling European merchants who met an unexpected death were thus buried in the colony, while British merchants normally would return to Britain for retirement before their final years, avoiding death in the colony.

European merchants, if defined in a narrow sense, mostly belonged to a small affluent class at the top of the society. But if we consider the broader definition of merchants to include other related occupations – like merchant navy seamen, artisans and shopkeepers, etc., who were less well-off than the typical elite merchant – then a much larger number of them were buried at the cemetery. Artisans and small-scale businessmen, who also made a living from selling, came from a diverse range of economic classes compared to the elite merchants. A substantial proportion of the dead buried in the cemetery in the early years were members of the merchant navy and their relatives.[23] They constantly travelled along the Chinese coast, but were an integral part of Hong Kong society.[24] Relatively few captains of merchant ships, like elite merchants, died and were buried in Hong Kong. Given that seventy-two captains and officers from merchant vessels were buried with headstones in the cemetery by 1860, perhaps hundreds, if not thousands, of ordinary seamen were buried in the colony.[25]

Unlike elite merchants or ship captains, many of the ordinary seamen died in destitution and ended up in nameless paupers' graves in the cemetery. Many of these poor whites were either unemployed merchant seamen, or policemen who had been dismissed for various offences.[26] Following sanitary improvement and the ending of the epidemics that had ravaged the military, poor Europeans outside the government forces like seamen or unemployed drifters constituted the majority of European deaths during the 1850s.[27] Their deaths were commonly associated with moral failings like drunkenness, so that the pauper's grave essentially became a stigma of being a failed colonist. A few unfortunate tradesmen also suffered the fate of a pauper's burial as they went bankrupt. Lim's work has cited the example of Frederick Funck, a merchant who drank himself to death in June 1848, dying on the verge of bankruptcy, and leaving behind a wife and a baby son.[28]

For the elite merchants, despite having a comfortable and often luxurious lifestyle, they were well aware of the death around them and how deathly the colony was. The tropical sun was thought to be a source of disease and death. But their anxieties did not merely come from the climate and disease, but also from the graves and burials that they witnessed all the time. Colonial administrator William T. Mercer wrote poems about how Chinese graves occupied all the hillsides so that there was not even enough space for the living.[29] This bears some similarity to how the British perceived India as a land of death in the nineteenth century. As suggested by David Arnold, India was not only perceived as a disease-ridden land with high white mortality; the highly visible deathscape of graveyards, burials and funerals across India was a recurrent feature of colonial literature.[30]

Hong Kong was no more than a place for making a fortune to most elite merchants. It was not a place for retirement or even for bringing one's family. A luxurious life was possible, but not a luxurious death. If the Victorian culture of extravagant funerals and burials was about displaying wealth and status, it would make little sense for British merchants to do so thousands of miles away from Britain. The early colonial community was volatile and small; the Protestant Cemetery itself was yet to be transformed into an impressive garden cemetery; and the Chinese in the colony were not considered an audience worth impressing. Displaying wealth in front of a small European community and an irrelevant Chinese majority meant little to the colonials compared with displaying their achievements back in the metropole.

Unlike in treaty ports like Shanghai, where the British focused on developing their commercial interests on foreign soil, Hong Kong had been ceded as a permanent colony. During its first two decades, as the government was still busy securing the young colony as a military station and logistical hub, efforts in developing it into a prosperous trading port were postponed. As evident in the cemetery fees policy, military state personnel were taken care of first in order to consolidate the colony's foundation. Thus, in these early years, poor European civilians, who drifted to the colony seeking opportunities, would hardly find Hong Kong as a welcoming place, and certainly not an ideal place to retire and die. Many, however, met an early death and had no escape. Wealthy merchants, despite making a fortune through Hong Kong, definitely had no intention to share the same fate and be buried in the colony.

Part 2 The role of Parsee, Jewish and Muslim merchants

In comparison with British merchants, it was the ethnic minorities of the colonial community who probably embraced their lives in the colony more. While British merchants always had a homeland to retire to once they had earned enough in the Far East, ethnic minorities, particularly Jews and Parsees, were fundamentally a mobile group in the empire often without a homeland. Despite having a small population, the Jews and Parsees in Hong Kong, who were mostly merchants, played an integral part in the colony's development throughout the nineteenth century. Their influences in the colony helped them to secure their own death spaces quite early on.

The Parsees were already playing a considerable role in the Canton trade long before the colonization of Hong Kong, having come with the East India Company to Canton in the eighteenth century.[31] A vast majority of the Parsee merchants in Canton and Hong Kong came from Bombay, where they were influential maritime merchants. The Parsees were a small community in Hong Kong.[32] They possessed, however, significant influence in its economy. According to the *Hong Kong Directory* for 1860, among seventy-three foreign firms, seventeen of them were owned by Parsees.[33] Their economic influence had already enabled them to obtain a Parsee Cemetery in Macau in 1829.[34]

In Hong Kong, the Parsee community was granted land for a cemetery in 1852, several years before the first burial even took place.[35] The cemetery was located directly south of the Protestant Cemetery, forming a close cluster with the Protestant and Catholic cemeteries. When Parsees came to China, they abandoned their traditional custom of using a 'Tower of Silence' for excarnation and adopted the practice of ground burial.[36] The cemetery was spacious considering the small number of Parsee burials; a building was erected in the cemetery where Parsees could practice various death rituals upon the body before burial.[37] Despite not being able to practice excarnation, the Parsee merchants were able to secure a spacious cemetery for their community just a few years after Protestants and Catholics.

Jewish merchants in mid-nineteenth-century Hong Kong mainly came from Bombay and Calcutta, with ancestry back in the Middle East.[38] There were also some British and American nationals who were ethnically Jewish. Prominent Jewish merchant families in nineteenth-century Hong Kong included the Sassoons and the Belilios, who started with the typical opium, cotton and tea trades, but later vastly expanded their businesses into property, banking and shipping.[39] In 1855, the Sassoon family purchased farmland in the Happy Valley for creating a cemetery. The Jewish Cemetery was granted by the government in 1857 with the first burial taking place that same year.[40] There were only eleven recorded burials throughout the 1860s and another eleven throughout the 1870s in the cemetery.[41]

Though most Muslims in nineteenth-century Hong Kong were policemen or soldiers, some were also merchants.[42] Just like the Parsees, Indian Muslims from Bombay participated in the Canton trade with the East India Company early on.[43] In 1858, a piece of land was granted to three Muslim men, most likely merchants, as a Muslim burial ground. The burial ground was soon closed in 1867 after a new 'Mahomedan Cemetery' in Happy Valley was granted to the Muslim community. The government funded the project and provided 2,000 dollars for the necessary work to be undertaken in developing the new Mahomedan Cemetery; bodies from the old Muslim burial ground were reinterred in the new cemetery.[44]

One could argue that these foreign merchants of ethnic minority background hailing from India or the Middle East, who were a mobile group within the empire, were more likely to treat Hong Kong as their permanent home and a place to die than the British merchants during the early colonial period. Jews and Parsees in particular, who lacked a homeland for their religious faith and ethnic identity, were more likely to treat a place that had provided them shelter and prosperity as home. Their intention to be buried in the colony properly brought them into negotiation with the colonial state for a decent cemetery for their community, and their economic strength enabled them to do so early on. This negotiating power for death spaces paved the way for Chinese and Eurasian businessmen to follow suit once they also developed a stronger attachment to the colony.

Part 3 Gradual prosperity and domesticity

Hong Kong experienced substantial economic growth throughout and after the 1860s. The acquisition of Kowloon in 1860 after the Second Opium War, the constant supply of cheap labour from China due to political upheaval during the Taiping Civil War, and the increasing investment from both Chinese and foreign merchants all added to the economic prosperity of the colony. Technological improvement in marine transportation and the opening of the Suez Canal in 1869 greatly eased travel between Europe and East Asia. It was safer and easier for Europeans to travel to Hong Kong. Instead of just having individual merchants embarking on a long and dangerous journey to the distant colony, it was now more common for them to travel with their families. A more domestic European community with a higher ratio of women and children began to develop.

This changing nature of the European community certainly had implications for death and burial. The Western cemeteries, particularly the Protestant Cemetery, acquired rich new meanings for the colonial community. The Protestant Cemetery was no longer merely a functional burial space for troops or a sad acre for colonists who died before their prime. The site had always been associated with melancholy, but during this period, new layers of meaning were also attached to the Protestant Cemetery, making it a desirable place to be buried.

Physically, the cemetery was transformed into a carefully tended garden similar to those popular among the middle and upper classes in Britain. Spacious garden cemeteries had already become a prevailing phenomenon in mid-nineteenth-century Britain. The rise of garden cemeteries in Britain on the outskirts of cities could be ascribed to both sanitary and cultural factors. With the rapid growth of urban populations, churchyard burials at city centres were becoming overcrowded and unsanitary. While sanitary factors certainly played a role, recent scholarship, however, has focused more on the cultural side of the story.[45] Philippe Aries and Lawrence Stone suggested the concepts of the 'death of the other' and 'affective individualism' to illustrate a major change in Western European thinking about the family and death since the eighteenth century. Stone's concept of 'affective individualism' explained 'the rise of familial attachment to a lover, child, spouse or parent' in the eighteenth century.⁴⁶ In the era of the 'death of the other', as periodized by Philippe Aries, there had also been increasing emphasis on individuals' personal relationships with the deceased in the West. Death was more often seen from the perspective of the losing of loved ones.⁴⁷ Such cultural and emotional changes could be reflected in cemetery design. Based on these concepts, archaeologist Sarah Tarlow has suggested the emotional significance of the garden cemetery. The deceased person and the dead body had growing affective emotional value for the living. The bereaved commonly felt that the resting place of the body should be comfortable and attractive. Furthermore, it became more important that the actual location of the dead should be 'visitable'. Private ownership of a spacious burial plot guaranteed that the bereaved could visit the dead anytime to mourn, reflect and commiserate.⁴⁸

The transformation of the Protestant Cemetery in Hong Kong to a garden design was very much associated with these cultural and emotional factors. The transformation took place a few decades later than the popularization of garden cemeteries in Britain, as a domestic European community was only gradually formed towards the late nineteenth century. The photograph in this chapter shows that the Happy Valley Protestant Cemetery during the late 1860s still had a rather simplistic design. It was a tranquil green space, but yet to be developed into a well-tended garden. The elegant garden design only came into being during the 1880s. As depicted by British military officer Henry Knollys in his travel writing, and as shown in photographs from the 1880s and 1890s, the cemetery was neatly decorated with tropical plants and water fountains.⁴⁹ Headstones and monuments became increasingly ornamental with sculptures full of symbolic meanings. Deceased children and women were interred under ornamental tombstones with angel sculptures. All these provided a feminine and affective aura for the cemetery. Living women and children would also visit the cemetery garden as a family unit either for memorial purposes or simply for recuperation in 'nature'. The cemetery thus became a domestic and intimate space where the dead could rest comfortably, while the family could visit their deceased loved ones and cultivate feelings for them.

While fourteen merchants and their family members were buried between 1845 and 1860 – most of them were sojourners – thirty merchants and their family members were buried between 1861 and 1875, as recorded by Patricia Lim. Here is evidence of a more domestic mercantile community, as there were seven women and six children among these thirty burials.⁵⁰ Nonetheless, a truly domestic mercantile community only really developed during the late nineteenth century. Towards the end of the century, a section of the cemetery was specifically reserved for long-term European residents. According to Lim, the section was reserved for those who had lived at least twenty-three years in Hong Kong and then died in their adopted home. In this section, there are 138 headstones representing 150 people, all of whom were buried between 1887 and circa 1910. These were indeed permanent European residents who wished to settle and die in the colony, rather than meeting an unexpected end before returning to Europe. Among the 138 headstones, twenty-one of them belonged to deceased merchants.[51] Within this settled European mercantile community is evidence of a considerable Scottish presence. As Jardine Matheson had been founded by two Scotsmen, William Jardine and James Matheson, a long line of Scotsmen duly worked for the company. Twenty-five Scotsmen were buried in this section were long-term European residents.[52] The Scots would continue to play a significant role in the development of the colony, not just commercially, but also politically.

Throughout the nineteenth century, Hong Kong remained a distant trading outpost in the eyes of most Britons, and was never a settler colony receiving substantial flows of British emigrants. But contrary to the harsh image depicted in the early years, Hong Kong was increasingly portrayed as a colony of leisure and opportunity. The vividness of colonial life in Hong Kong was increasingly depicted in the British media. Just next to the cemeteries was the Happy Valley Racecourse, which often featured in British popular culture as a place where extravagant colonial leisure activities took place.[53] The tropical environment was still deemed detrimental to Europeans in terms of both health and morality. Yet, the possibilities for comfort of colonial life were increasingly emphasized. A person of lower-middle-class background in Britain could expect an upper-middle-class lifestyle, with a nice house and multiple Chinese servants, if they chose to stay in Hong Kong. Having a family, constructing a home, growing old and finally dying in the colony were no longer objectionable to all European merchants. The cemetery, with its comfortable and affective aura, proves to be a reflection of the domestic European community.

Part 4 Emulation of Eurasian and Chinese business elites

When a Chinese died in nineteenth-century Hong Kong, his body would either be buried in a Chinese burial ground, which could be an official or unofficial one, or sent back to his ancestral homeland for burial. Throughout the nineteenth century, the latter course was much preferred. Despite the colonial state starting to regulate Chinese burials in 1856, official public Chinese cemeteries were not provided until the 1870s and 1880s.[54] These cemeteries were plain in design and often overcrowded, while the colonial state had the right to resume the land and exhume the bodies anytime. Most Chinese thus relied on various networks including their clans, guilds or regional associations to help them to send their bodies back to their ancestral home in case they perished in the city.

From the 1870s onwards, a philanthropic organization named Tung Wah Hospital emerged to cater for the Chinese dead. A vast system was set up to help transport the dying and deceased back to their ancestral homeland. Charitable cemeteries were also set up for those who could not be sent back. Tung Wah itself was an important socio-political institution for the emerging class of Chinese merchants to administer Chinese affairs. The Chinese merchant elites who ran Tung Wah also used the institution to represent general Chinese interests, mediate between the common Chinese and the colonial administration, and leverage their own power.[55] Among these Chinese affairs, the management of dead bodies was frequently the subject of contention between the colonial state and ordinary Chinese.

However, for this emerging class of wealthy Chinese merchants, there were apparently no burial sites in the colony that they regarded as fitting with their wealth and status. The Chinese business elites, many of whom were born and raised in Hong Kong, and who had made great fortunes there, had developed a growing attachment to the colony. Yet it had failed to provide them a decent final resting place. The state Chinese cemeteries were uninviting to them and bodies there were always subjected to exhumation. The Colonial Cemetery (the Protestant Cemetery), which theoretically had always been a state public cemetery, was de facto exclusive for European Christians and virtually excluded any Chinese burials throughout the nineteenth century. The Chinese merchant elites thus felt the necessity for a decent permanent cemetery for their own class. But pending a long process of petitioning, it was the Eurasian business elites who obtained a decent cemetery for themselves first.

The most iconic figure among this small yet influential group of Eurasian businessmen was Robert Ho Tung. Born to a Dutch merchant father and a Chinese mother, Ho Tung received a good English education in Hong Kong. He later worked as a comprador for Jardine Company and accumulated immense wealth.[56] In 1897, he was already reputed to be the richest man in the colony at the age of thirty-five.[57] In that year, Ho Tung and his brothers Ho Kom-tong and Ho Fook were able to buy a piece of land in Mount Davis from the government for the establishment of a cemetery for the Eurasian community. The government authorized such a 'Eurasian Cemetery' on the south-east slope of Mount Davis, and the place was officially known as Chiu Yuen Cemetery.[58] Apparently, Mount Davis was chosen as the site because Ho Tung's mother and a few Eurasians were already buried there amid the large number of Chinese burials. Ho Tung and his brothers wished to claim a separate space in Mount Davis exclusively for their family. In 1899, Ho Tung requested the government to alter and fix the boundary of the Chiu Yuen Cemetery, since the boundary between the vast number of existing Chinese graves and his intended private cemetery was unclear.[59]

Ho Tung's intention to have a distinct burial site for his family and few other Eurasian families had two possible meanings. First, he was differentiating Eurasians from the vast number of Chinese burials there. Second, he wished to have a private cemetery for his family, walling off their family burials from the crowded burial ground for Chinese commoners. While the cemetery owed its existence to a certain extent because Eurasians could not integrate well into either the Chinese or European community, the cemetery would never have been created if an influential Eurasian business elite had not emerged. Without the immense wealth and social influence of Ho Tung, such a private cemetery could not have come into being. Throughout its history, the cemetery had been managed privately and was only reserved for prominent Eurasian families, while a vast number of lower-class Eurasians would never make it there. Chiu Yuen Cemetery was therefore, in effect, more of a private cemetery than a cemetery devoted to the general Eurasian population of Hong Kong.

By obtaining this spacious private cemetery, Eurasian business elites could design their burial spaces and tombstones free from government restrictions, which they could hardly do in crowded state Chinese cemeteries. Throughout the colonial period, the government regulated Chinese burials not just in terms of burial depth, but sometimes also the width and length of burial plots. Some Chinese had previously complained to the government that the regulated size of burial plot was far too small, as Chinese coffins were normally larger than European ones.[60] Large moon-shaped graves could not possibly exist in the crowded state Chinese cemeteries. Inside Chiu Yuen Cemetery, large moon-shaped graves were placed well apart from each other. Ho Kom-tong, Ho Tung's half-brother and in fact probably a full Chinese by ethnicity, had deep knowledge of Feng-Shui.[61] He designed his own burial plot in the cemetery, ensuring that its location and direction provided the best possible Feng-Shui.[62] Most of these Eurasian business elites, who were buried in the cemetery throughout the twentieth century, emphasized their Chinese cultural heritage through adopting

Chinese burial practices. They were able to carry out such practices freely and to a much greater extent than Chinese commoners buried in state cemeteries. This paved the way for other Chinese business elites to follow suit and press the government for a decent permanent cemetery.

The Chinese business elites, who had already gained considerable sociopolitical influence through institutions like Tung Wah, were slowly invited into the colonial administration to a limited extent. A few utilized their position to demand burial spaces for themselves. Wei Yuk, a locally born and educated prominent businessman, like Ho Tung, became a successful comprador at a young age. He was appointed as a member in the Legislative Council in 1896. In 1901, he voiced his demand to have a private burial ground for his family within a state Chinese cemetery. The government, however, rejected his demand, claiming that he had already obtained 2,267 square feet for burial purposes previously and could not possibly ask for more.[63] Wealth and status could enable these Chinese businessmen to enjoy certain privileges, but such privileges were not unlimited.

Another influential Chinese merchant, Lau Chu Pak, was the most assertive figure in pushing for Chinese burial rights. Similar to Wei Yuk, he was born and educated in Hong Kong, and later became a Legislative Council member. During his time on the colonial Sanitary Board, he first raised the concern in 1909 that the Colonial Cemetery had no right to ban Chinese death practices and burials.[64] This was certainly met with a strong backlash by some European members in the board. In the end, Lau lost the vote, but the government revised the law. Chinese practices like joss-sticks and firecrackers were allowed in a small section of the Colonial Cemetery, while the remaining large section of the cemetery was still reserved for Christian burials where such funerary practices were prohibited.[65] Throughout the debate, Lau emphasized that 'the better class of Chinese' needed and deserved a decent cemetery as they had made Hong Kong their permanent home.

The term 'better class of Chinese' was often adopted by Chinese business elites in distinguishing themselves from Chinese commoners, as well as being used by the colonial population in differentiating the Chinese. These Chinese business elites, who mostly received a Western education and worked closely with the colonial administration, portrayed themselves as 'progressive' in contrast to the 'backward' Chinese masses. As some of them were born and educated in Hong Kong, and all of them made a fortune in the colony, more and more of them considered Hong Kong as their permanent home and wished for a permanent burial in the city. In 1913, the Chinese Permanent Cemetery was finally granted to them. Instead of choosing to have their body sent back to their ancestral homeland for burial just like most of the Chinese commoners, their decision to be permanently buried in the colony reflected their attachment to Hong Kong.

Part 5 The question of 'emotional authenticity'

Throughout this chapter, we have seen how wealth enabled merchants of different ethnic backgrounds to obtain decent burial spaces from the colonial state. A hierarchy existed, however, given that certain ethnic groups were granted a cemetery well before others. Parsee and Jewish merchants were given a cemetery in the 1850s while Chinese businessmen did not obtain one until the early twentieth century. As Parsee and Jewish merchants were also regarded as part of the foreign colonial community, Chinese merchants, throughout the nineteenth century, were still mostly seen as 'the other'. Elite Chinese businessmen put forward a more 'civilized' and 'progressive' image of themselves in order to be treated differently from lower-class Chinese, but they barely dissolved the fundamental racial dichotomy in colonial society.[66] Chinese elites were able to emulate the European colonials in the realm of death, but during their lifetime, they still faced distinction and separation as the norm.

The gaining of death spaces by the Chinese business elites by no means implied that their ostentatious death practices gained approval and respect from the colonial community. Discursively, their funerary practices were consistently challenged. The Western colonial discourse pinpointed that Chinese death practices lacked consistency and emotional authenticity.[67] Such discursive attack enabled the European colonials to continuously challenge the legitimacy of Chinese funerary practices, no matter how wealthy the Chinese merchants became. Chinese elites did sometimes respond to these attacks and engaged in debates. As a result, there was an ongoing discursive contest over the issue of death practices, just as there was spatially. The discursive battle would also directly influence the spatial politics of burial, as an attack on the value of death practices would threaten the legitimacy of burial spaces.

Brenda Yeoh's work on the contest of space in colonial Singapore illustrates similar debates in death practices that directly influenced the spatial politics of death. In colonial Singapore, Chinese merchants gained their own private cemeteries long before the Chinese business elites in Hong Kong did, having carved out land outside the municipal limit as de facto private cemeteries as early as the 1820s.[68] However, by the 1880s, when the colonial state needed to initiate urban development, serious conflict over space took place. The Europeans could not comprehend why the Chinese would choose to reserve favourable land on top of hills for the dead while the living dwelt on low swampy ground. It was the exact opposite of the colonial practice of residing at hill stations for their cooler and cleaner environments, while using the low swampy ground as cemeteries. This echoes back to the colonial imagery of deathscape in tropical Asia mentioned earlier. Burials were everywhere; and the Chinese, in the European mind, certainly misplaced their emphasis on the dead over the living.

Chinese merchants in Singapore used very similar language to those in Hong Kong, referring themselves as the 'better class of Chinese'.[69] The Chinese mercantile community in Singapore attempted to counter state sanitary measures or urban development and protect their burial sites by drawing up arguments based on religious beliefs. They cited Chinese sages to argue for the inviolability of geomancy, hoping that religious arguments might prove beyond the restraint of a secular colonial state.[70] Colonial officials however were never convinced by the religious sincerity of the Chinese merchants. They cited what happened in Qing China to counter the Chinese merchants' arguments, suggesting that ancestral temples were also summarily torn down for government projects in Qing China. The common practice of storing remains in urns for relocating burial spots was also cited to undermine the necessity of permanent Chinese burial grounds.[71] All these were used to suggest that the Chinese had no real feelings against removing graves.

In the broader discourse, sinologists and missionaries working in China had written about how Chinese utilized their beliefs in geomancy to bargain for interests. Both Ernst Johann Eitel and Edwin Joshua Dukes, who wrote extensively about Feng-Shui, remarked on how Chinese took advantage of the Europeans through their beliefs of Feng-Shui. Eitel concluded in his study that Feng-Shui 'possesses an extraordinary amount of flexibility. It may be turned and twisted by skilful manipulation to suit almost any combination of circumstances.'[72] These works by sinologists were more than just academic discourse as colonial officials would seek their knowledge in understanding and critiquing Chinese beliefs.

Back in Hong Kong, when Lau Chu Pak was petitioning for a permanent cemetery at the turn of the century, someone used Confucian beliefs to argue against Lau's argument in an article in the *Hong Kong Daily Press*. The writer first pointed out that Lau must be a follower of Confucius as he prominently supported building a Confucian Temple in Hong Kong. He then quoted Confucius saying that places of burial should not be made to resemble a pleasure garden. Rather they should be brought into harmony with those who weep and mourn... To feast in luxurious apartments of the dead is an insult to the memory. More suited is some rugged height unfitted for the plough, where the pure and simple homage of the heart can be substituted for these vain frivolities.[73]

Such arguments directly pinpointed that Lau's demand for a decent cemetery lacked religious grounds and consistency. The writer also pointed out the lack of emotional sincerity in ostentatious Chinese burials, as Confucius had taught the Chinese that 'pure and simple homage of the heart' should be preferred over 'vain frivolities'.

From this example, we could see that arguments employed by the colonials against Chinese mercantile elites were not simply based upon a religious dichotomy of European Christian sacredness against 'pagan' Chinese practices. Instead, the colonials sought to interpret Chinese beliefs themselves, and challenge the consistency and sincerity of Chinese practices based on their interpretations. Ultimately, in most cases, British colonials criticized the affluent Chinese for placing too much emphasis on the dead over the needs of the living, and that many Chinese had also 'used' the dead for their interests, instead of being sincere in commemorating them.

Criticism of ostentatious death practices and spaces also took place concurrently in Victorian society against the wealthy. While the middle and upper class in nineteenth-century Britain were expected to spend a great deal on funerals and burials, the practice nonetheless provoked criticism. Funeral reforms in the 1850s pinpointed the greed of funeral undertakers, and urged for simpler funeral plans for the working class. Extravagant funerals and ostentatious burials were seen by some as snobbish exhibition rather than a genuine expression of loss.[74] In late-nineteenth-century Hong Kong, British colonials no longer monopolized wealth, and many Europeans in the colonial community were poorer than the elite Chinese merchants. Witnessing the opulence of the Chinese mercantile community and the growth in their social influence, Europeans felt negative about their ostentatious practices that often occupied much of the public sphere. But as the colonial state gradually conceded in the spatial politics of death, Europeans used emotional authenticity and religious sincerity as discursive weapons against the wealthy Chinese elites. Chinese merchants were able to emulate the Europeans in terms of wealth and burial spaces. Yet at the turn of the century and for some decades after, their death practices and spaces were hardly acknowledged as sacred and emotionally genuine.

Finally, how funerals, particularly funeral processions, were carried out in the colony might reaffirm such discourse. From a survey of newspapers sources reporting funeral processions in Hong Kong, as well as in another major treaty port, Shanghai, large Chinese funeral processions for wealthy individuals were a common spectacle. Large funeral processions within the European colonial community, in contrast, were mainly state public events. These widely reported Western funeral processions were generally for state officials or military personnel, and were regarded as solemn state commemorations with social and political values. In contrast, large-scale Chinese funeral processions, often in the very same streets, were simply represented as unabashed displays of wealth.[75] Later in the early twentieth century, when certain Chinese elites who were part of the colonial administration died, they were given a state funeral procession. Those funerals had a myriad of Chinese and Western elements, and they were much respected and valued by the European colonial community.[76] Compared to Chinese funeral processions for wealthy individuals irrelevant to the colonial community, these state funerals for Chinese elites tied to the colonial administration were acknowledged as solemn and respectable.

Conclusion

Travelling afar and interacting with other cultures were elements of a mercantile life. In the nineteenth century, being a merchant within the British Empire often involved living in a distant and alienating land. While immense wealth could be earned by foreign merchants along the China coast, a sense of home took longer to develop. The issues of death and burial were direct reflections of the foreign merchants' attitudes and level of attachment to the colony of Hong Kong. Through studying the development of cemetery landscapes and the discourses surrounding death and burial, we can better understand the changing attitudes of various mercantile groups in the colony. As more and more of them started to identify Hong Kong as their home, funerals and burials became expressions of status in the city. This was even more important for the Eurasian and Chinese business elites, who faced an uphill struggle to attain status and recognition in the colony.

The display of wealth was another major element of being a successful merchant. This display was not confined to life itself, but followed after one's death or the death of a loved one. Such display, however, was not always welcomed by others, but was often seen as materialistic and lacking emotional authenticity. For the Chinese business elites, who had more to prove, their display attracted criticism from the Europeans. European colonials criticized ostentatious Chinese funerary practices in various ways, including by claiming that ostentatious display was at odds with 'genuine' Chinese beliefs. During the turn of the century, Chinese business elites were awarded burial privileges that had been previously denied to them. Although wealth enabled them to emulate the Europeans in burial spaces, racial boundaries were far from being completely transcended, and Chinese death practices continued to be judged differently. Chinese business elites had to continuously contend with colonial attitudes, as the differences across cultures – rather than the universality of human emotions – were stressed.

6

Charlotte Jane:
National symbol and global reality

Annette Bainbridge

The ship *Charlotte Jane* is both a national and regional symbol in New Zealand. The ship's story is linked with the founding of Christchurch, which is New Zealand's third largest city and the main city of the Canterbury region. Her name is commandeered frequently in Christchurch, whether it is for a boutique hotel, a new quay at the Port of Lyttelton, a popular restaurant, or a recent art exhibition. However it is notable how little is known about her generally, particularly in New Zealand popular history. Even the most recent historical examination of her role contains little information about the ship's career after she had brought emigrants to the Canterbury colony in 1850.[1] She remains just a name, symbolically linked with a particular narrative of colonial history that is fast becoming outdated.

In stark contrast, the real career of *Charlotte Jane* is an intriguing example of a process of globalization that gathered pace in the mid-nineteenth century. She can be firmly placed in the context of Victorian Britain's technological, industrial, commercial and imperial expansion. *Charlotte Jane* was built by one of Britain's most innovative ship builders, and she sailed under the command of captains who were practitioners of the most modern navigational techniques possible at the time. She took part in several key aspects of empire building, including the transportation of both British colonists to various colonies around the world, and British troops whose job was to assert imperial dominance and British political might.

The story of the *Charlotte Jane* is important for three specific reasons. The first is that it firmly embedded the nascent colony of Canterbury, and the islands of New Zealand, into the rapid commercial expansion of global trading networks. This directly contradicts one of the central mythologies of the creation of Canterbury, and its urban hub Christchurch. This myth claimed that the new society being created in New Zealand was an attempt to escape from the consequences of mass globalization and industrialization and that moral worth and godliness alone were the motivating factors behind the creation of the colony.

Second, her story reminds us that the growth of Western activity in East Asia took place in a wider moment of change, and against a global backdrop that also included European and later Japanese expansion into the Pacific region. This was an international ship that was very much of her time, and her time would be one of the most dynamic eras in recent human history.

Third, the story of *Charlotte Jane* illustrates the 'connectivities' at the core of this volume, notably through the case of William Alt, who served as a crewman on the vessel from 1853 to 1858. Moreover, *Charlotte Jane* demonstrates how akin to individuals profiled in this book, a single ship facilitated commercial, personal and imperial links between Britain, East Asia, Australasia and the Pacific during the mid-nineteenth century.

The myth of the 'Pilgrims'

When *Charlotte Jane* sailed into Lyttelton Harbour, Canterbury, in December 1850, she sailed into New Zealand history and myth. 'From henceforward the age of the colony will be described as dating from the arrival of the Charlotte Jane', the local newspaper stated triumphantly.[2] *Charlotte Jane* was one of the 'First Four Ships' that brought settlers to create a model Anglican colony in Canterbury, New Zealand. These emigrants sailed under the auspices of the Canterbury Association and the leadership of John Robert Godley, a young Irish squire who had become deeply involved with the High Anglican Tractarian movement whilst at Oxford.[3] The capital city of the new colony would even be named Christchurch in a tribute to his Oxford College.[4]

Godley, and his more disreputable partner, former convicted criminal Edward Gibbon Wakefield, had a specific vision for this new colony. Years later, in 1916, New Zealand historian Henry Wigram summarized that vision by stating that Canterbury was to be 'a new settlement… peopled by the sons and daughters of the Church of England, a chosen band, to pioneer the cause of religion and education in the vast unoccupied territories of the Southern Seas'.[5] Modern New Zealand historian Gordon Ogilvie has agreed that their purpose was to 'plant overseas a society that would carry on the values of an England increasingly threatened by industrialism and revolution at home'.[6]

It was no coincidence that these particular pioneers would come to be referred to as 'the Pilgrims'. The use of this term reflected past historical models of colonization, such as the Pilgrim Fathers of America, sailing to Plymouth on the *Mayflower* to practice their own 'purified' interpretation of Christianity in a new land. There were also traces of an even earlier history in the name. It seemed particularly apt that these pilgrims were going to Canterbury, and like their medieval counterparts, must overcome adversity, as well as the stresses and strains of a difficult journey, in order to prove themselves worthy of the promised land. Events that occurred on their journey therefore took on a strong religious resonance. For instance, the arrival of the First Four Ships in Port Lyttelton within the space of a few days of each other, after being separated at sea for several months, was seen as a positive religious omen for the success of this Anglican venture.[7] However, newspapers from other parts of New Zealand which had less of a stake in promoting the myth of the Pilgrims were more inclined to put this coincidence merely down to 'the perfection of navigation' and 'the masterly skill of British seamanship'.[8]

From the beginning then, *Charlotte Jane* and her passengers were meant to represent a specific kind of new colony based on godliness, hard work, thrift, and moral character. As the *London Times* put it in 1851, 'A slice of England cut from top to bottom was despatched in September last to the Antipodes.'[9] The newspaper considered this attempt at colonization to be 'a deliberate... solemn

Figure 8 The *Charlotte Jane*. James Edward Fitzgerald, watercolour on paper, 1850.
Source: James Edward Fitzgerald watercolour, Canterbury Museum, New Zealand.

and devoted pilgrimage to a temple erected by nature for the good of all-comers, blessed with strong limbs and courageous hearts'.[10]

This colony would not be based upon increasing commercialization and industrialization, expanding global opportunities, or the desire to rid the mother country of undesirable surplus population. It was considered important therefore to differentiate Canterbury in emigration literature from the Australian colonies of New South Wales and Tasmania with their convict histories and unabashed grasping of economic expansion. To this end, Edward Wakefield provided written descriptions of exactly the type of settlers that the Canterbury Association did not want: 'paupers, vagabonds and sluts;... your middle class of broken down tradesmen, semi-swindlers and needy adventurers;... men of desperate fortunes and young reprobates spurned or coaxed into banishment'.[11] The implication was that settlers fitting these descriptions would probably feel themselves more at home in Australia.

Even the design of the advertising for emigrants to Canterbury reflected the idealization of the new settlement. New Zealand historian, Patricia Thomas, has analysed the typography of posters advertising emigration. She concluded that the use of gothic influenced fonts reflected the way in which 'part of the attraction of New Zealand was its characterisation as a place set in the past' and its ability to become a 'perfected vision of the contemporary imperfection' that was industrialized England.[12]

The strong ideals behind the Canterbury colonial venture were acknowledged during Christchurch's centennial celebrations in 1950 which centred on the arrival of the First Four Ships. The souvenir booklet for the occasion lauded the respectability and moral worth of the original settlers and noted that the Canterbury settlement was not designed to be 'a place for all and sundry to come with the aim of getting rich quick', rather 'it was to be a community representing the best elements in English society of their day'.[13]

The pilgrims supposed moral worth was such that it enabled their descendants to claim 'social superiority over those who followed'.[14] Even as late as the 1970s and 1980s, some Christchurch denizens gained a certain amount of social status by claiming their ancestors arrived on the First Four Ships. The myth of the pilgrims was an integral part of the Canterbury psyche. In 2000, Governor-General Sir Michael Hardie-Boys would describe the pioneers as 'hard working, practical people – a mix of builders, tradesmen, craftsmen, professionals, workers, farmers – who established for all who came after them a way of life... they found swampland, and bequeathed a city'.[15]

However all myths, no matter what original basis they might have had in truth, involve considerable distortions of reality. The myth of the arrival of *Charlotte Jane*, bearing the honoured pilgrim fathers to populate and civilize an empty land, bears little resemblance to the reality of the nascent colony of Canterbury in 1850. Yet, despite this, before the late twentieth century, the pilgrims' 'imagined, highly localised version of the past was never seriously contested, even though it was constructed by a relatively small number of cultural leaders and Pilgrim descendants'.[16] More recently, historians have contested this myth and challenged older interpretations of the colonial narrative.

Much as early New Zealand historians such as Henry Wigram would have liked to think of the Pacific as 'vast unoccupied territory', it was, of course, no such thing. The dominant narrative of the First Four Ships had to struggle against the obvious counter-narrative of the existence of the indigenous Ngai Tahu people in the South Island of New Zealand and the need to negotiate with them for land.[17]

Equally problematic was the fact that several great farm estates already existed on the Canterbury Plains, some of which would be immediately visible to anyone looking out over this supposedly virgin land just waiting to be settled. To further puncture the pilgrim narrative of creating an Anglican settlement from scratch, those farms were owned by mainly Scots Presbyterian settlers or Australian speculators.[18]

Without the existence of these people already on the Canterbury Plains, the pilgrims would have had a difficult task merely surviving their first year. The pilgrims had to rely mainly on food supplied by John Deans, a Scots Presbyterian farmer, as well as Māori from the outlying villages.[19] An English-language newspaper for Māori readers emphasized the vulnerability of the settlers and the economic opportunities occasioned by their arrival. 'These settlers will be able to do little or nothing for themselves during the approaching seed time. Let not our Māori friends forget that they will want bread and that these colonists have gold to give in exchange... Now is the time for our Natives to prosper.'[20]

It also must have been particularly galling to the Anglican settlers that until churches could be built for them to worship in they were forced to request the use of outbuildings on John Deans' farm for their Sunday services.[21] Nor did Deans and the other settlers already in Canterbury fit easily into the rather rigid class structure that Godley and Wakefield had wanted to export to the new colony.[22]

The Anglican pilgrims' founding myth was continually challenged by the presence of these already established settlers who were referred to as 'the forty niners', and the Ngai Tahu labourers without whom the pilgrims might not have survived.[23] Thus, this myth of the First Four Ships carrying the Anglican pilgrims across the seas, to fulfil their destiny by creating a colony based on moral worth and godliness, rather than greed and opportunity, would always rest on flimsy ground. However possibly the biggest challenge to the symbolic and idealized narrative of the First Four Ships were the real-life careers of the ships themselves. In the myth of the Canterbury pilgrims, *Charlotte Jane* leaves her settlers to their divine purpose and sails off over the horizon, no longer needed now that she has fulfilled her role in the story. She is a mere cipher and an unworldly one at that.

The *Charlotte Jane* and the global networks of empire

The history of the real *Charlotte Jane*, by contrast, places both ship and new colony firmly into the intense commercialism of the imperial global trading networks of the nineteenth century and the rapid industrialization of mid-century Britain. *Charlotte Jane* was built in the shipyard of William Patterson of Bristol in 1848.[24] Patterson was an important figure in the technological development of the Victorian ship-building sector and had previously worked with Isambard Kingdom Brunel on the Great Western Railway in 1838.[25] Patterson was at the forefront of innovations in engineering and ship-building techniques that would allow the world to become more globally connected than ever before. *Charlotte Jane* was built for James Thompson and Company of London to be used on East India trade routes.[26] Even her design by Patterson reflected this reality, her hull being 'bluff-bowed for the East India' trade winds, and critics would note the 'excellence of her materials and workmanship'.[27] From her beginning she was, both by design and intention, an integral part of the economic expansion of the British Empire.

Her first captain was appropriately experienced in the global networks of the empire. Captain Alexander Lawrence had previously commanded *Lady Clarke* which had voyaged to Adelaide and Sydney, as well as having sailed the usual trade routes to 'Madras and Bengal'.[28] Lawrence was born in the Scottish fishing port of Arbroath in 1813, and like many men from such backgrounds went to sea as a mariner.[29] He possessed a comprehensive knowledge of the Pacific, as well as being a practitioner of the new methods of sailing and navigation that were transforming the speed of global commerce. Merchant navy captains with an eye for opportunity realized that those trading companies who could deliver their goods to and from their intended destinations the fastest would inevitably have the competitive edge. Alexander Lawrence was one of the far-sighted commanders who acknowledged that 'owners and masters were looking for ways to make faster, shorter passages', and he was happy to take risks accordingly.[30]

Lawrence became commander of *Charlotte Jane* in 1848, and successfully carried a group of 264 new settlers to Port Jackson, Australia in the same year. The *Sydney Morning Herald* announced that 'His Excellency the Governor has directed it to be notified for general information, that the Ship Charlotte Jane… arrived on the 8th [October]'.[31] The next year, Lawrence and *Charlotte Jane* were back on the Asian trade routes, and luckily there exists a written description of this journey, in the form of Julius Berncastle's book, *A Voyage to China*, published in 1850.

Berncastle provides a passenger's-eye picture of *Charlotte Jane*, stating that she was 'built at Bristol, of teak, sails well, and is very handsomely fitted up,

Figure 9 Captain and Mrs Lawrence.

Source: Dr A. C. Barker photograph, Dr A. C. Barker Collection, Canterbury Museum, New Zealand.

with great height between decks and excellent ventilation'.[32] Her well-ventilated interior would be remarked upon by other commentators, thus suggesting that it was unusual enough to be worthy of note. He also places *Charlotte Jane* firmly into contemporary imperial trading networks, as he had joined the ship at Bombay where she was loaded with cotton, and then sailed with her to China where they were 'to take in tea for London'.[33] While Berncastle recalled that the cargo of tea was not ready when they docked in China, so they sailed without it, the memoirs of another British merchant in China, William Melrose, states the ship did take some of his tea back to London where it was sold successfully.[34] Perhaps the discrepancy came about if Berncastle was absent ashore when the tea was loaded on board.

If this transaction was a solid example of imperial trade links, the majority of the crew for this voyage were also representative of the empire. Most of the men were Lascars, and Berncastle noted that 'all orders to the crew are given in Hindustanee, the Serang and Tindals, who are like boatswains amongst them, being the only persons who understand English; this gives the voyage quite an oriental finish'.[35] This language barrier was to have unfortunate results later in the journey. Berncastle's description gives a flavour of the way both the empire and 'the Orient' were seen as almost romantically exotic by many British people.

Berncastle also provides insight into Captain Lawrence's character, describing him 'a most excellent navigator and experienced seaman.' Lawrence's experience was such that during the voyage he was called upon to testify to a committee in Singapore about ways in which British shipping could be protected from dangerous natural features in the Straits of Malacca. In order for more Western ships to sail in Asian waters, safe shipping lanes, on what Berncastle referred to as the 'high road to China', had to be established quickly.[36] The opinions and experience of a commander such as Lawrence were integral to the creation of successful shipping networks in that area of the globe.

Perhaps the best illustration of Lawrence's traits as a captain, though, was to come through Berncastle's description of an incident that occurred on the way to China. The Lascar sailors had been out in bad weather the whole night, securing the sails. They came down in the morning for a hot breakfast only to be ordered by the mate to go off to another job. 'One and all of them refused to go on with the work, and came off… to complain to the Captain, as it appears they had done to the Serang, without his giving a due consideration to their reasonable demand.' The mate or Serang 'being the only one who understood their language… reported it as an act of open mutiny.' Cutlasses were called for and the 'mutiny' was suppressed by force.[37]

In the aftermath, it became obvious why Captain Lawrence was considered a strict, but fair disciplinarian. Attempts at mutiny were obviously taken seriously, but Lawrence also seems to have realized that there was more to this story than he had been told by the mate. What happened next has been described in a recent study of Lascar mutinies. 'In a classic show of punishment, one of the mutineers was tied up in preparation for a flogging before being given a last minute reprieve. The captain then addressed the crew's original complaint promising that their meals would not be interrupted again. The serang, meanwhile, was summoned to the quarterdeck and reprimanded for ignoring the concerns of his Lascars.'[38] Berncastle alludes to aspects of Captain Lawrence's personality – his insistence on fairness as well as discipline, his common sense in dealing with people, and his willingness to embrace innovations in traditional sailing and navigation techniques – that would once again come to the fore in his next voyage, when Lawrence sailed *Charlotte Jane* into Antipodean history.

By the middle of 1850, *Charlotte Jane* was back from China and resting Thames-side in the East India Docks, loading cargo and settlers for the voyage to New Zealand. She, along with the other three ships scheduled for the Canterbury run, *Randolph*, *Cressy* and *Sir George Seymour*, were described as 'fine ships... much superior to emigrant ships in general'.[39] Despite this vote of confidence, when *Charlotte Jane* weighed anchor off Plymouth on 7 September, things on the ship were 'in dire confusion' and supplies had been left behind. The reason for this haste was simple. Captain Lawrence was so convinced of the effectiveness of the new methods of navigation that he made a wager with the masters of the other three ships that he would make it to Port Lyttelton, Canterbury, in under 100 days. So determined was he to win this bet that he risked the possible wrath of his passengers by leaving port before all their supplies were fully loaded.[40]

In sailing *Charlotte Jane* to the Antipodes, Lawrence utilized the new sailing technique created by John Towson, known as The Great Circle Track method. This involved 'going around Cape San Roque on the Brazilian Coast and using it as a departure point for the high southern latitudes'. New tacking techniques meant that ships were able to deal with the strong westerly winds of the Southern Hemisphere known as the 'Roaring Forties'. However these winds could still pose a threat to heavily laden ships carrying large numbers of emigrants and sometimes the tactic could force ships to sail too far towards the cold southern latitudes.[41]

Edward Ward, a passenger on the 1850 voyage to Canterbury, wrote a humorous description of daily life on board *Charlotte Jane* while she was buffeted by these infamous westerlies. 'Dinner was an awful scramble... part of my dinner was eaten on the floor and part on the table... for small dishes [you] must exercise the art of harpooning, and shooting flying, as potatoes, salt and bread etc, come swimming past.'[42] Sleeping was just as difficult as eating, with Ward being woken in the night by 'a shower' composed of 'a bottle of ink, a bottle of eau de cologne, my watch and a shoe' falling on his head.[43]

To Ward, a young man with a sense of humour, we owe an equally vivid description of attempts to perform the genteel ritual of afternoon tea in *Charlotte Jane*'s cabins. Using military metaphors, he wrote about how the gentility was shattered by 'the battalions of cockroaches careening about... deploying over the tea tray, countermarching upon the slices of cake, enfilading the butter and scaling the jampot'.[44] However uncomfortable the effects of the buffeting winds (and invasions of cockroaches) were on the passengers, the captain was right to be confident in the new sailing methods – *Charlotte Jane* made landfall in under 100 days.[45] Lawrence won his wager with the other captains.

For all his willingness to take risks, Lawrence appears to have been respected as a fair and decent captain. Once the first four ships arrived in Lyttelton, Lawrence's vessel was the only ship that had no desertions recorded.[46] He had been strict with his crew, with Edward Ward noting that at one point during the voyage the sailors were 'discontented at being allowed no grog'.[47] However Lawrence was also careful to encourage entertainments that would allow his men to blow off steam in a controlled fashion, such as the popular on-board boxing matches.[48]

The cabin passengers on *Charlotte Jane* had admiration for him, but there were numerous incidents during the voyage in which steerage passengers showed their resentment at being treated as servants by the wealthy elite on board.[49] The nascent, egalitarian colonial spirit was already beginning to loosen traditional social structures. At one point the strongbox with guns was brought up on deck to symbolically represent the captain's absolute authority and quell mutinous rumblings.[50] This dramatic gesture had less effect on the protesting passengers than the far more serious threat to deprive them of hot dinners which caused resistance to collapse almost immediately.[51]

Despite these problems all the settlers arrived safely at their destination and Captain Lawrence remained on good terms with many of the pioneers for the rest of his life. A local newspaper praised his 'unceasing attention to the wants of all' on board the ship, and overall he seems to have been remembered fondly by his passengers.[52] He would visit New Zealand again, many decades later after his retirement, and be photographed relaxing in the garden of Alfred Barker, *Charlotte Jane*'s former doctor.[53] Barker's first home in Canterbury, an A-frame hut, sported a canvas roof made from a damaged sail salvaged from *Charlotte Jane*, a gift from Captain Lawrence.[54]

In December 1850, however, there was no question of retirement. *Charlotte Jane* was re-victualled and repaired in Lyttelton and then sailed for Port Jackson, Australia. After picking up cargo there, she seems to have left in mid-April for London.[55] Meanwhile an incident had occurred that must have devastated the crew. On 8 April 1851, the *Sydney Morning Herald* reported on the inquest of the ship's cook, Richard Wootton, who died after cutting himself while chopping infected meat.[56] It was a sobering reminder that the dangers on board a Victorian ship could come as much from inadequate storage of food, and lack of medical understanding of the causes of infection, as from the sea itself.

In late 1851, Lawrence sailed *Charlotte Jane* back to Adelaide, Australia. It was a voyage with some worrying moments for passengers, with one woman recording that on 18 December, the weather was 'squally and violent' with 'some sails carried away and damaged'.[57] By January, the weather had turned fine and on 15 January 1852, a local newspaper, the *Sydney Morning Herald*, would note the safe arrival in harbour of 'the barque *Charlotte Jane*, 720 tons, Laurence [*sic*] Master, from London'.[58] It was the first ship to have arrived that year 'from England... with government passengers'.[59] These included the first group of emigrants to reach South Australia from the Shetland Islands. 'They were 55 in number, of whom 25 were single women' according to a local newspaper, so this group was particularly welcome in a colony that still had a gender imbalance.[60]

After offloading his human cargo, Lawrence supervised the re-loading of the ship. He was also forced to follow up a case of desertion when Robert Murray, the new ship's cook, ran off to get married. More populous colonies such as Sydney and Adelaide were often the scene of desertions, because it was easier to hide in a larger population than a small, new settlement like Canterbury. However, Murray was unsuccessful at evading capture and was forced back to the ship by the local magistrate despite the pleas of his new wife.[61]

The voyage back to London that year would involve great financial responsibility for Lawrence because, as the *South Australian Register* noted when describing 'the particulars of the Charlotte Jane's cargo', it was 'valued at no less a sum than 238,000 pounds'.[62] *Charlotte Jane* had arrived at the perfect time to take advantage of a financial boom in the Australian colonies, after the discovery of gold had attracted international interest. She had been chartered by 'the South Australian Mining Association' and consequently would carry back to London 'one of the most valuable cargoes ever despatched from this province. Besides about 40,000 pounds worth of copper, she takes something more than 48,300 ozs. of gold.'[63] A local newspaper reported that 'the ship sailed Monday evening [for London] with a fair wind, the crew and passengers in high spirits; among the latter are 16 successful gold-diggers, with their treasure on board.'[64]

Captain Lawrence was obviously considered trustworthy by both the mining company and the insurers who were underwriting the voyage. It is also evident that this trust was shared by his crew. A local newspaper commented that 'the seamen, who received their wages in advance, evinced their confidence in the commander by placing their money in his charge during the voyage to England'.[65]

The next year, Lawrence again transported gold back from the Australian goldfields to Britain. He had already safely brought out '30,000 pounds in specie for the Bank of Australasia'.[66] Now he was being entrusted with more gold to take back to London. In recognition of the temptations inherent in carrying such a rich cargo, Lawrence made some changes to his ship for the voyage home. For the first time, *Charlotte Jane* was advertised in Adelaide newspapers as a 'well-armed' ship. Lawrence also wanted to minimize risk by sailing to England as fast as possible, so he guaranteed that the ship would only take as much 'dead weight' as would 'put the ship in good ballast and sailing trim', and touted for only 'light freight' to be taken on board.[67] Some of his crew would be newcomers this time, with Lawrence advertising in the newspaper for 'a Baker and a Butcher' wanting to go back to England, presumably to fill vacancies in those offices on board ship.[68] No doubt with such a rich cargo, any applicants were rigorously screened.

The increasing financial importance of the Australasian trade route was about to pay handsome dividends for Captain Lawrence. In late 1853, he was transferred to *Orient*, a ship intended to sail solely on Thompson and Company's Orient Line service to Australia.[69] He would eventually go on to become the owner of his own successful shipping firm, A. Lawrence and Company in the City of London.[70] William Russell assumed command of *Charlotte Jane*. Under his tenure, the ship became involved in another key role in the expansion and consolidation of British imperial might: the transport of troops.

Charlotte Jane crewman William Alt: From naval cadet to East Asian merchant

In February 1854, *Charlotte Jane* was commandeered as a transport ship to move troops to Barbados. The letters from one of her crewmen, William Alt, described this voyage which was notable for the ship becoming 'becalmed for three days'.[71] Alt was himself an example of the rich possibilities opening up for British people of all social backgrounds in the global networks of the empire. His family had fallen on hard times and he became a young officer in training in the merchant navy. He ended up creating a successful trading company at Nagasaki, Japan, at the age of only nineteen, exporting tea and importing ships and military supplies. His experiences were truly international, encompassing: visiting many destinations on the imperial trade routes whilst in the merchant navy; his apprenticeship in mercantile trade in Shanghai; the creation of the above-mentioned Alt & Co. in Nagasaki; and finally his marriage in Adelaide, Australia. These international connections in his life mirrored the international network of empire in which the *Charlotte Jane* functioned. She was the main ship on which he served.[72]

Transporting over 160 troops was not easy for a ship the size of the *Charlotte Jane*, and Alt writes how even Captain Russell was forced to give up his cabin and sleep somewhere else on the ship.[73] However, she completed her mission successfully, and the Caribbean beaches seem to have been a pleasant diversion for the crew, with Alt using the time to seemingly singlehandedly invent the sport of body-surfing.[74]

By May the ship was back in South Australia. The *South Australia Register* updated its daily reports on 'Vessels in Harbour' and noted amongst the new arrivals the presence of the 'Charlotte Jane... Russell, Master'.[75] William Russell had safely brought yet another group of settlers to their new life in the Antipodes. These Australian settlers obviously appreciated the efforts of *Charlotte Jane*'s captain. Through the unusual gesture of writing an open letter to a newspaper, a group of sixteen passengers offered Russell, 'our most sincere thanks for the great kindness we have experienced from you, and for your unvaried gentlemanly conduct to all on board during our passage from London to Adelaide'.[76]

This impression that Russell was an extremely generous and competent captain is echoed in Alt's letters. Alt describes a captain who had a profound sense of responsibility towards the young men in his crew. Russell ensured they kept up with the education that would enable them to advance in the merchant navy by lending them 'books and charts' as well as 'a quadrant' and teaching them navigation.[77] He also appears to have looked after their moral welfare, with Alt noting that his captain encouraged him to go to church on Sundays, write to his family regularly and kept him away from strong spirits and grog. After arriving in Adelaide in 1854, *Charlotte Jane*'s crew found that prices of regular goods had gone up so 'the captain has raised the men's wages per month'.[78] It was a practical gesture from a humane commander.

In November 1854, they arrived back in the English Channel. The voyage from Adelaide had taken 'nearly four months' and there were further delays before landing, as they were stuck, 'becalmed and waiting for a breeze', just off the Lizard Peninsula. Captain Russell sensibly kept his young officers in training busy with navigation lessons through the frustrating days of waiting.[79]

The next year would see *Charlotte Jane* sailing to Malta.[80] Alt's letters also provide evidence that *Charlotte Jane* was chartered by the French for use as a troop transport and supply ship to the Crimean Peninsula.[81] The Crimean War was a significant event in the history of both French and British attempts to extend their sphere of influence in the Eastern Mediterranean and the Ottoman Empire. Ottoman authority was crumbling and the British and French were determined to prevent the Russian Tsar absorbing Ottoman territories into his empire. This meant that the *Charlotte Jane* was once again playing a role in attempting to expand and consolidate Britain's imperial network.[82]

This voyage was particularly poignant for Alt, as his brother 'Harry had been killed on 18 June 1855' in a battle on the Crimea. Alt was able to go ashore and see where the fighting had taken place. The site was 'hard and rocky' and he described the terrain as 'sown with rifle bullets'. Alt also provides a description of the difficulties of keeping shipping functioning in such an inhospitable environment. Getting supplies ashore was slow and arduous, as *Charlotte Jane* was 'frozen out half a mile' so only smaller loads could be taken on shore at a time. One of the main supplies carried on the ship was hay for the army's horses and unloading it was a drawn out process. It probably did not help that the crew 'were frozen to death' and their boots had to be thawed from their feet at the end of the day. Nor, psychologically, could they have been encouraged by the fact that the harbour they anchored in contained 'any number of wrecks'. There were some moments of beauty that helped break the grimness of the scene. Alt noted that 'all the rigging was like spun glass – icicles etc'. Despite this, and a few opportunities for the inevitable wartime looting that came their way, it is almost certain that *Charlotte Jane*'s crew were happy when their Crimean task was finally over and they were back on the warmer eastern trade routes.[83]

In 1857, *Charlotte Jane* was sent to Shanghai with paying passengers and cargo. According to Australian historian Ian Welch, the American Mission in Shanghai noted that 'the ship Charlotte Jane arrived yesterday from England, and brought back one of our oldest scholars (now a youth of twenty-four) who has filled a government situation in Jamaica for about two years, and more recently has visited England and France'.[84] The career of this young Chinese man, who had been given a Western education, effectively demonstrates the global reach of empire and nineteenth-century trading links, as well as the profound changes they could bring (for good or ill) to the lives of ordinary people.

Alt's life was about to be changed too, after this voyage. His letter of 15 August 1857 tells how the *Charlotte Jane* moved on from Shanghai to collect some cargo. The ship was forced to wait until the tea arrived and Alt was not happy to be 'lying here in this heathenish place'.[85] He was obviously experiencing some culture shock, writing that 'By the time we leave China I shall certainly have had quite enough of the celestial empire for one voyage'.[86] However the 'celestial empire' had obviously not had enough of Alt. He was offered a job by a Portuguese merchant in Shanghai and Captain Russell, solicitous of Alt's welfare to the last, urged him to accept, pointing out that 'if I staid with him he could not hold out to me any prospect of fortune' whereas he had excellent chances for advancement and enrichment through accepting such an offer.[87] As is noted in the Introduction of this volume, Alt would later become a major figure in the European merchant community in Japan, setting up business in Nagasaki.[88]

The final voyages

Evidence for the next few years of *Charlotte Jane*'s career is somewhat sketchy compared with her earlier years. It is hard to tell whether the evidence for her final voyages has just been lost, or whether it is possible that the years of constant voyaging, particularly to challenging places like the Crimean Peninsula, had taken their toll on the ship's physical structure, meaning that she spent more time in dock. Certainly, there might have been problems with the ship. In February 1862, the *Times of London* reported that *Charlotte Jane* had been scheduled for a voyage to Victoria, a port city on Vancouver Island in Canada, to deliver people and supplies to some unnamed goldfields. Obviously, news had spread of her successful runs as a gold transport ship from Australia. However, the clipper ship, *Lockett*, a 'fine vessel', the paper informed its readers, would now 'be despatched instead of the Charlotte Jane'. The reason for her inability to make this voyage was not stated.[89]

Charlotte Jane seemed to be back on form by 1864, when she would make yet another voyage to the Antipodes, travelling to New Zealand for the first time since 1850. This time her destination would not be the province of Canterbury, with its now-bustling city of Christchurch having been planned around the central point of what was to be an Anglican Cathedral.[90] The pilgrims, despite having been joined by a decades' worth of settlers of all denominations, were still insisting that Anglicanism was the literal and figurative centre of the city.

Charlotte Jane, however, would not be sailing back into Lyttelton to disturb, or consolidate, the pilgrim myth. Rather, she was bound for the province of Southland, at the southern reaches of New Zealand's South Island.[91] Southland, with its main town of Invercargill and navigable harbour of Bluff, had been settled by mainly Scottish Presbyterian emigrants who were only too happy to take advantage of imperial trading networks to bring economic activity to their area.

There were other far-reaching changes on board *Charlotte Jane*. From this voyage onwards, William Russell was no longer her captain. There is evidence that he may have been transferred to *Athelston*, a ship which had then sailed for Singapore.[92] Captain Lobbett became the new commander of *Charlotte Jane*.[93] There is little evidence available about his career on *Charlotte Jane* apart from this voyage to New Zealand. His journey to Southland in 1864 was varied, with 'a fine passage to the Cape and severe weather the remainder of the voyage'.[94] His cargo was a fascinating example of the goods both needed, and wanted, to make a financially and socially successful colony.

Charlotte Jane carried basic necessities of daily life including foodstuffs such as barley, split peas, castor oil and sago. Trade and agricultural implements such as steel spades, shearing tools, weighing machines, horseshoes and nails, chains and iron bars were also in evidence. For those homesick for a taste of England there was Yorkshire bacon and hops from Kent. The more financially well-off of the colony could take their pick from luxury items such as French brandy, chocolate, glassware and pianos. Also available were billiard table fittings for the gentlemen and 'Eau de Cologne' and 'all the fashionable perfumes' for the ladies.[95]

When *Charlotte Jane* was unloaded in Bluff Harbour, all of these goods, and more, were removed from the ship. However, she was also carrying another special cargo that would play a leading role in the future prosperity of this small colony. By this time newspapers all over New Zealand were already speculating on the effect that railways would have on the colonial economy. The *Nelson Examiner* was not alone when it published an article pleading for the government 'to spare no effort that... railway lines may be speedily in operation, for we are convinced that a large spirit of commercial enterprise will be evoked by the openings of these railways for traffic'.[96] The cargo of *Charlotte Jane* would be an integral part of kick-starting this process of railway building in Southland because she was carrying 'three locomotive engines' and 'two engineers... to put the engines and carriages together'.[97] These locomotive engines seem to have travelled in some kind of prefabricated parts which were then to be reassembled. It was a time-consuming process, and so unusual that descriptions of it even made the Australian newspapers. On 11 August, the *Melbourne Argus* reported that 'the landing of... railway locomotives... commenced' from the ship the previous day. The paper noted how:

> the small engine for the passenger carriages was the first landed, the next being the largest of the three – the goods train locomotive. This engine is between 12 and 14 tons weight, independent of its rolling gear, internal and external fittings. The landing of both was carried out safely and satisfactorily. Captain Walff, of the Oscar, barque, which is lying in port wind-bound, placed his officers and crew at the disposal of Captain Lobbett... Captain Lobbett being short-handed.[98]

It was obviously an operation of great engineering skill and patience to get these massive locomotives safely onto land. It was also an impressive feat of seamanship for Captain Lobbett to have brought a ship burdened with such heavy weight, safely from Britain to the other side of the globe. The newspapers' comment on *Charlotte Jane* being short-handed is interesting. Had she been reduced to a more skeleton crew in the interests of transporting the tremendous weights on board, or was this symptomatic of a larger problem with the ship?

The arrival of these locomotives meant that the *Charlotte Jane* should have played a major role in the beginnings of New Zealand's rail industry. However the Southland Provincial Council squandered the opportunity presented by the new engines. They over-extended their finances by attempting to create a railway not just from the Port of Bluff to the city of Invercargill, but also onwards to the goldfields.[99] They also succumbed to the offer of cheaper railway infrastructure, and accepted contractor J. R. Davies's assurances that wooden railway lines would be the sensible solution.[100] The wooden lines quickly 'crushed and splintered' and in dry weather sparks set them alight.[101] The Southland Council was bankrupted by this fiasco.[102]

It is, perhaps, fitting, that in 1864 *Charlotte Jane* was part of a development that was intended to steer New Zealand and its economy towards the future and not just because she had been part of the country's beginning. For the career of the trading ship, *Charlotte Jane*, was about to come to an abrupt end. The ship, which had been at the cutting edge of shipping technology less than twenty years before, was now less desirable, especially when compared with the new steamships that were starting to populate the shipping industry.

Captain Lobbett and his crew made one final, recorded trading voyage to Singapore in early 1865, and then sailed home to Falmouth Harbour.[103] There is no subsequent recorded explanation as to why *Charlotte Jane* was sold to a foreign buyer and her British registry formally closed.[104] The ship's eventual fate is unknown. According to one uncorroborated report, a ship named *Charlotte Jane*, under the command of a Captain Richards, visited the Marshall Islands in 1868.[105] It is difficult to determine if this was the same ship that had previously traversed the globe multiple times.

The *Charlotte Jane*: A global story

In one small corner of the world, the province of Canterbury, and its main city of Christchurch, *Charlotte Jane* is still remembered, but for one achievement: sailing safely into Lyttelton Harbour on a warm summer's day in December 1850 with the so-called Canterbury Pilgrims on board, a band eager to create a colony that would be a 'slice of England', only better.[106] They did not succeed, although not for want of trying. However, even if the legend of the pilgrims has few supporters these days, it is a shame that the entire story of their ship is not widely known in New Zealand. As a national symbol, *Charlotte Jane* is flat and one-dimensional; she is a glorified taxi that only exists to deposit the settlers in their new land, then disappear over the horizon again so that Canterbury can safely get on with, well, becoming Canterbury.

One issue that New Zealand has had to contend with, then as now, is a deep sense of geographical, and thus perceived social and economic isolation. The story of the pilgrim fathers does nothing to alleviate this, but oddly enough, a narrative that puts not them, but their ship, centre stage, would help address this issue of isolation, whether real or imagined. From the beginning, *Charlotte Jane* was part of a world story. She was built for trade and transport in international waters. Through her voyages, and those of other ships like her, the far-off colony of Canterbury became part of an integrated world of trade, commerce and culture. Perhaps now when the effects of modern globalization are being examined, questioned and critiqued, it is time in New Zealand to move on from the national and local myth, and reassess and remember the global reality.

Whether she continued sailing, or was sold for scrap, the story of *Charlotte Jane* is the story of the imperial and global economic expansion that occurred in the mid-nineteenth century. Through the transportation of colonists and troops, the building up of new trade routes and new methods of transport and navigation, and the facilitation of cultural exchange on a global scale, *Charlotte Jane* was part of an imperial system that influenced and determined the shape of the modern world. Her crew and passengers were innovators, traders, opportunists, entrepreneurs and idealists. They travelled to and from all the corners of the globe from Britain to Barbados, from Singapore to Australia, from China and Hong Kong to New Zealand. While there is much to find disturbing about the imperial ethos that drove many of their actions, the contribution of *Charlotte Jane* and other trading ships of the nineteenth century towards the creation of our modern global economy must be acknowledged.

7

Dreams of expanding the British Empire: The life of George Windsor Earl

Ranald Noel-Paton

George Windsor Samuel Earl: a sonorous name, and a remarkable life, but few have heard of him. He was one of a band of young British men who ventured to Asia and Australasia seeking to forge careers, make fortunes and help to build the British Empire. He was a man of both vision and enterprise which seemed at one time to mark him out as a future leader in imperial affairs in Southeast Asia and Australia. But his name does not rank today in the annals of the empire which he sought so hard to serve. Although the cognoscenti of the Royal Geographical Society (RGS) and the Royal Asiatic Society and other scholars may be aware of his life and achievements, only recently has the *Oxford Dictionary of National Biography* contained an entry for him.[1] Russell Jones, a scholar of East and Southeast Asian languages, refers to him generously:

> We as academics should recognise him as a member of the band of amateur scholars who were our predecessors in the 18th and 19th centuries; William Marsden, Sir Stamford Raffles, John Leyden, John Crawford and many others. Earl was unquestionably a scholar and strikingly prolific writer. The range of languages which he is said to have mastered would not discredit a modern professional scholar in this field; Dutch, French, German, Spanish, Bugis, Bajan and Malay. His interests were legion and included navigation, law, agriculture, geography, and ethnography. He wrote pamphlets, translated books, and published articles in some of the leading scholarly journals of the day. His subjects ranged from discussion of the possibility of settlements in Australia and elsewhere to recondite ethnographical studies which were to be quoted with some respect by ethnologists later in the century. He was a man of his time and shared many of the prejudices of European scholars in the 19th century. Yet he showed an empathy with the people of the Indonesian region which was not

universal. A Portuguese who knew Earl well referred in a note after Earl's death to his respect for the Malays and linked his name in this with that of Raffles, which is no mean compliment.[2]

I give Jones's comment by way of introduction and would add only that George Earl was more than just a scholar; he was a man of action and enterprise. This chapter will follow the life of Earl to demonstrate how that action and enterprise played out within the context of British imperial expansion in Southeast Asia and Australia during the early nineteenth century. Like his son-in-law, William Alt, Earl left Britain while in his early teens to make a living on the sea, sailing to India and back on an English East India Company vessel. Furthermore, like Alt and several others profiled in this volume, Earl maintained an abiding interest in maritime commerce. Nonetheless he distinguished himself with his focus on expanding British trade explicitly for the benefit of the British Empire. As a key figure in British colonialism in Australasia, he thus complements the stories of those, examined by Annette Bainbridge, who developed New Zealand's Canterbury colony. Like Rutherford Alcock, the British diplomat examined by Sano Mayuko, Earl penned numerous books and articles, many focused on aiding British imperial enterprises in Australia and Southeast Asia. He also wrote extensively about the places he visited and lived in Southeast Asia and Australia. Indeed as a chronicler of his travels, experiences and observations, Earl may have left his most significant legacy, crafting accounts that richly detailed aspects of culture, society and language in insular Southeast Asia, accounts still consulted by historians today.[3]

Born in London in 1813, Earl was one of three children, their mother being a lady of private means and their father, a Royal Navy captain. He later resigned his commission and joined the East India Company as an owner/master of the barque, *Aurora*. He was an ambitious, mercurial, colourful character whose life was decidedly adventurous. Although absent for much of Earl's life, he nevertheless seems to have imbued his son with a spirit of adventure. Fourteen years old when his father died, he had received a reasonably good education in two London schools where he demonstrated a lively intelligence. But this was not enough to keep him at school. Determined to follow his father's footsteps, he joined the East India Company as a midshipman and sailed on one of their vessels to Calcutta and back. This proved a transformational experience from which he benefitted ever after.

The Britain to which he returned was ablaze with talk of the Swan River settlement in Western Australia. This was heralded as a virtual land of milk and honey. It was just the sort of project to fire his imagination, and at the end of

Figure 10 George Samuel Windsor Earl, *c.* 1860.
Source: Ranald Noel-Paton.

1829, aged sixteen, he sailed for the Swan River in the first wave of settlers. But there was no immediate land of milk and honey. Conditions were hard and the odds were stacked against a single teenager becoming a successful settler.

Eastern Seas: 1832–5

After two and a half years, Earl decided to leave Western Australia, embarking on what was to become the seminal period of his life. His time there had not been fruitless. He had learned much about land and personnel management, as well as navigation. He single-handedly sailed a dinghy 200 miles along the coast of Australia from Perth to report on a crisis in the outlying settlement of Augusta. Earl collected people with the same energy and enthusiasm as he collected information. His curiosity and seeming encyclopaedic interest were inexhaustible. At this time, he started to record his experiences, carefully chronicling his life to allow us to consider it today.

In Fremantle, he met up with Captain Walter Pace, owner of considerable acreage in the Swan River area. He had also commanded *Medina*, a large standard ship of the Britain-Australia trade. Obviously prosperous and educated, with knowledge and experience of seafaring and commerce in Asian and Australian waters, he was just the sort of person with whom Earl liked to spend time. They became good friends and Earl learned much from him.

Pace also owned the Dutch schooner, *Monkey*, and he invited Earl to join him on a forthcoming voyage. He was to be a sailor rather than a passenger, acting effectively as first mate. It was the beginning of an eventful two and a half years of sailing the Java and China seas, the Gulf of Thailand and the Straits of Malacca, but not all on the *Monkey*. Her crew comprised natives of the whole East Indian region and this was where Earl started to learn the local languages. On this voyage they sailed via Java, Anjer, Batavia (Jakarta) to Sourabaya, whose residents were widely known for their fine wood and shipbuilding skills. There, *Monkey* was to have a major overhaul, but Earl moved on, sailing via Batavia and Sumatra to Singapore, where he arrived one year after leaving Western Australia.

He had with him a letter of introduction to a Dr José d'Almeida, whom Earl described at the time as a 'Portuguese merchant from Oporto'. This hardly did justice to possibly the most prosperous and influential man in Singapore. d'Almeida found Earl to be an interesting and energetic young man. Earl fully reciprocated this regard and was greatly influenced by him. d'Almeida encouraged all his interests in the area; its people, languages, natural resources, trade and commerce. He also spent much time with ships' masters and navigators who knew well the waters of Southeast Asia.

Not yet twenty-one, Earl found Singapore a stimulating and thrilling place. It owed its existence to the competition for colonial expansion among European countries. Britain, whose trade with China was growing rapidly at that part of the nineteenth century, sought to expand its dominion in what was then generally called the Indian Archipelago. There was also the desire to obstruct the Dutch, whose interests in the region were immense.

After some local coastal trading voyages, Earl embarked on a journey to establish a regular trading link with an independent Chinese colony in Borneo. d'Almeida made him captain of a trading schooner, *Stamford*, which was to sail through Dutch-dominated waters. This added uncertainty to the voyage as Dutch policy was to prohibit any trade not sanctioned by Dutch officials. Earl was reportedly the first Briton to venture into this part of Borneo to pursue trade. His trip was reasonably successful and while there he became the first Englishman to visit the gold mines of the Sinkawan-Montradok region. He made several other voyages on the *Stamford* to Java and Malacca. During all these journeys he kept copious notes, which provided the basis for his later publications, particularly for his famous book, *The Eastern Seas* (dedicated to Dr José d'Almeida and explained more fully below). After two and a half years in the region, he was becoming a considerable authority.

Preparations: 1835–8

Earl travelled back to Britain five years after leaving for the new settlement at the Swan River. The intervening period had been a truly formidable experience. In the middle of 1837, at the age of twenty-five, he produced *The Eastern Seas*, which became a bestseller.[4] Essentially a travel book, it had wide appeal, especially for readers interested in adventure, exploration and discovery. I possess Earl's own copy, for it bears his signature, various penciled scribblings, drawings and notes. Written in a compelling style, the book contains sections dealing with politico-economic matters and British imperial policy and also offers endless criticism of Dutch colonial practices. The readership included members of the Royal Geographical Society, Royal Asiatic Society, senior politicians and government ministers. The latter were especially important as the area was one of particular sensitivity and complexity for British interests. *The Eastern Seas* established Earl as a Western authority on matters relating to the Indian Archipelago and the intense Anglo-Dutch rivalry in the region. It did not touch, however, on certain contemporary Australian affairs with which Earl was soon to become involved. Here a brief piece of history is relevant.

Some fifty years had passed since the British first colonized Australia with the settlement at Botany Bay in 1787. The Union Jack had been raised then on the southern coast and at Swan River, but in the context of British imperial plans, the entire northern shore of that vast continent was unprotected. From the moment Earl had left Western Australia in 1832, he had been exposed to the politics and imperial machinations surrounding the Indian Archipelago. He noted the growing interest of the French in the region as well as the increasing prosperity and influence of Singapore.

Sir Stamford Raffles was appointed Lieutenant-Governor of Java in 1811, where his governance had been a conspicuous success due to his policies of efficient, honest administration, encouragement of trade, establishment of fair taxes and dues, as well as the minimizing of bureaucracy and red tape. He had intended to make Java the centre of an eastern insular empire, in which task he would have succeeded had it not been handed back to the Netherlands by the British in 1816, to the disgust of British traders. The next year, Raffles was appointed Lieutenant-Governor in Sumatra, where his administration was characterized again by his philosophy, ever mindful of Dutch plans to oust British trade and influence and thus establish complete control throughout the Indian Archipelago.

In 1819, he persuaded the Sultan and the Temengong of Johore, the two rulers of the state which included Singapore, to cede that unpopulated island to the East India Company. Settlement and development proceeded immediately. Situated at a critical point on the trade routes between Europe and China, this turned out to be a stroke of imperial acumen that outmanoeuvred the Dutch. Five years later in 1824, Britain and the Netherlands signed a treaty ensuring the security of the island state and, theoretically at least, giving access for British traders to the eastern parts of the Indonesian archipelago controlled by the Dutch.

All this had happened only fifteen years before George Earl arrived in Singapore. Apart from his scholarly pursuits, his guiding passion was trade. It provided the vehicle for all his other interests. Earl never met Raffles, who died in 1826, but he hero-worshipped him and his philosophy, which shaped him and underpinned his own vision and ambition. Rajah Brooke, another distinguished Englishman of the time and a friend of Earl, began his career in Sarawak in 1838 declaring, 'I go to carry Sir Stamford Raffles' views in Java over the whole Archipelago.'[5]

The vision which overwhelmed Earl was of a second Singapore based on the northern shore of Australia, complementing in every way its partner to the north. This vision was in fact not original even if Earl were to refine and develop it. The proposal for a strategic and commercial emporium on the north coast appears to have been made first by a British trader, William Barnes, who had originally been employed by the East India Company. For a few years in the early 1820s, Barnes had been trading between the Moluccas and New South Wales. He communicated his view to the Colonial Office in London that the establishment of a settlement (he suggested the Gulf of Carpentaria) on the Australian north coast would bring considerable commercial advantage and would strike a blow against the aggressive expansion of the Dutch.

Barnes's proposal was noticed by the East India Trade Committee, an organization of traders concerned with Britain's commercial interests in Asia. Having endorsed it, the committee brought it to the attention of the Parliamentary Under Secretary of the Colonial Office, who in turn consulted Captain Philip Parker King, the Naval Hydrographer, and a man who had recently surveyed the Australian north shore. Although Barnes had recommended the Gulf of Carpentaria, Parker King favoured Port Essington, with a superb natural harbour, on the western side of the Cobourg Peninsula.[6] The Colonial Office had to depend on two surveys, Parker King's and the 1803 survey made by Matthew Flinders, the well-known navigator and explorer. The main difficulty was that no one in the Colonial Office had any good knowledge of these two places or even precisely where they were. In reality Barnes's recommendation to them was correct but was just an opinion, while Parker King's was evidence-based.

Lord Bathurst, Secretary of State for War and the Colonies, and Sir John Barrow, Secretary for the Admiralty and an ardent imperialist, both accepted the argument in principle: that such a settlement would be of benefit to British trading in general; would provide a much-needed port for naval and merchant shipping tackling those seas and especially the Torres Straits. Finally, it would be of great strategic value for the protection and furtherance of British colonial interests. The go-ahead was given. In 1824, HMS *Tamar* and the transport ship, *Countess of Harcourt*, sailed from Sydney bound for Port Essington. Unable to find a supply of water there, the commander, Captain James Gordon Bremer, proclaimed possession of the territory and sailed on to Melville Island a short distance to the west.

Things did not go well and two years later the settlement was relieved and moved to Raffles Bay on the east side of the Cobourg Peninsula. This too failed and was relieved in 1829, leaving the north shore, in the minds of many British officials, again unprotected from the imperial forays of other nations. The whole affair seems to have been a complete muddle, which indeed it was, but it is easy to forget the immense difficulties caused by isolation, poor communications, lack of knowledge and lack of experience. These first, ambitious attempts failed but the arguments and potential remained.

Five years later in 1835, the project of a north shore settlement began to dominate George Earl's life. Newly back from Singapore, he was aware of the two failed settlements but was certain that mistakes had been made. He was convinced that the interests of the British Empire would be well served by a thriving trading settlement strategically placed on the north shore. He believed that fertile soil existed; certain crops like cotton, coffee and pepper would flourish; imported labour would be available; rice would be grown, buffalo introduced and trade developed with surrounding islands. Energetically he built up contacts, established relationships with the Royal Geographical Society and became a member of the Royal Asiatic Society while simultaneously completing *The Eastern Seas*. He now spoke French, Dutch, German, Spanish and various Southeast Asian regional dialects. He met and lobbied people endlessly. Historian Jim Allen describes his position like this:

> One sees Earl in 1835 as a young, intelligent, capable man, dogmatic and with a singleness of purpose which enabled him to make enemies as well as friends. Above all however, he alone possessed the experience and first-hand knowledge to pursue the ventures to which he now turned, the establishment of the third British emporium on the north coast of Australia.[7]

In 1836, Earl sent a copy of his first published work, advocating new British colonies in Australia, to Lord Glenelg, then Secretary for War and the Colonies.[8] Senior government and naval personnel, including Captain John Washington, Secretary of the Royal Geographical Society, advocated such plans. Earl's *The Eastern Seas*, available since 1837, added to the increasing support for this new venture, as did the continuing threat of an expanding French, Dutch, or even American presence in the region.

After much debate, supporters began to appeal to the Treasury to approve an expedition. Initially this was not forthcoming. The Chancellor of the Exchequer at the time was not impressed by the arguments and stated he would not seek parliamentary approval for funding what he saw as the re-establishment of settlements which had only recently been abandoned. Those in favour of the project were not to be denied, however, and Sir John Barrow, First Lord of the Admiralty, who particularly championed the cause, came to an agreement with Lord Minto, the First Sea Lord. They resolved that the settlement would be classified under the naval concept of 'warships in commission' and funded through the Admiralty's budget. Parliamentary approval was not required.

This clever strategy allowed the project to proceed but not without further objections, which were later to prove fatal. The Treasury was determined not to find itself funding, by default, future liabilities. Initially the project was allowed to proceed for strategic reasons, and approval was not given for commercial development. Earl's superiors chose Port Essington with its fine harbour, well suited to naval purposes. Earl believed the settlement should have been established at Raffles or Barkers Bay, opposite Croker Island in the Bowen Straits. That site was infinitely preferable for a settlement destined to be centred on commerce as it was more accessible for all types of shipping and closer to the Torres Straits shipping lanes. Nonetheless under the circumstances Earl was in no position to argue and gave his full support. His inclusion in the expedition was considered necessary and he was appointed 'linguist' and 'draughtsman', two positions which hardly did justice to his knowledge and experience. But this detail did not concern him so long as he was a member of the expedition.

We know that Earl and Sir James Brooke (Raja Brooke) were well acquainted. Brooke had been impressed by Earl's *The Eastern Seas*, especially the section which dealt with Borneo. In fact, the Secretary of the Royal Geographical Society had thought that Earl should accompany Brooke on the expedition he was planning to survey Australasian waters. His talents would have made a formidable contribution but his mind was on northern Australia. C. A. Gibson-Hill, the historian and one-time director of the Raffles Museum in Singapore (now the National Museum of Singapore), commented that Brooke could never have taken George Earl with him for the following reason: 'Enthusiasm, ability and intelligence are not endearing characteristics and Brooke was so obviously a man who did not like competition. Earl might have survived the trip but Brooke would have been miserable.'[9]

Port Essington, 1838–44

In February 1838, HMS *Alligator*, a twenty-eight gun warship, accompanied by HMS *Britomart*, sailed from Plymouth under the command of Sir James Gordon Bremer. The ships arrived in Sydney in late July. Over the following two months detailed plans and the acquisition of necessary supplies had to be finalized and approved by Sir George Gipps, the colony's governor. The expeditionary fleet consisted of the two ships which had come from Britain plus the 450-ton barque, *Oronto*, the schooner, *Essington*, and HMS *Beagle*, which was to be based for her surveying duties at Port Essington. The Admiralty had dispatched *Beagle* to Australia following its second surveying expedition to South America, a voyage on which Charles Darwin served as naturalist. Some 300 people had to be provided for basic prefabricated housing, tools and equipment of every sort; tropical fruit trees and seeds from the Botanical Gardens in Sydney; the frame of a church gifted by the Bishop of Australia; material for a hospital, barracks and storerooms; every sort of suitable stores, medicines, clothing and textiles; and finally cows, sheep, pigs and poultry. Each ship was packed to the gunwales. On 17 September 1838 the fleet sailed down the long inlet of Port Essington.

The task of finding the precise location of the settlement commenced immediately and a few days later, the chosen site was named Victoria after the new queen. Feverish activity accompanied the first few months. Work on the pier and the range of buildings were the priority; stores, workshops, outhouses had to be created; land prepared for animals and agriculture; wells sunk for water supply; friendly contact established with the Aboriginal population.

In addition to his involvement with the physical work at the settlement, Earl prepared for the first exploratory voyage to Kissa in the Serwatty Island group off the north coast of Timor. He was to establish relations with the islanders, spreading the news of Port Essington and the potential for trade. He and his crew sailed on *Essington* one month after their arrival there and returned with a cargo of nineteen buffalo, sixteen pigs, a hundred sheep, and a number of banana stems, coconuts and seeds for planting in the colony's garden.

Shortly afterwards, Sir James Gordon Bremer himself sailed HMS *Britomart* to Dili, about 400 miles off and the nearest European settlement to Port Essington. Again this was a flag-waving exercise to spread the word. While there, he was able to communicate with the East India Company's resident in Singapore confirming developments and requesting him to disseminate as widely as possible the news and the potential for trade. Earl accompanied Bremer throughout, his knowledge of language and local customs making him a key adviser. Bremer was received at Dili and elsewhere with full honours due to his senior rank and position. He had already proclaimed that he had taken possession of the entire northern coast of Australia on behalf of the queen. The Union Jack and its flagstaff had been erected with suitable ceremony at the top of Cape York on the journey from Sydney to Port Essington.

Meanwhile work on the infrastructure of Victoria was being completed. Final touches were made to the main buildings, the hospital, the smithy and the victualing store. Victoria Square around which many of the houses were built looked rather like an English village. An impressive pier was completed, almost fifty yards in length (the outline of which can still be seen today). The gun batteries were under construction and the guns themselves, five 18-pounders and four 6-pounders, were ready to be installed at Adam Head overlooking the harbour. Victoria was of course a garrison, a naval station for which Admiralty funds had been provided. At the same time, it had to provide an acceptable home for the men, women and children of the settlement who were almost completely cut off from the rest of the Anglo-European world. The rains had provided good conditions for the gardens to flourish and settlers were encouraged to grow vegetables like cabbage and pumpkin. The soil was reasonably rich, and bananas, oranges and lemons were starting to grow.

With the settlement established, expeditions took place around the Cobourg Peninsula and beyond as far as possible. Earl busied himself with his navigational, botanical, zoological and ethnographical interests. He almost obsessively recorded everything of note, always traveling with his books and papers, sending back much material to those parties with whom he was connected. At the same time, he would not shirk a duty or an opportunity to help or be involved in any activity at the settlement. He was no doubt a popular and easy-going man, if opinionated and irrepressible.

In spite of the formal designation of Port Essington, trade in all its colours was in the forefront of Earl's mind. His expectation was that crops like cotton and sugar cane would be grown. Cattle would be reared and horses raised to sell on the Indian and Chinese markets. Profitable trepang (sea cucumber) fisheries would be established to supply the Chinese market. Labourers would be drawn from surrounding islands to provide manpower for agricultural development. Merchant shipping would call on its way to and from the Torres Straits. This was the plan.

All these matters had been addressed in the published material given to the Secretary for War and the Colonies in 1836. Widely read, this work was responsible for much of the early interest in what materialized as the Port Essington project, even though Earl had specified 'in the vicinity of Raffles Bay', not Port Essington.[10] However, eight months after the founding fleet had arrived there, Sir James Gordon Bremer, the commander, felt satisfied that the new settlement was well and truly established and that this had been made known far and wide. He decided to return to Sydney, taking Earl with him, to report on the colony's progress to the Governor of New South Wales. In spite of the British Government instruction that Port Essington should be only a naval garrison, Bremer and Earl had expected that orders throwing open Port Essington for settlers would have been listed. They were keenly disappointed to find that this was not the case. In fact Sir George Gipps had received notice from the Secretary of State in London that he was not to encourage permanent settlement at Victoria, nor to grant permanent title to any adjacent land. It was a naval garrison.

This was a blow from which they would not recover; who would invest in Victoria/Port Essington with this sort of constraint? Bremer brought every pressure he could bear on the governor that permission to invest was absolutely vital to future success. A compromise of sorts was achieved with the concept of 'permissive occupancy' being available, but this was neither attractive nor understandable. There were too many alternatives for investment; freehold land was easily available around Sydney and in New South Wales. After two previous settlements had failed, there was little confidence that Port Essington would succeed. Port Essington then lost its main champion when Sir James Gordon Bremer was appointed Commander in Chief of the Indian Station and took command of the 74-gun HMS *Wellesley*. He never returned to Victoria. In November 1839, just over a year after its founding, a great hurricane struck Port Essington with brutal force. The settlement was devastated, the desolation complete.[11] Earl arrived back after the event and joined the valiant efforts to rebuild both infrastructure and morale.

Nonetheless over the following nine years, the settlement's decline was slow and relentless. A few ships came and went each year, more often out of distress rather than for trade. Ill health and lassitude took its toll, the main diseases being malaria and dysentery. Deaths occurred regularly and the fundamental failings became more and more apparent. The settlement was in the wrong place. It was too far off the main shipping routes, and the long inlet of the harbour, 18 miles from the sea, made access difficult. Its potential for trade was also harmed by colonial government policy and punitive Dutch commercial policies. These poor prospects deterred Chinese, Malays and Europeans alike from settling and investing in property. Effectively, Earl's vision of a trading emporium to rival Singapore was emasculated.

The settlement proved itself as a safe haven for ships in distress, and the presence of warships, either on station or in the vicinity, had greatly reduced piracy across thousands of square miles. In the final analysis the whole project was a case of high hope but, in practice, a failure. Yet the seeds had been sown: some twenty years after Port Essington was abandoned in 1849, a hundred miles away to the west, the foundations were laid for the town of Palmerston. In 1911, it was renamed Darwin.

Change of Circumstances: 1844–7

George Earl was not at Port Essington during the five years before it was abandoned. Yet he did not avoid the endemic malaria and dysentery which finally caused his evacuation to Britain on sick leave. However, just before leaving he was appointed Magistrate and Commissioner for Crown Lands. It is unclear if he intended to return after regaining his health. While recuperating back home and armed with all his books and research papers, he began to produce a series of articles to be published in Singapore in the *Journal of the Indian Archipelago and Eastern Asia*. He also prepared a paper for the Royal Geographical Society which was published in the society's journal late in 1845.[12] His major task was to complete and arrange for publication his book, *Enterprise in Tropical Australia*. It appeared in 1846 and was a wide-ranging commentary on the geographical features of the Cobourg Peninsula; its soil, seasons, climate and trading potential, both there and in other similar colonial areas of Australia.[13] He also prepared another paper for the Royal Geographical Society, 'On the Aboriginal Tribes of the Northern Coast of Australia'.[14]

Another matter was put to Earl's ever-agile mind. Britain in the 1840s was in the middle of a railway building boom. In 1844, British investors were attracted to the colony of New South Wales as a potential site for railway investment. In 1845, three companies were formed in London for such construction and one of these companies approached Earl to seek his support and involvement. Examining their financial interests, he confirmed this potential and undertook to take the matter further on their behalf when he returned to Sydney.

Other than this, his literary work took up most of his time, but neither this nor his questionable health prevented him from falling in love with Clara Siborne. When they met, she was only sixteen, exactly half his age, and came from an elite Anglo-Scottish family. She was captivated by him, unusual as he was – known to Ministers of the Crown, governors, admirals, senior people in all walks of life, as well as Malay seamen and Chinese traders. They were married at Trinity Church, the parish church of Upper Chelsea, in April 1846, exactly one year after his return to Britain. Much recovered from his illness, Earl was obliged to return to duty, so he and his young wife sailed for Australia one month after their wedding. Arriving in Sydney four months later, he met up with the Governor and Colonial Secretary in order to learn the latest news of Port Essington. As Commissioner for Crown Lands, he needed to clarify his duties there and also in connection with the new colony of North Australia for which Queen Victoria had just granted the charter.

Also with their approval, he progressed as far as possible the question of railways for New South Wales. This proved disappointing. While there was considerable local interest, there was also clearly a need for more investigation – accurate surveys, traffic forecasts and expected return on capital. Earl had to conclude that the interest of his London principals was premature and advised them accordingly. This development did take place some years later but did not involve him. As for Port Essington, the doubts and uncertainties continued, but it was not only the Northwest monsoon which delayed his return there.

Fairly soon after arriving in Sydney, Earl learned that his wife was pregnant. It was out of the question for him to go to Port Essington so an enforced stay in Sydney was necessary. Earl continued with his research and writing, as well as the duties required of him as the Colonial Secretary. He was also engaged in geological work. During his earlier days sailing in Asian waters, Earl developed theories relating to the geology of Southeast Asia. While the islands of the eastern Indonesian archipelago differ in structure and elevation from Australian territory, there were patterns of similarity which, when taking account of relatively shallow seabed characteristics (compared to the great depths and trenches existing at the eastern rim), suggested an ancient connection between Australia and Asia. He argued that the direction of the mountain ranges of the Malay Peninsula and Sumatra is identical with the ranges in Australia. As already mentioned, Earl submitted to the Royal Geographical Society a complex paper, which was read at a general meeting of the Society in 1845 just after his wedding. He was not the first to suggest that Australia had been linked to Asia or that the Ural Mountains are an extension of the Malayan and Cambodian ranges to the northwest, as those of Australia are an extension to the southeast.

But he refined the case in the context of mineral wealth, including gold, known to exist in the northwest Asiatic ranges, and therefore, he anticipated in the Australian southeastern extension as well. Mineral wealth, particularly gold, was an issue of momentous importance. Earl knew when he submitted this paper that gold nuggets had been discovered in the Blue Mountains of New South Wales. At the time, he advised colonial authorities to carry out a mineralogical and geological assessment in secret, so as to avoid a harmful gold rush. After his paper was read at the Royal Geographical Society, it was disputed by Mr (later Sir) Roderick Murchison and others. This opposition was published in the journal, *London Athenaeum*, in June 1845, after the newly married Earls had sailed for Australia. The relevance of this will appear later.

A daughter was born to Earl and his then eighteen-year-old wife Clara in June 1846 in Woolloomooloo, at that time a garden suburb of Sydney. Six months later, when the baby and mother were deemed fit to travel, the Earls sailed from Sydney to Singapore via Hong Kong. Their intention was to learn the latest news of Port Essington and then decide on their plans. The news could not have been worse and within a week or so Earl decided there would be no onward travel. The best advice was that a return to Port Essington, especially with wife and baby, would be out of the question.

Law Agent: 1847–52

Within seven weeks of arriving in Singapore, Earl had taken up the life and position of a permanent resident; his name is given in the 5 April 1847 edition of the *Straits Times* as a member of the grand jury at the April Quarter Sessions. Now thirty-four years old, he continued to research crops and plants growing in Singapore and the Malay Peninsula to determine which might prove profitable in tropical Australia. His friendship with the Logan brothers, Abraham and James Richardson (J. R.), became close. J. R. Logan was the founder and editor of the *Journal of the Indian Archipelago and Eastern Asia* to which Earl contributed many articles. Not infrequently he wrote for the *Singapore Free Press*, of which J. R. was also the editor until it was bought by Abraham, who himself became editor. *The Free Press* was arguably the most important independent newspaper in Singapore.

The Logan brothers were also law agents in Singapore and after eighteen months they invited Earl to join their firm to practise as a law agent. His appointments and connection with Port Essington ended in 1849 by which time he had established himself as a successful member of Singaporean society. Law agents were involved in virtually every aspect of commercial and administrative life. The city state was a hive of activity. The political scene was vibrant if complicated, under a governor who reported to the Government of India in Bengal.

Earl was in his element. In addition to his law agency work, he prepared and published in J. R. Logan's journal seven papers during 1851 and 1852. He also made many contributions to the *Free Press*, which were of course unnamed. The year 1852 saw the amicable division of the Logan brothers' Law Agency. J. R. returned to Penang where he would take over the editorship of the *Pinang Gazette* and set up his own law agency practice. A monument outside the Law Courts in Georgetown today bears tribute to his service to Penang society. His brother, Abraham, remained in Singapore, where he continued to be a major force in the city's affairs.

Gold: 1852–6

These changes coincided with a decision by the Earls to return to Britain for a visit. George Earl's health was deteriorating again, giving cause for concern. Six years had passed since their wedding and departure for Australia. Clara's father had died and they wished to see family and friends as well as introduce their daughter, Elisabeth (Annie), who was about to turn five years old. They arrived back in England in the winter of 1852 to great joy among their families. At the age of thirty-nine, Earl should have been in the prime of life, but he was not. His illness diminished his energy, spirit and enthusiasm.

Nonetheless he focused on completing a work long in preparation, *The Native Races of the Indian Archipelago; the Papuans*.[15] This was the key anthropological study of the Papuan people and would remain the standard reference for several decades. He had planned a sister volume, *Brown Tribes of the Moluccas, Timor and Celebes*, but this never materialized, the result, I believe, of his indisposition and also what was to be the only serious quarrel of his life.

The issue was gold. As already mentioned, his paper published and read at the Royal Geographical Society in 1845 had indicated the presence of gold in Australia. This had been disputed and formally opposed, his detractor being Roderick Murchison, later to be knighted as president of the society. In 1851 in Singapore, Earl learned that the discovery of gold in New South Wales had been publicized. He also heard of the written claims by and for Murchison that he was the first to have anticipated the existence of gold in New South Wales and Victoria. In view of what had transpired five years earlier, this seemed to Earl plagiarism and dishonesty of the worst sort, made more awkward by the plagiarist being a man of high esteem.

Although Earl's case was compelling, he sought only to set the record straight. He sent several letters to Lord Colchester, the then president of the Royal Geographical Society whose replies were courteous and constructive. Under the circumstances it was probably not possible for him to correct the situation, but he did agree that Earl could publish the correspondence. This accordingly took place in 1853.[16] The very public dispute was probably why Earl never sought to become a member of the society, although he had been a close friend of its secretary. But there was an interesting and unexpected result.

The issue caught the eye of the head of a London firm, Hyde Clarke & Associates, which had acquired the domestic and imperial rights to manufacture and sell the Berdan Pan, an ore-crushing machine used in the extraction of gold. The availability of such a machine was extremely timely and Earl was offered the position of Australian representative of the company. Earl was nothing if not an optimist, and with a wife and child, he was always conscious of the need to make money.

He accepted the offer, aware that to be a salesman was a distinct change of direction. It meant relocating to Australia, but the chance of prosperity in a country he loved. The period in Singapore had been a success. He had established himself as an agent, administrator, writer and commentator. Yet he had walked away from this with no apparent purpose other than to restore his good health. The year back in Britain had seen him in poor health. He wrote no papers or essays and, achieving little, was a shadow of his former self.

The Australian venture revived his spirits and energy. He absorbed rapidly the disciplines of his new trade and sailed with Clara and Annie to Sydney, accompanied by a consignment of Berdan Pans. They arrived in January 1855. His appointment was met with considerable interest as he was well known in the country. He made an agreement with a Melbourne firm, Samuel & Co., to handle storage and delivery of all pans sold. He marshalled as much press and publicity as possible and embarked on a sales campaign like no other. There was plenty of competition, but the Berdan was apparently a first-class product. Earl travelled widely. Shortly after his arrival he was in the goldfields of Bendigo and Ballarat in Victoria, demonstrating and making sales, mostly in Victoria but also in New South Wales. By the middle of that year of 1855, seven months after his arrival, the Berdan Pan was becoming an established tool employed in the Australian goldfields. Those months had been a veritable blitzkrieg which may have worn him out. His health deteriorated and the old anxieties recurred: his health, a stable life for his wife and child, their future.

Government Service: 1856–9

Earl decided that they had to return to Singapore to re-establish himself as a law agent and advocate, at both of which had a proven and successful record. On 19 July 1855, he and his family sailed from Sydney and after an adventurous voyage arrived in Singapore six months later. Immediately, he set himself up under his own name as an advocate and law agent. He was still well known and it seemingly did not take him long to reinforce the respect in which he had been held. Singapore's business world had multiplied during his three-year absence and the demand for advice and litigation was widespread.

Having launched the Berdan Pan business in Australia, Earl retired from that full-time commitment. However, he considered that the machine would be suitable for crushing antimony, tin and coconuts for their oil, and he was able to make more sales in Sarawak and Malacca before parting formally from the company. Earl never knew how successful he had been. Thirty years later figures showed that 335 machines were in use in Australia alone. He had helped to introduce the most successful, long-lasting mining and milling machinery to Australia and the East Indies.

The success of his law business and the slow decline in his health led him in June 1857 to join government service as Sitting Magistrate for Singapore. This was a senior position and it marked the final break with the sort of life he had been living over the previous thirty years. Frequent bouts of malaria had weakened him, although his intellect remained undiminished. His prime consideration as ever was the long-term welfare of his wife and child. One year after becoming Magistrate he was appointed third Assistant Resident at Singapore, Resident being the vernacular for a regional governor. While this does not sound entirely impressive, it was a senior post and one which was normally open only to regular officials of the Indian Administration recruited in Britain under covenant. Earl was an exception.

His performance in fulfilling the roles of Magistrate and Assistant Resident was exemplary and marked him out as a safe pair of hands. His responsibilities were not easily carried out, especially at tense times for the British Empire in Asia. Concern was generated by the 1857 Indian Rebellion (Mutiny), strained relations with the Qing amid the Second Opium War, Chinese merchants in Penang, piracy at sea, as well as rumours of a planned uprising among Indian convicts sent from India. There were also problems between the Singapore Administration and the Government of India, and in addition, between Singapore's merchant community and the East India Company.

Furthermore, there was at this time an increasingly vociferous campaign in Singapore for an end to rule of the colony by imperial authorities based in India. A Reform League, comprised of many of Earl's friends, emerged. Earl's government position prevented him from supporting them openly, although it was known that in *The Eastern Seas*, published twenty-five years earlier, he was the first to advocate in print the separation of the Straits settlements from the Government of India. He instead urged that they be made a Crown Colony answerable to London. At the end of 1863, the British government instructed Sir Hercules Robinson, Governor of Hong Kong, to report on the Singapore situation. His recommendation was that this transfer of government should take place.

On another matter, George and Clara Earl decided that their daughter Annie should return to Britain for schooling. Just after her tenth birthday in 1857, she travelled alone, in the care of friends. She would not see her parents again for six years.

Government Service, Penang and Province Wellesley: 1859–64

In 1859 Earl transferred to Penang, where he would serve as Assistant Resident. Apart from an obvious interest in promotion, it is not entirely clear why he left an admirable position in Singapore. Perhaps he thought it was too tame for him or too routine. Penang and the Province Wellesley area, for which he became responsible, was large and required extensive travel in country districts, often to neighbouring Malay States. His new position included that of Police Magistrate. Both positions had been held by men who had died. The position was thus not ideally suited to a middle-aged man whose health had been undermined over the previous twenty years.

The early 1860s took their toll on Earl with burdensome fieldwork which would have taxed the strength of even a young and fit man. Yet in the midst of his demanding work schedule he found time to pursue his intellectual interests. Wearing his ethnological hat, he published in the *Transactions of the Ethnological Society of London* a paper, 'On the Shell-mounds of Province Wellesley in the Malay Peninsula'. This involved strenuous field research work to study the habits of past generations. He also published, in 1861, *Topography and Itinerary of Province Wellesley* in the Pinang Gazette Press, owned by his friend J. R. Logan. In 1863 his article 'A Handbook for Colonists in Tropical Australia' was published in the *Journal of the Indian Archipelago*.[17]

Another important legacy of his literary work was his creation of the name 'Indonesia'. He felt that a single area name should apply to all the islands of the Indian Archipelago (itself one of many names) and also to the peoples who lived there. In an article published in Logan's journal in 1850 he had proposed the name 'Indo-nesian' or 'Malay-unesian'.[18] J. R. Logan preferred the former and, with Earl, changed it slightly to 'Indonesia' and 'Indonesian'. Earl is generally credited as 'the man who named Indonesia' and Logan should be credited for publicizing it.

Final Tide: 1864–5

The return from Britain of the Earls' daughter Annie, now aged sixteen, was the start of a sublimely happy period. She no doubt lit up their lives, but it was not to last for long. Eight months later Earl suffered a stroke. Tired, ill and worried about his job, he soldiered on, able to do only office and administrative work. Two months later his condition had worsened and the Standing Medical Committee in Penang instructed that he was to leave the Straits immediately to go on sick leave for twelve months. Ideally he should have returned to Britain, as his wife and daughter wished, but no suitable booking was available. With Clara and Annie, Earl sailed from Singapore in January 1864 bound for Adelaide.

This was a fateful turn of events. On board their ship was William Alt, on his way home to Britain from Japan. Then aged twenty-three, he fell in love with the sixteen-year-old Annie, and she with him. While the Earls remained in Adelaide, Alt sailed on to Britain, returning to Adelaide seven months later. The couple were married on 15 September 1864 at Trinity Church, Adelaide, and sailed shortly afterwards to Nagasaki, where Alt operated his business.[19]

Annie never saw her father again. Although only seventeen when she married, she would soon show herself to be an ideal wife for William, illustrated by the fact that setting off to live in Japan did not trouble her unduly. She and William lived for four years in Nagasaki and later in other cities in Japan. She bore him four children while in Japan and four more after their return to Britain in 1871. They were married for forty-four years.[20]

One month after the marriage in Adelaide, George and Clara returned to Penang. He appeared to have made a complete recovery, regaining his spirits and energy. He took up his old position in government in January 1865, but after only a few weeks was laid low with an attack of dysentery which left him supine and jaded. With his usual dedication he tried to return to his duties. He even had a final flourish with his dream of an Australian north shore capital city. One month before he died, Earl submitted a substantial and definitive paper to his old friend Sir Dominick Daly, Governor of South Australia and Northern Territories, who was still responsible for the project. But he was a broken man. The Penang Medical Officer wrote that 'only his wonderfully sanguine and buoyant spirit' kept him alive. He also stated that no medical treatment could save him if he chose to remain in the tropics.

Earl recognized that his days were numbered. He hurriedly made arrangements for Clara to leave for Japan to stay with their daughter and booked his own passage home to England. His ship, *Shantung*, sailed from Penang on 7 August 1865 and he died on board two days later. His body was returned to Georgetown and interred in the Christian cemetery on 10 August. His death was listed in newspapers in Penang, Singapore, Sydney and Adelaide. No announcement was made in Britain. *The South Australian Register* of 27 November 1865 carried a lengthy obituary, believed to have been written by Sir Dominick Daly.[21]

Earl was always on the leading edge of the development of the British Empire in Southeast Asia and Australia; yet, he never witnessed the fulfilment of his endeavours, particularly in the creation of a successful colonial settlement in northern Australia during his lifetime. Nonetheless, his key role in championing colonial enterprises has led historian R. H. W. Reece to declare: 'The [residents of] the City of Darwin should rightly claim Earl as their own Raffles.'[22]

Editorial Note: This chapter is a synopsis of Ranald Noel-Paton's monograph, *An Eastern Calling: George Windsor Earl and a Vision of Empire*. London: Ashgrove Publishing, 2018. In that work, Noel-Paton draws extensively on the over forty published articles and books as well as unpublished personal records of George Windsor Earl of which space does not permit to be fully included here. However, all are listed, along with other source material, in the reference section of *An Eastern Calling*.

Notes

Introduction

1. An early and influential look at the emergence of the treaty port system is John K. Fairbank, *Trade and Diplomacy on the China Coast: The Opening of the Treaty Ports, 1842–1854*, two volumes (Cambridge, MA: Harvard University Press, 1953). The role of merchant houses and their lobbying in this story was notably explored in Michael Greenberg, *British Trade and the Opening of China, 1800–1842* (Cambridge: Cambridge University Press, 1951), and more recently in works such as Glenn Melancon, *Britain's China Policy and the Opium Crisis: Balancing Drugs, Violence and National Honour, 1833–1840* (Aldershot: Ashgate, 2003); J.Y. Wong, *Deadly Dreams: Opium, Imperialism and the Arrow War (1856–1860) in China* (Cambridge: Cambridge University Press, 1998).
2. A pioneering work in English on the development of the treaty port regime in Japan is W.G. Beasley, *Select Documents on Japanese Foreign Policy, 1853–1868* (London: Oxford University Press, 1955).
3. Such works on China include: Rhoads Murphey, *The Treaty Ports and China's Modernization: What Went Wrong?* (Ann Arbor, MI: University of Michigan, Center for Chinese Studies, 1970); Billy K. L. So and Ramon H. Myers, eds., *The Treaty Port Economy in Modern China, Empirical Studies of Institutional Change and Economic Performance* (Berkeley: University of California, Berkeley, Institute of East Asian Studies, 2011). On Japan, Shinya Sugiyama, *Japan's Industrialization in the World Economy, 1859–1899: Export Trade and Overseas Competition* (London: Athlone Press, 1988); Catherine L. Phipps, *Empires on the Waterfront: Japan's Ports and Power, 1858–1899* (Cambridge, MA: Harvard University Asia Center, 2015). A valuable study of diplomacy in the 1850s and 1860s is Michael Auslin, *Negotiating with Imperialism: The Unequal Treaties and the Culture of Japanese Diplomacy* (Cambridge, MA: Harvard University Press, 2004).
4. Pär Kristoffer Cassel, *Grounds of Judgment: Extraterritoriality and Imperial Power in Nineteenth-Century China and Japan* (New York: Oxford University Press, 2012); Isabella Jackson and Robert Bickers, eds., *Treaty Ports in Modern China: Law, Land and Power (Routledge Studies in the Modern History of Asia)* (London: Routledge, 2016).
5. Peter Ennals, *Opening a Window to the West: The Foreign Concession at Kobe, Japan, 1868–1899* (Toronto: University of Toronto Press, 2014); Cole Roskum,

Improvised City: Architecture and Governance in Shanghai, 1843–1937 (Seattle: University of Washington Press, 2019).

6   Robert Nield, *China's Foreign Places: The Foreign Presence in China in the Treaty Port Era, 1840–1943* (Hong Kong: Hong Kong University Press, 2015); J.E. Hoare, ed., *Culture, Power & Politics in Treaty Port Japan, 1854–1899: Key Papers, Press and Contemporary Writings: Volume 1: Historical Perspectives* (London: Renaissance Books, 2018).

7   Hugh Cortazzi, ed., *Victorians in Japan: In and around the Treaty Ports* (London: Bloomsbury Academic Collections, 2012 (originally published by Althone Press, 1987); Ruth Rogaski, *Hygienic Modernity: Meanings of Health and Disease in Treaty-Port China* (Berkeley: University of California Press, 2004); Mary Tiffen, *Friends of Sir Robert Hart: Three Generations of Carrall Women in China* (Crewkerne, UK: Tiffania Books in association with Queen's University Belfast, 2012); Donna Brunero and Stephanie Villalta Puig, eds., *Life in Treaty Port China and Japan* (London: Palgrave Macmillan, 2018).

8   We note that Donna Brunero and Stephanie Villalta Puig have employed this approach in their recently published edited volume, *Life in Treaty Port China and Japan*.

9   David Lambert and Alan Lester, 'Imperial Spaces, Imperial Subjects', in *Colonial Lives across the British Empire*, ed. D. Lambert and A. Lester (Cambridge: Cambridge University Press, 2006), 1–31.

10 Alan Lester, 'Imperial Circuits and Networks: Geographies of the British Empire', *History Compass* 4, no. 1 (2005), 124–41; Zoë Laidlaw, *Colonial Connections 1815–45: Patronage, the Information Revolution and Colonial Government* (Manchester: Manchester University Press, 2005).

11 John Darwin, 'Orphans of Empire', in *Settler and Expatriates: Britons over the Seas*, ed. Robert Bickers (Oxford: Oxford University Press, 2010), 329–45.

12 'Important News from China: Latest Position of Affairs at Canton – Great Alarm among British Residents', *New York Times*, 25 March 1857, 1.

13 Sherard Osborn, *The Past and Future of British Relations in China* (Cambridge: Cambridge University Press, 2014), 11–14.

14 Charles Richardson's private correspondence is reproduced in: Robert S.G. Fletcher, *The Ghost of Namamugi: Charles Lenox Richardson and the Anglo-Satsuma War* (Amsterdam: Amsterdam University Press, 2019). The following paragraphs draw on this material.

15 Reference here is to the personal correspondences of William John Alt, 1853–65. Hereafter, each specific reference to the letters will be given as WA (for William Alt), followed by the date, place where written, the recipient (if known) and the file number of the digitized collection. The editors thank Tessa Montgomery, a direct descendant of William Alt, for generously allowing access to the original

letters. Mrs. Montgomery kindly donated the letters to the Sainsbury Institute for the Study of Japanese Arts and Cultures (Norwich, UK), which coordinated with the Art Research Center, Ritsumeikan University (Kyoto, Japan) to digitize them to expand scholarly access. The original letters are now held by the Nagasaki Museum of History and Culture.

16 WA to Mother, 20 November 1853 (WA08-013a, WA08-013b). For example, an earlier Robert Hellyer, an ancestor of this book's co-editor, carved the figurehead for *Cutty Sark*, launched in 1869. Royal Museums of Greenwich, https://collections.rmg.co.uk/collections/objects/14752.html (accessed 15 March 2020).

17 E. Cleere, *Avuncularism: Capitalism, Patriarchy, and Nineteenth-century English Culture* (Stanford: Stanford University Press, 2004).

18 WA to Mother, Port Adelaide, 30 May 1854 (WA10-001b).

19 C.L. Richardson to C. Richardson, 6 August 1853, in Fletcher, *Ghost of Namamugi*, 135.

20 WA to Aunt, Shanghai, 6 November 1857 (WA08-011a).

21 WA to Mother, Shanghai, May 1858 (WA07-003a).

22 WA to Mother, Port Adelaide, 30 May 1854 (WA10-001b).

23 WA to Balser, Nagasaki, 31 March 1863 (WA03-12-01a).

24 L. Davidoff, *Thicker than Water: Siblings and Their Relations, 1780–1920* (Oxford: Oxford University Press, 2012).

25 E. Cleall, L. Ishiguro and E.J. Manktelow, 'Imperial Relations: Families in the British Empire', *Journal of Colonialism and Colonial History* 14, no. 1 (Spring 2013): online http://doi.org/10.1353/cch.2013.0006

26 For example, Alt sent a £50 draft to his mother in March 1859 (WA07-018) and mentioned £100 sent home in letters posted from Nagasaki on 28 September 1862 (WA04-005_01a) and on 29 April 1863 (WA03-011a).

27 WA to Frances (sister)? Nagasaki, 17 February 1863 (WA03-001b).

28 Using money from another branch of the family to invest in settlement real estate, Richardson profited from the dramatic growth of Shanghai's population in the early 1860s, as refugees fled the countryside for the relative safety of the treaty port. See: Fletcher, *Ghost of Namamugi*, 22–3.

29 Contemporary press accounts of Richardson's death described him as being on the verge of retiring to England, but it seems likely his trip to Yokohama was connected to setting up new business there. See: Fletcher, *Ghost of Namamugi*, 26–7.

30 WA to Mother, 3 February 1860, Nagasaki (WA03-015a).

31 Upon the abolition of slavery in 1833, the firm received compensation money from the British taxpayer for its connections to Caribbean plantations.

32 The development of Alt's tea export business is explored in detail in Robert Hellyer, *Green with Milk and Sugar – When Japan Filled America's Tea Cups* (New York: Columbia University Press, 2021), 36–49.

33 WA to Mother, Nagasaki, 28 September 1862 (WA04-005-01a).
34 WA to Frances (sister)? Nagasaki, 17 February 1863 (WA03-001a).
35 WA to Frances?, Nagasaki, 17 February 1863 (WA03-001b).
36 Richardson followed the course of the Crimean War closely, for example, and because that great conflict had an East Asian dimension, too – culminating in the 1854 siege of Petropavlovsk – Richardson and his father could both share news from their respective ends of the conflict.
37 WA to Mother, Shanghai, 20 September 1863 (WA03-005a).
38 Alt's business activities in Nagasaki during the 1860s are examined more fully in Robert Hellyer, 'Mid Nineteenth-Century Nagasaki: Western and Japanese Merchant Communities within Commercial and Political Transitions', in *Merchant Communities in Asia, 1600–1980*, ed. Yuju Lin and Madeleine Zelin (London: Pickering and Chatto, 2014), 159–76.
39 Michele Blagg, 'Gold Refining in London: The End of the Rainbow, 1919–1922', in *The Global Gold Market and the International Monetary System from the Late 19th Century to the Present: Actors, Networks, Power*, ed. Sandra Bott (Houndmills, Basingstoke, UK: Palgrave Macmillan, 2013), 91; B. Mountford and S. Tufnell, eds., *A Global History of Gold Rushes* (Oakland, CA: University of California Press, 2019).
40 Arguably his most significant work is George Windsor Earl, *The Eastern Seas: Or, Voyages and Adventures in the Indian Archipelago, in 1832-33-34* (London: W.H. Allen, 1837).
41 The editors also regrettably did not have access to Elisabeth Alt's memoirs, written late in her life. Elisabeth Alt, 'Some Memories of Elisabeth Christiana Fernhill Alt (née Earl)', unpublished manuscript, National Library of Australia.
42 While the merchant press of the time was inclined to emphasize the transformative impact of external actors on a 'static' and 'timeless' 'Orient', scholars have long stressed the significance of internal dynamics in shaping the changes that now occurred throughout the treaty port world. See, for example: Takeshi Hamashita, 'Tribute and Treaties: Maritime Asia and Treaty Port Networks in the Era of Negotiation, 1800–1900', in *The Resurgence of East Asia: 500, 150 and 50 Year Perspectives*, ed. Giovanni Arrighi, Takeshi Hamashita and Mark Selden (London: Routledge, 2003), 17–47.

Chapter 1

1 For the peculiar processes of his unusual promotion from the Consular service to the Diplomatic service, see Sano Mayuko, *Orukokku no Edo: Shodai eikoku koshi ga mita bakumatsu nihon* (Alcock's Edo: Japan in the Bakumatsu Period, as seen by the First British Minister) (Tokyo: Chūōkōron-shinsha, 2003), 28–35.

2   His first appointment was, in fact, consul at Fuzhou, but for some personnel complications mainly due to miscommunication between London and Hong Kong, he was first sent to Amoy and spent his earliest days in China there. (These processes were traced through a broad survey of documents mainly in the British Foreign Office files [hereafter FO] FO 17/85, 87, 88, 89, and FO 682/1977/127, held in The National Archives, UK [hereinafter, NA]).

3   For the moment, the reliable studies on Alcock's life in English, though being separate short articles and not a comprehensive volume, were written by the late Sir Hugh Cortazzi. These include 'Sir Rutherford Alcock, Minister to Japan, 1859–62' and 'Alcock returns to Japan', in *British Envoys in Japan, 1859–1972*, ed. Hugh Cortazzi et al. (Kent: Global Oriental, 2004), 9–21 and 33–8. There are other, more recent articles mentioning some aspects of Alcock's work, such as: Andrew Cobbing, 'A Victorian Embarrassment: Consular Jurisdiction and the Evils of Extraterritoriality', *International History Review*, 40, no. 2 (2018): 273–91; Andrew Hillier, 'Bridging Cultures: The Forging of the China Consular Mind', *Journal of Imperial and Commonwealth History*, 47, no. 4 (2019): 742–72. Besides, not to mention, his profile is found in the *Oxford Dictionary of National Biography*. Alexander Michie's *The Englishman in China during the Victorian Era: As Illustrated in the Career of Sir Rutherford Alcock*, 2 vols. (Edinburgh: William Blackwood and Sons, 1900) has been regarded as the only biography of Alcock by a contemporary; the work is, of course, important but needs to be read carefully as it contains not a few inaccurate elements of information. I published the aforementioned 2003 book in Japanese mainly focusing on Alcock's time in Japan. I am currently preparing Alcock's critical biography, which is forthcoming from Minerva Press (Kyoto, Japan).

4   For a brief note for readers' information, Alcock had been a young, promising surgeon, before he had to give up that career because of the illness which deprived the free movement of his arms and fingers. After retirement from the diplomatic service, he was still active for more than a quarter century in various honourable positions in London, not only relative to Asian affairs but also in the medical field.

5   Alcock to Bonham, 14 December 1848, FO 228/91, NA.

6   Based on his appointment to the newly created position in Japan in 1858, it was in 1859 that he actually arrived in the country.

7   FO 228/50 and 52, NA.

8   'List of British residents at the port of Shanghae on the 1st day of January 1847, taken from the registry kept at the consulate', FO 228/76, NA.

9   FO 228/64 and 76, NA.

10 A typical communiqué is Alcock to Davis, 10 June 1847, FO 228/77, NA.

11 FO 228/131, 146, NA.

12 From Alcock to Bonham, 2 February 1854, FO 228/176, NA.

13 Alcock's appointment to Japan was not only based on his ability but entangled with many other elements including the finances of the Foreign Office (for the purpose of keeping down the total personnel costs for the Far Eastern Service). This is beyond the scope of this paper but will be made clear in detail in my planned biography of Alcock.
14 Alcock to Hammond, 22 February 1859, FO 391/1, NA.
15 For more details of these initial occurrences in Nagasaki and Edo, see Sano, *Orukokku no Edo*, 22–55.
16 For the relatively novel view on the Japanese diplomacy of this era with the emphasis on the autonomy and high administrative ability of shogunate officials, see Mitani Hiroshi, *Perii raikō* (The Arrival of Perry) (Tokyo: Yoshikawa Kōbunkan, 2003); Sano Mayuko, *Bakumatsu gaikō girei no kenkyū: Ōbei gaikokan tachi no shōgun haietsu* (Diplomatic Ceremonial in the Bakumatsu Period: Western Diplomats' Castle Audiences with the Shogun) (Kyoto: Shibunkaku, 2016).
17 Tokyo Daigaku Shiryō Hensanjo, ed., *Bakumatsu gaikoku kankei monjo* (Collection of Documents on late-Edo Period Foreign Relations), vol. 20 (Tokyo: University of Tokyo Press, 1972), 709–11.
18 Tōzenji still exists near Shinagawa Station in Tokyo, although the temple's premises have been much diminished compared with Alcock's time.
19 Rutherford Alcock, *The Capital of the Tycoon: The Three Years' Residence in Japan*, vol. 1 (London: Longman, Green, Longman, Roberts, & Green, 1863), 102–5.
20 The US consul-general soon joined, and the French representative arrived three months later. The Dutch consul visited Edo periodically but kept his nation's major legation in Nagasaki, where the Dutch had maintained a factory since the early seventeenth century. These four countries formed the initial diplomatic corps in the shogun's capital. The Russian government established its legation in Hakodate as early as 1858, but the location was too far away to be part of the activities around Edo and Yokohama.
21 J. E. Hoare, *Japan's Treaty Ports and Foreign Settlements: The Uninvited Guests 1858–1899* (Surrey: Japan Library, 1994), 6–7. See also Sano, *Orukokku no Edo*, 73–94. While the merchants rapidly built their business in Yokohama, the foreign consulates first operated in Kanagawa across the bay. However, their distance from the people they were assigned to protect and administer proved too inconvenient, and the consuls could not continue it practically. From a year later, they gradually accepted the reality, and gave up their 'legal' footings in Kanagawa and moved to Yokohama.
22 For example, Grace Fox, *Britain and Japan 1858–1883* (Oxford: Oxford University Press, 1969), 60–1.
23 Tokyo Daigaku Shiryō Hensanjo, ed., *Bakumatsu gaikoku kankei monjo*, vol. 22, 539–43. See also Fukuchi Genichirō, *Kaiojidan* (Reflections on the Past) (Tokyo: Ozorasha, 1993 (facsimile edition of Tokyo: Min'yusha, 1894 original), 23–5; Sano, *Orukokku no Edo*, 84.

24 Sano, *Orukokku no Edo,* 76–80.
25 Alcock to Malmesbury, 13 July 1859, FO 46/3, NA.
26 Alcock, *The Capital of the Tycoon,* 137.
27 Ibid., 3.
28 Malmesbury to Alcock, 1 March 1859, FO 46/2, NA.
29 Alcock, *The Capital of the Tycoon,* 139.
30 Alcock to Malmesbury, 14 July 1859, Parliamentary Papers, Session 1860, vol. LXIX (Accounts and Papers: State Papers-China; Japan; Syria), 25.
31 Alcock, *The Capital of the Tycoon,* 140.
32 Ibid.
33 Some later developments of the Yokohama question that typically verify this prospect are mentioned in the same chapter of his book. Alcock, *The Capital of the Tycoon,* 142–4.
34 For details, see Sano, *Orukokku no Edo,* 173–92.
35 Alcock to Hammond, 19 August 1861, FO 391/1, NA (Underlines by Alcock)
36 For details, see Sano, *Orukokku no Edo,* 146–57, 198–206. A remarkable cultural significance of this mission was first unveiled in Haga Tōru, *Taikun no shisetsu* (The Tycoon's mission) (Tokyo: Chuokoronsha, 1968).
37 Michie, *The Englishman in China during the Victorian Era,* vol. II, 77.
38 Russell to Alcock, 8 August 1864, FO 46/42, NA.
39 Typically, Alcock to Russell, 18 November 1864, FO 46/47, NA.
40 Hammond to Alcock, 26 January 1865, FO 46/52, NA.
41 Alcock to Russell, 15 March 1865, PRO 30/22/50, NA.
42 For details of the deep-rooted social class-based prejudice by which the nineteenth-century British consuls suffered and the actual situation, see D. C. M. Platt, *The Cinderella Service: British Consuls since 1825* (London: Longman, 1971). Alcock's unexceptional promotion from the Consular to the Diplomatic Service opened the same path for his successors, namely Harry Parks and Ernest Satow.
43 Alcock to Russell, 15 March 1865.
44 Russell to Alcock, 7 April 1865, FO 17/420, NA.
45 Alcock to Russell, 1 December 1865, FO 17/432, NA.
46 Mainly in, FO 17/448, 450, 451, and 452, NA.
47 Alcock to Clarendon, 12 February 1867, FO 17/474, NA.
48 The records of these visits are included in the files FO 17/475 and 476, NA.
49 See, mainly, FO 17/477, 571 and 572, NA.
50 Banno Masataka, *Kindai Chūgoku gaikō-shi kenkyū* (A Study of the History of Modern Chinese Diplomacy) (Tokyo: Iwanami shoten, 1970), 238.
51 Alcock to Stanley, 16 April 1868, FO 17/572.
52 Alcock to Stanley, 22 January 1868, FO 17/572.

53 The Alcock Convention – its contents and the drafting processes – are explained by Nathan A. Pelcovits in his legendary *Old China Hands* (New York: King's Crown Press, 1948), and also covered from a more Chinese point of view in Mary Clabaugh Wright, *The Last Stand of Chinese Conservatism: The T'ung-chih Restoration, 1862–1874* (Stanford: Stanford University Press, 1957). The Japanese historian Banno Masataka followed them in the 1970s: Banno, *Kindai Chūgoku gaikō-shi kenkyū*; Banno, *Kindai Chūgoku seiji gaikō-shi* (History of Politics and Diplomacy of Modern China) (Tokyo: University of Tokyo Press, 1973). Immanuel C. Y. Hsu, 'Late Ch'ing Foreign Relations, 1866–1905', in *Cambridge History of China,* volume 2: *Late Ch'ing, 1800–1911, Part 2,* ed. John K. Fairbank and Kwang-Ching Liu (Cambridge: Cambridge University Press, 1980), 70–141 does also briefly mention the Alcock Convention. After that period of scholarly interest, the Convention does not seem to have attracted substantial academic attention until recently. A doctoral thesis in Chinese, 'The New Treaty between China and Britain in 1869 and the Sino-British Relations', by Fei Wei, East China Normal University (2004), is the newest and a rarely dedicated study on this convention, but I must confess that I have not had a chance to read this thesis (in Chinese) except for its English abstract.

54 The text of the convention was published as a Command Paper: *China. No. 1 (1870). Despatch from Sir Rutherford Alcock Respecting a Supplementary Convention to the Treaty of Tien-tsin, Signed by Him on the 23rd of October, 1869* (London: Harrison and Sons, 1870).

55 FO 17/579, NA. See also Pelcovits, *Old China Hands,* 72–85.

56 Pelcovits, *Old China Hands,* 65.

57 FO 17/581, NA.

58 Granville to Wade, 10 August 1871, FO 17/546, NA.

59 Alcock to Clarendon, 28 October 1869, in *China. No. 1 (1870).*

60 Alcock to Clarendon, 30 September 1869, FO 17/578, NA.

61 Alcock to Clarendon, 7 December 1869, FO 17/579, NA.

62 Pelcovits, *Old China Hands,* 74.

63 Manchester Chamber of Commerce to Foreign Office, 15 January 1870, FO 17/579.

64 Foreign Office to the Chambers of Commerce in UK, 20 January 1870, FO 17/579.

65 Memo by Hammond, 11 February 1870, FO 17/579.

66 *China. No. 1 (1870).*

67 Alcock to Clarendon, 11 March 1870, FO 17/547, NA.

68 For example, Alcock to Clarendon, 4 February 1870, FO 17/547.

69 Alcock to Clarendon, 26 April 1870, FO 17/548, NA.

70 Wei, 'The New Treaty between China and Britain in 1869 and the Sino-British Relations' (abstract).

71 Hsu, 'Late Ch'ing Foreign Relations, 1866–1905', 76–8.
72 Platt, *The Cinderella Service*, xiii.
73 Symbolically, he is known to have taken action to materialize Japan's first participation in a world expo in the occasion of the International Exhibition in London, 1862, to introduce Japanese cultural objects there, and created an origin of *Japonisme* in Europe. See Sano, *Orukokku no Edo*, 193–234. Alcock's own second and last major book was: *Art and Art Industries in Japan* (London: Virtue and Co., Limited, 1878).
74 Platt, *The Cinderella Service*, xiii.
75 Pelcovits, *Old China Hands*, 300–2.
76 Markus Mössalang and Torsten Riotte, 'Introduction: The Diplomats' World', in *The Diplomat's' World: A Cultural History of Diplomacy, 1815–1914*, ed. Markus Mössalang and Torsten Riotte (Oxford: Oxford University Press, 2008), 7.
77 P. D. Coates, *China Consuls: British Consular Officers, 1843–1943* (New York: Oxford University Press, 1988), vii.

Chapter 2

1 The original document is preserved today at the UK National Archives (FO 881/541).
2 William G. Beasley, *Great Britain and the Opening of Japan 1834–1858* (London: The Japan Library, 1995), 31–54.
3 As noted in the introduction, Mackenzie had loomed large in the early career of Charles Lenox Richardson at Shanghai.
4 Antoinette Cheney Crocker, *Frank Woodbridge Cheney: Two Years in China and Japan* (Worcester, MA: Priv. print. by Davis Press, 1970), 53.
5 William McOmie, 'The Frigate *Askold* and the Opening of the Russian Settlement at Nagasaki', *Crossroads: A Journal of Nagasaki History and Culture* 4 (Summer 1996): 1–32.
6 Myōgyōji, which accommodated the Nagasaki British Consulate from June 1859 to July 1865, remained like an oasis of Japanese culture while the foreign settlement developed around it. The buildings rented by the British no longer exist, but the temple still functions on the original site to this day.
7 Rutherford Alcock to C. Pemberton Hodgson, 13 June 1859 (FO 262/7).
8 *The London Gazette*, 25 February 1859.
9 C. Pemberton Hodgson, *A Residence at Nagasaki and Hakodate in 1859–1860* (London: Richard Bentley, 1861), 30.
10 Ibid., 111.
11 C. Pemberton Hodgson to Rutherford Alcock, 15 June 1859 (FO 262/7).

12 C. Pemberton Hodgson to the Foreign Office, 7 July 1859 (FO 46/5).
13 Taniguchi Ryōhei, 'Mrs Mary Elizabeth Green', (unpublished Japanese manuscript, May 2010).
14 Ernest Satow, *A Diplomat in Japan* (Oxford: Oxford University Press, 1921), 22.
15 Kuwata Masaru, *Kindai ni okeru chūnichi Eikokugaikōkan* (British Diplomats in Japan, 1859-1945), (Kobe: Mirume Shobō, 2003), 307-8.
16 From a biographical sketch published in the *Illustrated London News*, 26 October 1861.
17 George S. Morrison to the Foreign Office, 19 January 1859 (FO 46/5).
18 Ibid., 17 August 1859 (FO 46/5).
19 Ibid., 7 September 1859 (FO 46/5).
20 George S. Morrison to Rutherford Alcock, 11 January 1860 (FO 262/18).
21 'Report on British Trade at Nagasaki for 1859' (FO 262/18/32-5).
22 'Port of Nagasaki: Exports During Half Year to 30 June 1859' (FO 262/18/70).
23 A native of Aberdeenshire, Glover arrived in Nagasaki in September 1859 to assist Kenneth R. Mackenzie in the local branch of Jardine, Matheson & Co. He established Glover & Co. in 1862 and went on to serve as a prime contributor to Japanese modernization. For more on Glover, see Shinya Sugiyama, 'Thomas B. Glover: A British Merchant in Japan, 1861-1870', *Business History* 26, no. 2 (1984): 115-38; Alexander McKay, *Scottish Samurai: Thomas Blake Glover, 1839-1911* (Edinburgh: Canongate, 2012).
24 As outlined in the Introduction, William J. Alt arrived in Nagasaki in late 1859 and established Alt & Co. the following year, achieving stunning successes in the early trade and collaborating closely with Mitsubishi founder Iwasaki Yatarō. The grand house he built in Nagasaki is the oldest building of Western-style stone construction in Japan, designated today as a National Important Cultural Property. For more on the former Alt House, see Brian Burke-Gaffney, *The Former Alt House: Biography of a Nagasaki Landmark* (Nagasaki: Flying Crane Press, 2020).
25 'In the Matter of the Foreign Location' (FO 262/18/141-2).
26 'Regulations for British Subjects in the Port and Harbour of Nagasaki', *Nagasaki Shipping List and Advertiser*, 14 August 1861.
27 M. Paske-Smith, *Western Barbarians in Japan and Formosa in Tokugawa Days, 1603-1868* (Kobe: J.L. Thompson and Co., 1927), Appendix No. 15, 386-408.
28 'Land Regulations for the Port of Nagasaki in Japan' (FO 262/173/153).
29 'Allotment of Land' (FO 262/19/61).
30 George S. Morrison to Rutherford Alcock, 13 October 1860 (FO 262/19/49-54).
31 Terry Bennett, *Photography in Japan 1853-1912* (Tokyo: Tuttle Publishing, 2006), 41-51.
32 'General Report on the Trade of Nagasaki in Japan for the Year 1860' (FO 262/29/39-47).

33 George S. Morrison to Rutherford Alcock, 13 April 1861 (FO 262/29/90-8). Modern-day Minamiyamate is the site of Glover Garden, where the former Alt, Glover and Ringer family houses are preserved along with other nineteenth-century buildings.
34 William J. Alt et al to A.A. Annesley (acting consul), 30 June 1861 (FO 262/29/154-5).
35 George S. Morrison to Rutherford Alcock, 29 May 1861 (FO 262/29/125-6).
36 Rutherford Alcock provides a detailed account of both the overland journey and the attack on the British Legation in his book *The Capital of the Tycoon: A Narrative of a Three Years' Residence in Japan*, vol. II (New York: Harper & Brothers, Publishers, 1863), 61–158.
37 George S. Morrison to Edward St. John Neale, 4 April 1863 (FO 262/60/7-8).
38 FO 262/60/81-5. The Nagasaki British Consulate moved to another rented building at No. 9 Higashiyamate in 1865. Renamed the Belle Vue Hotel, Green's Hotel served as one of the most popular Western-style accommodations in Nagasaki until closing in 1920.
39 'Statement of Mr. Glover', 12 July 1863 (FO 262/60/144-5).
40 'Statement of William Willis M.D.', 24 July 1863 (FO 262/60/153).
41 *The Oxford Journal*, 16 February 1867.
42 RG 11/1086.
43 After leaving Green's Hotel in 1865, the Nagasaki British Consulate moved to another rented building at No. 9 Higashiyamate and then, in 1882, to the former premises of Frazar & Co. at No. 6 Ōura, a choice waterfront lot in the heart of the foreign settlement. The fine brick and stone building erected on the lot in 1908, which remains to this day as a National Important Cultural Property, housed the consulate until the attack on Pearl Harbor on 8 December 1941. For more on the former Nagasaki British Consulate, see Brian Burke-Gaffney, *The Former Nagasaki British Consulate, 1859–1955* (Nagasaki: Flying Crane Press, 2019).

Chapter 3

1 Hirose Shizuko, 'Bakumatsu ni okeru gaikoku guntai Nihon chūryū no tancho' (The Beginning of the Stationing of Foreign Troops in Japan in the Bakumatsu Period), *Ochanomizu shigaku* (Bulletin of the Department of History, Ochanomizu University) 15 (1972): 8–42, 83; Hora Tomio, 'Igirisu Furansu ryōkoku guntai no Yokohama chūton' (British and French Troops Stationed in Yokohama) in *Bakumatsu-ishinki no gaiatsu to teikō* (Foreign Pressure and Japanese Resistance during Bakumatsu and Meiji Restoration Periods) (Tokyo: Azekura-shobō, 1977), 7–146; Ishii Takashi, *Meiji ishin no kokusaiteki kankyō, zotei* (The International

Contexts of the Meiji Restoration), enlarged and revised edition. (Tokyo: Yoshikawa Kōbunkan, 1966); Nakatake (Hori) Kanami, 'Bakumatsu-ishinki no Yokohama Eifutsu chūtongun no jittai to sono eikyō: Igirisu gun o chūsin ni' (The Conditions Surrounding the Stationing of British and French Troops in Yokohama and Their Influence – A Focus on the British Troops), *Yokohama Kaikō Shiryōkan kiyō* (Yokohama Archives of History Review) 12 (1994): 1–32; Yokohama Kaikō Shiryōkan ed., *Shiryō de tadoru Meiji-ishinki no Yokohama Eifutsu chūtongun* (Collection Sources Related to the British and French Troops Stationed at Yokohama) (Yokohama: Yokohama Kaikō Shiryōkan, 1993); Yokohama Kaikō Shiryōkan ed., *Yokohama Eifutsu chūtongun to gaikokujin kyoryūchi* (The British and French Troops Stationed in Yokohama and the Foreign Settlement) (Tokyo: Tokyo-dō shuppan, 1999); Yokohama-shi ed., *Yokohama shishi* (The History of Yokohama City), vol. 2 and vols. 3-2 (Yokohama: Yokohama-shi, 1959, 1963).

2 'Letter from N. P. Kingdon to his mother, 12 May 1863', transcribed in Yokohama Kaikō Shiryōkan ed., *Shiryō de tadoru Meiji-ishinki no Yokohama Eifutsu chūtongun*, 126–7.

3 Ministère des Affaires Etrangères, correspondence politique, Japon, vol. 9, Duchesne de Bellecourt to Drouyn de Lhuys, no. 262, 30 June 1863.

4 Despatches from US Minister to Japan, vol. 4, Duchesne de Bellecourt to Pruyn, 5 May 1863, Encl.1 to no. 24, Pruyn to Seward, 8 May 1863.

5 The National Archives (UK) [TNA:] Foreign Office General Correspondence, Japan (FO 46)/34, Neale to Maj-Gen Brown, 12 May 1863, Encl.5 to no. 69, Neale to Russell, 12 May 1863.

6 TNA: FO 46/34, Maj-Gen Brown to Neale, 19 May 1863, Encl.2 to no. 83, Neale to Russell, 27 May 1863.

7 TNA: FO 46/40, de Grey & Ripon to Maj-Gen Brown, 9 September 1863, Encl.2 to Lugard to Hammond, 9 September 1863.

8 Letter from J. Smyth to his father, 13 June 1864 from the J. Smyth collection. Courtesy of the Smyth family and held at the Yokohama Archives of History. By the end of June the huts were complete (Ibid., 28 June 1864); Nakatake (Hori) Kanami, 'Bakumatsu no Yokohama Igirisu chūtongun shikan no shokan: Dai 20 rentai dai 2 daitai Sumisu chūi no shokan, 1–3' (Letters of J. Smyth, Lieutenant of the 2nd Battalion, 20th Regiment from 1863 to 1866), *Yokohama Kaikō Shiryōkan kiyō* (Yokohama Archives of History Review) 34, 36, 37 (2016, 2019, 2021).

9 TNA: FO 46/43, Neale to Russell, no. 11, 30 January 1864.

10 Hora, 'Igirisu Furansu ryōkoku guntai no Yokohama chūton', 47–9.

11 For more on soldiers' mortality in mid-nineteenth century Hong Kong, see Reports from Hong Kong on mortality of troops in China, in *British Parliamentary Papers, China 27* (Shannon, Ireland: Irish University Press, 1971), and Bobby Tam's chapter in this volume.

12 *Japan Times' Daily Advertiser*, 18 September 1865.

13 *Japan Times*, 17 November 1865.
14 'A Memoir of F. Davies', in the collection of the National Army Museum; Oyama Mizuyo, trans., 'Dai 20 rentai gungakutaiin Davies no shuki' (Memoir by F. Davies, a Military Band Member of the 20th Regiment), in *Shiryō de tadoru Meiji-ishinki no Yokohama Eifutsu chūtongun*, ed. Yokohama Kaikō Shiryōkan, 101–2.
15 Tim Carew, *The Royal Norfolk Regiment* (London: Hamish Hamilton, 1967), 64. There are similar descriptions in other Regimental histories. See Jonathan Sutherland and Diane Canwell, *The Holy Boys: A History of the Royal Norfolk Regiment and the Royal East Anglian Regiment, 1685–2010* (Barnsley, South Yorkshire: Pen & Sword Military, 2010), 66–7.
16 'Death of Mr H. J. Vincent', *Japan Weekly Mail*, 2 November 1907; Nakatake (Hori) Kanami, 'Moto Igirisu chūtongun heishi, Vincent-ke no haka' (The Family Tomb of Vincent, a British Soldier Stationed in Yokohama), *Kaikō no hiroba* (Brochure of the Yokohama Archives of History)115 (February 2012): 6–7.
17 *Japan Times' Daily Advertiser*, 18 September 1865.
18 William Hunter, *Chronicle & Directory for China, Japan, & the Philippines for the Year 1872* (Hong Kong: Daily Press Office, 1872), 153.
19 Patricia McCabe, *Gaijin Bochi, the Foreigners' Cemetery Yokohama, Japan* (London: Bacsa, 1994), 78.
20 Japan Gazette Co. Ltd., *'Japan Gazette' Yokohama semi-centennial* (Yokohama: Japan Gazette Co., 1909), 39.
21 Ibid., 51.
22 *Japan Times' Daily Advertiser*, 22 January 1866.
23 *Japan Weekly Mail*, 6 March 1875. British soldiers were called 'red corps' or 'the redcoats' for their red-coloured uniform.
24 'Caspar Brennwald Diary', in the possession of DKSH. This English translation is from *Shiryō de tadoru Meiji-Ishinki no Yokohama Eifutsu chūtongun*, 131. Also see the chapter by Fukuoka Mariko and Alexis Schwarzenbach in this volume.
25 Ernest Satow, *A Diplomat in Japan* (Philadelphia: J. B. Lippincott, 1921), 163.
26 *Japan Herald*, 25 October 1862.
27 John R. Black, *Young Japan; Yokohama and Yedo*, vol. 1 (London: Trubner, 1880), 174. Charles Lenox Richardson, the victim of Namamugi, had himself served in the Shanghai Volunteers: Robert S.G. Fletcher, *The Ghost of Namamugi: Charles Lenox Richardson and the Anglo-Satsuma War* (Folkestone: Renaissance Books, 2019), 15–16.
28 *Japan Times*, 6 April 1866. The newspaper reported that 'the Mounted Volunteers may trace their existence to a suggestion made by Major Meares two years and a-half ago'.
29 *Japan Times' Daily Advertiser*, 9 January 1866.
30 *Japan Times' Daily Advertiser*, 6 March 1866.

31 *Japan Times*, 9 March 1866.
32 Max von Brandt, *Dreiunddreissig Jahre in Ost-Asien. Erinnerungen eines deutschen Diplomaten* (A German Diplomat's Thirty-three Years in East Asia), vol. 2 (Leipzig: Georg Wigand, 1901).
33 Hara Kiyoshi and Nagaoka Atsushi, trans., *Doitsu kōshi no mita Meiji-ishin* (Max von Brandt, Dreiunddreissig Jahre in Ost-Asien [Thirty-three Years in East Asia]) (Tokyo: Shin-jinbutsuōraisha, 1987).
34 Hakoishi Hiroshi, 'Kaisetsu: Meiji ishin to Fon Buranto, (An Explanation: the Meiji Restoration and Max von Brandt)' in *Doitsu to Nihon o musubu mono: Nichidoku shūkō 150nen no rekishi* (Relations between Germany and Japan: 150 Years of Friendship between Germany and Japan), ed. Kokuritsu Rekishi Minzoku Hakubutsukan (Sakura: Kokuritsu Rekishi Minzoku Hakubutsukan, 2015), 58.
35 Black, *Young Japan*, vol. 1, 368–9.
36 E. S. Benson, an American resident in Yokohama. The Japanese local government left the management of the policing to a foreigner holding the title of the Director of Land and Police. The first director was Martin Dohmen, the Dutch interpreter of the British Consulate (term: 1867–1868), and the second was Benson, (1868–1877).
37 *Japan Gazette*, 30 January 1875.
38 *Japan Weekly Mail*, 6 March 1875.
39 Yokohama Bōeki Shimpō-sha, *Yokohama kaikō sokumen shi* (Another Aspect of the History of the Opening of the Port of Yokohama) (Yokohama: Yokohama Bōeki Shimpō-sha, 1909), 123–4; Morita Chūkichi ed., *Yokohama seikō meiyo kagami* (A Directory of Successful Individuals in Yokohama) (Yokohama: Yokohama shōkyō shimpō-sha, 1910), 92–3.
40 *North China Herald*, 9 July 1864.
41 *Yokohama Mainichi Shimbun* (Yokohama Daily News), 12 June 1872. This was the first daily Japanese newspaper launched in Yokohama in 1871.
42 *Yokohama Mainichi Shimbun*, 19 December 1873.
43 Suzuki Jun, 'Ran-shiki, Ei-shiki, Futsu-shiki: Shohan no "heisei" dōnyū' (The Introduction of Dutch-style, British-style and French-style 'Military Systems' in Various Domains) in Yokohama Kaikō Shiryōkan ed., *Yokohama Eifutsu chūtongun to gaikokujin kyoryūchi*, 213–46.
44 Hora, 'Igirisu Furansu ryōkoku guntai no Yokohama chūton', 141.
45 Kishi Motokazu, 'Ishinki no Yokohama chūton Igirisu guntai tettai mondai; "Gaiatsu" to chūōshūken katei no tokushitsu' (The Withdrawal of British Troops from Yokohama in the Meiji Restoration Period: 'Foreign Pressure' and the Process of Centralization of Power and Authority) *Nihon rekishi* (Journal of Japanese History) 377 (1979): 69–87.
46 TNA: FO 46/109, Parkes to Clarendon, no. 116, confidential, 28 May 1869. Parkes called Sanjo 'the Prime Minister'.

47 TNA: FO 46/109, 'Minutes of interview between Her Majesty's Minister and the Ex-Prime Minister Iwakura Uhioyei no Kami', 7 June 1869, Encl. to no. 131, Parkes to Clarendon, 12 June 1869.
48 Kishi, 'Ishinki no Yokohama chūton Igirisu guntai tettai mondai', 85-fn.27, 86-fn.49.
49 Richard Sims, *French Policy towards the Bakufu and Meiji Japan 1854–95* (Richmond, Surrey: Japan Library, 1998), 93–6.
50 Kokaze Hidemasa, 'Eifutsu chūtongun tettai-ki no kokusai kankei: fubyōdō jyōyaku taisei no saihen o meguru Igirisu to Nihon' (The International Circumstances Surrounding the Withdrawal of British and French Troops: Relations between Britain and Japan during the Revision of the Unequal Treaty System) in *Yokohama Eifutsu chūtongun to gaikokujin kyoryūchi*, ed. Yokohama Kaikō Shiryōkan, 309–35.

Chapter 4

1 The authors would like to thank Lea Haller, Monika Burri, Roman Wild and Denise Ruisinger for their valuable comments on this chapter.
2 Saitō Takio, 'Gaishō gawa kara mita Meiji zenki no Yokohama bōeki' (Trade in Yokohama Seen from the Perspective of Western Firms), *Yokohama Kaikō Shiryōkan kiyō* (Yokohama Archives of History Review) 6 (1988): 121.
3 Dai Nippon sanshi kaichō Danshaku Matsudaira Masanao yori tokubetsu kai'in Siber Wolff Shōkai ate shōjō (Certificate of Commendation from the Director of the Dainippon Silk Foundation, Baron Matsudaira Masanao, to Siber, Wolff & Co.), dated on 29 May 1903. In possession of DKSH Holding Ltd. On the importance of the US market, see Giovanni Federico, *An Economic History of the Silk Industry, 1830–1930* (Cambridge: Cambridge University Press, 1997), 61–78; Ishii Kanji, *Nihon sanshi gyō bunseki* (An Analysis of the Japanese Silk Industry) (Tokyo: Tokyo Daigaku Shuppan-kai, 1972), 19–56.
4 Friedemann Bartu, *The Fan Tree Company: Three Swiss Merchants in Asia* (Zürich: Diethelm Keller Holding Ltd., 2005); Jürg Wolle, *Expedition in fernöstliche Märkte. Die Erfolgsstory des Schweizer Handelspioniers DKSH* (Expeditions in Far-Eastern markets. The Success Story of the Swiss Trading Pioneer DKSH) (Zürich: Orell Füssli, 2009); Andreas Zangger, *Koloniale Schweiz. Ein Stück Globalgeschichte zwischen Europa und Südostasien (1860–1930)* (Colonial Switzerland. A Piece of Global History between Europe and Southeast Asia) (Berlin: transcript, 2014); for today's activities of the company, see www.dksh.com (accessed 15 April 2018).
5 On the history of Swiss trading houses, see among others, Christof Dejung, *Die Fäden des globalen Marktes. Eine Sozial- und Kulturgeschichte des Welthandels am Beispiel der Handelsfirma Gebrüder Volkart 1851–1999* (The Threads of the

Global Market. A Social and Cultural History of Global Trade Based on the Example of the Trading House Volkart Brothers) (Köln: Böhlau, 2013); Zangger, *Koloniale Schweiz*; Lea Haller, *Transithandel. Die Rolle des Kleinstaats im globalen Kapitalismus* (Transit Trade. The Role of the Small State in Global Capitalism) (Berlin: Suhrkamp, 2019).

6   On the importance of silk as Japan's main export commodity, see Shinya Sugiyama, *Japan's Industrialization in the World Economy, 1859–1899: Export Trade and Overseas Competition* (London: Athlone Press, 1988); Yasuhiro Makimura, *Yokohama and the Silk Trade: How Eastern Japan Became the Primary Economic Region of Japan, 1843–1893* (Lanham: Lexington Books, 2017).

7   See article 'Schifffahrt' in Historisches Lexikon der Schweiz, http://www.hls-dhs-dss.ch/textes/d/D14054.php (accessed 15 April 2018); Walter Zürcher, *Schweizer Flagge zur See. Die Geschichte der schweizerischen Hochseeschiffahrt* (The Swiss Flag at Sea. The History of Swiss High Sea Shipping) (Bern: Benteli, 1986). Some Swiss trading houses such as the Basler Handelsgesellschaft or André & Cie. owned ships but did not run them under Swiss flags. We thank Lea Haller for this insight.

8   On Jardine Matheson, see John McMaster, *Jardines in Japan 1859–1867* (Groningen: V.R.B. Offsetdrukkerij, 1966); Ishii Kanji, *Kindai Nihon to Igirisu shihon: Jardin Matheson shōkai o chūshin ni* (Modern Japan and British Capital: The Case of Jardine Matheson) (Tokyo: Tokyo Daigaku Shuppan-kai,1984). Ishii points out that while Western trade in Japan in its earliest period from 1859 to around 1866 was almost completely occupied by giant British trading firms such as Jardine, Matheson & Co. and Dent & Co., more and more smaller trading firms began trading in Japan's treaty ports from the mid-1860s and came to undermine the monopoly of the British firms, helped by the development of banking and steamship-mailing systems in East Asia (Ishii, ibid., 157–75). However, Ishii gives no details over each individual case of those smaller-scale trading firms.

9   On the establishment of diplomatic relations between Switzerland and Japan, see Paul Akio Nakai, *Das Verhältnis zwischen Japan und der Schweiz. Vom Beginn der diplomatischen Beziehungen 1859 bis 1868* (The Relationship between Japan and Switzerland. From the Beginning of Diplomatic Relations in 1859 to 1868) (Bern: Haupt, 1967); Nakai Akio, *Shoki Nihon Suisu kankeishi: Suisu Renpō Monjokan no Bakumatsu Nihon bōeki shiryō* (History of Early Swiss-Japanese Relations: Sources on Japanese Trade in the Bakumatsu Period Held in the Swiss Federal Archives) (Tokyo: Kazama Shobō, 1971).

10 The typescript was made by the late Prof. Thomas Immoos of Sophia University in Japan, probably in view of the company's 100th anniversary in 1965. The diaries were first used in the anniversary publication SiberHegner und Co. ed., *Hundert Jahre im Dienste des Handels, 1865–1965* (Hundred Years in the Service of Trade) (Zürich: SiberHegner Holding, 1965). Up to the present, the project has completed

its translation of selected parts of the diary from 1862–7, and this is now published as: Yokohama-shi Furusato Rekishi Zaidan (Historical Foundation of Yokohama City) and Burenwaldo Nikki Kenkyū-kai (Study Group of the Brennwald's Diary), eds., *Suisu shisetsu dan ga mita Bakumatsu no Nihon: Brenwaldo nikki 1862–1867 (Japan during the Bakumatsu Period: Seen by the Swiss Mission Brennwald's Diary 1862–1867)* (Tokyo: Bensei Shuppan, 2020).

11 The Brennwald diaries consist of five volumes covering the periods of 10 October 1862–14 December 1863, 16 December 1863–3 May 1866, 4 May 1866–5 December 1867, 11 August 1870–30 June 1873, 3 July 1873–8 February 1878. Further volumes covering the period from December 1867 to August 1870 may have existed but do not survive. The diaries of Caspar Brennwald will be abbreviated as DCB.

12 A total of 247 letters are held by the Zentralbibliothek, MS Z II 349; 80 letters are held by the corporate archives of the Diethelm Keller Holding in Zurich, DKH C 3 1, DKH C 3 2. The authors would like to thank Diethelm Keller Holding for granting them access to both the Siber letters and the Brennwald diaries.

13 The research project is located at Lucerne University's School of Art and Design, https://www.hslu.ch/de-ch/hochschule-luzern/forschung/projekte/detail/?pid=124 (accessed 29 January 2018). The transcription was made in 2017 by Dr Alexandra Bloch-Pfister, Münster, Germany, jointly financed by the Lucerne University and the National Museum of Japanese History.

14 Thereafter, he led the Swiss branch of Siber & Brennwald. See entry 'Hermann Siber' in Historisches Lexikon der Schweiz, http://www.hls-dhs-dss.ch/textes/d/D30929.php (accessed 15 June 2018).

15 For the balance sheet, see Hermann Siber to Gustav Siber, henceforth HS to GS, 12 May 1867, ZBZ Ms Z II 349. The corporate archives of Siber & Brennwald and its successors are held by Diethelm Keller Holding in Zurich.

16 For theoretical approaches to commodity trading houses, see Marten Boon, 'Theoretical Approaches to Commodity Trading Companies', Paper delivered at the conference, Commodity Trading Companies in the First Global Economy, 1870–1914, Rotterdam, 5–6 February 2017; for transnational approaches to Swiss history, see www.transnationalhistory.ch (accessed 30 April 2018).

17 See entry 'Caspar Brennwald' in Historisches Lexikon der Schweiz, http://www.hls-dhs-dss.ch/textes/d/D30913.php (accessed 15 April 2018). The fact that Caspar Brennwald was an orphan can be deduced from his diary which invokes letters from a stepmother but not from any other parent. See, for instance, DCB, 17 July 1863. The diary also includes a reference to a visit to the father's grave, DCB, 16 August 1865.

18 In his diary, Caspar Brennwald remembers trips to France and Portugal, see, for instance, DCB, 24 July 1863, while a document summarizing his career in the DKH archives also mention stations in Italy, see [Lebenslauf Caspar Brennwald], July 1899, DKH, C 3 156.

19 Brennwald repeatedly remembered the disappointment in Aarau in the summer of 1862 when in Japan, see DCB, 2 August 1863; 16 March 1864; 11 May 1864. He also fondly remembered his former employer as 'Papa Hunziker', see DCB, 18 December 1862.
20 DCB, 10 October 1862.
21 See entry 'Aimé Humbert-Dorz' in Historisches Lexikon der Schweiz, http://www.hls-dhs-dss.ch/textes/d/D4537.php (accessed 15 April 2018).
22 See DCB, 20 December 1862; 19 April 1863.
23 For further details of the mission, see Nakai, *Das Verhältnis zwischen Japan und der Schweiz*, 45–114.
24 On the restrained foreign policy of the shogunate during this period, see Yokohama Kaikō Shiryōkan, ed., *Brenwaldo no Bakumatsu Meiji Nippon nikki* (Brennwald's Diary in Japan of the Bakumatsu and Meiji Periods) (Tokyo: Nikkei-BP, 2015), 30–3; Michael Auslin, *Negotiating with Imperialism: The Unequal Treaties and the Culture of Japanese Diplomacy* (Cambridge, MA: Harvard University Press, 2006), Chapter 4.
25 See Kaspar Brennwald, *Bericht über den Seiden-Export von Japan* (Report on the Silk Exports of Japan) (Bern: Schweizerisches Handels- und Zolldepartement, 1863); ibid., *Bericht über den Thee-Exporthandel Japans und den Exporthandel Japans im Allgemeinen* (Report on the Tea Export of Japan and the Export Trade of Japan in General) (Bern: Schweizerisches Handels- und Zolldepartement, 1863).
26 Kaspar Brennwald, *Notizen über die Seidenzucht in Japan* (Notes on Silk Rearing in Japan) (Bern: Schweizerisches Handels- und Zolldepartement, 1864). See also DCB, 16 May 1863; 7 July 1863. Upon his return to Switzerland, Caspar Brennwald also published a general report on the Swiss trading mission to Japan, see Kaspar Brennwald, *Generalbericht betreffend den kommerziellen Theil der schweizerischen Abordnung nach Japan* (General Report Relating to the Commercial Part of the Swiss Delegation to Japan) (Bern: J.A. Weingart, 1865).
27 See DCB, 6 February 1864.
28 See DCB, 8 July–10 November 1864.
29 For the first time this idea is recorded in DCB, 28 April 1864. For offers to work for Swiss trading houses, see DCB, 23 January 1865; 9 May 1865; 23 June 1865, 14 July 1865.
30 See entry 'Hermann Siber' in Historisches Lexikon der Schweiz, http://www.hls-dhs-dss.ch/textes/d/D30929.php (accessed 15 April 2018).
31 See Silvio Honegger, *Gli Svizzeri di Bergamo. Storia della comunità svizzera di Bergamo dal Cinquecento all'inizio del Novecento* (The Swiss of Bergamo. History of the Swiss Community in Bergamo from the Sixteenth to the Nineteenth Century) (Bergamo: Edizioni Junior, 1997), 96.

32 On the Italian silk industry of the nineteenth century, see Federico, *An Economic History of the Silk Industry*, 7–29. On the Zurich silk industry in the first half of the nineteenth century, see Walter Bodmer, *Die Entwicklung der schweizerischen Textilwirtschaft im Rahmen der übrigen Industrien und Wirtschaftszweige* (The Development of the Swiss Textile Industry in the Context of Other Industries and Parts of the Economy) (Zürich: Berichthaus, 1960), 304–8.
33 For instance, they were one of the main providers of raw silk to the Thalwil-based Schwarzenbach silk manufacturer in the 1870s, see ZBZ, MS Schwarzenbach 791.1, 41.
34 On pébrine and its effects on the global silk industry, see Federico, *An Economic History of the Silk Industry*, 36–41; from the mid-1870s and 1880s, more Japanese raw silk was exported directly to France (Marseille) and the United States: Yokohama-shi, ed., *Yokohama shishi* (History of Yokohama City), vol. 3-I, 'Meiji zenki no Yokohama' (Yokohama in the Early Meiji Period) (Yokohama: Yokohama-shi, 1961), 470–3; Ishii, *Nihon sanshi gyō bunseki*, 40–51.
35 HS to GS, 13 October 1862, ZBZ Ms Z II 349. For Hermann Siber's education, see SiberHegner, *Hundert Jahre im Dienste des Handels*, 12.
36 HS to GS, 21 October 1862, ZBZ Ms Z II 349.
37 See HS to GS, 5 November 1862, ibid.
38 See HS to GS, 1 January 1863, ibid.
39 See, for instance, HS to GS, 22 November 1862 or 23 March 1863, ibid.
40 Initially the idea was to go to China, see HS to GS, 26 January 1863, ibid. The possibility of going to Japan first appears in HS to GS, 4 December 1863, ibid. The last letter from London is HS to GS, 17 December 1864, DKH C 3 1.
41 DCB, 24 July 1865.
42 See SiberHegner, *Hundert Jahre im Dienste des Handels*, 12.
43 DCB, 11 August 1865.
44 DCB, 5 September 1865.
45 See DCB, 10 November 1865.
46 DCB, 20 November 1865.
47 See HS to GS, 10 September 1867, ZBZ Ms Z II 349.
48 See DCB, 2 October 1865, 27 November 1865.
49 See DCB, 18 November 1864, 26 November 1865, 29 November 1865.
50 See DCB, 28 November 1865.
51 DCB, 27 November 1865.
52 See DCB, 27 November 1865.
53 Circular, 28 November 1865, facsimile in SiberHegner, *Hundert Jahre im Dienste des Handels*, p. 14; DCB, 28 November 1865.
54 See DCB, 2–12 December 1865.
55 See DCB, 21 October 1865. 14 February 1866.
56 This process lasted for more than a year and only ended in March 1867. See DCB, 15 March 1867.

57 See DCB, 3 September 1866; SiberHegner, Hundert Jahre im Dienste des Handels, 15, 32.
58 On the establishment of Yokohama by the Tokugawa regime, see Simon Partner, *The Merchant's Tale: Yokohama and the Transformation of Japan* (New York: Columbia University Press, 2017); Makimura, *Yokohama and the Silk Trade*; Yokohama-shi ed., *Yokohama shishi*, vol. 2: 'Kaikō ki no Yokohama' (Yokohama in the Period of Its Port-Opening) (Yokohama: Yokohama City, 1959); Yokohama-shi Furusato Rekishi Zaidan (Historical Foundation of the City of Yokohama), ed., *Yokohama: rekishi to bunka* (Yokohama: Its History and Culture: Memorial Edition of the 150-Year Anniversary of the Port's Opening) (Yokohama: Yūrindō, 2009), 156–91.
59 For the distance to Edo, see Makimura, *Yokohama and the Silk Trade*, xvii.
60 DCB, 1 May 1866.
61 See HS to GS, 27 July 1866, ZBZ Ms Z II 349.
62 DCB, 23 October 1866.
63 The shipment went to a company named Arles, Dufour. See HS to GS, 31 October 1866, ZBZ Ms Z II 349.
64 See DCB, 16 December 1866.
65 DCB, 23 January 1866.
66 See HS to GS, 11 July 1866, ZBZ Ms Z II 349; and, for Grisons, HS to GS, 12 May 1867, ibid.
67 On the market for silkworm eggs, see Federico, *An Economic History of the Silk Industry*, 38–9. The Tokugawa shogunate prohibited the export of silkworm eggs for the first years after the ports' opening in 1859, for fear that their too rapid export would damage the production of raw silk in Japan. In 1864, the prohibition was lifted, but even thereafter the Japanese authorities tried to control silk exports. See: Yokohama-shi, ed., *Yokohama shishi*, vol. 2, 506–11, 593–8; vol. 3-I, 62–165; Suzuki Yoshiyuki, *Kaiko ni miru Meiji ishin* (The Meiji Restoration as Seen through Cocoons) (Tokyo: Yoshikawa Kōbunkan, 2011), 11–46.
68 Nakai, *Das Verhältnis zwischen Japan und der Schweiz*, 121.
69 HS to GS, 22 August 1868, DKH C 3 1. They were purchased from the Sendai domain. The commercial relations between Siber and this domain in 1868 will be examined in more detail below.
70 See Andreas Zangger, 'Schweizer Seidenhändler in Japan' (Swiss Silk Merchants in Japan), in *Kirschblüte & Edelweiss. Der Import des Exotischen* (Cherry Blossom & Edelweiss. Importing the Exotic), ed. Michaela Reichel and Hans Bjarne Thomsen (Baden: hier + jetzt, 2014), 135.
71 See Albert Jost, *Charles Rudolph & Co. 50 Jahre Rohseidenimport* (Charles Rudolph & Co. 50 Years of Importing Raw Silk) (Zürich: Desco Handels AG, 1939), 65.
72 Hermann Siber took up Japanese lessons in May 1866, see HS to GS, 10 May 1866, ZBZ Ms Z II 349.

73 HS to GS, 11 July 1866, ibid.
74 HS to GS, 28 May 1866, ibid.
75 HS to GS, 28 May 1866, ibid.
76 On the importance of tea, see Sugiyama, *Japan's Industrialization in the World Economy*, 140–69.
77 See HS to GS, 27 July 1866, ZBZ Ms Z II 349.
78 See DCB, 15 May 1871. On the importance of coal, see Sugiyama, *Japan's Industrialization in the World Economy*, 170–212.
79 See HS to GS, 5 January 1868, ZBZ Ms Z II 349.
80 For more on early Japanese immigration, see Ikuko Torimoto, *Okina Kyūin and the Politics of Early Japanese Immigration to the United States, 1868–1924* (Jefferson, NC: McFarland, 2017), 23–9; 33–48.
81 HS to GS, 12 August 1866, ZBZ Ms Z II 349.
82 See DCB 26 October 1865, 27 October 1865. On taffachellas ('bunte schmalgestreifte Baumwolltücher'), see also Nakai, *Das Verhältnis zwischen Japan und der Schweiz*, 117.
83 See, DCB 11 November, 13 November, 17 November 1865.
84 See, for instance, DCB 16 December 1873, black cloth; 5 December 1873 blue cloth; 5 December 1867 red cloth.
85 See, for instance, HS to GS, 12 May 1867, ZBZ Ms Z II 349.
86 'Militärtuch'. See, for instance, DCB, 10, 28 April 1867, 19 December 1872.
87 'Motsubashi' would mean 'Hitotsubashi', the family name borne by Yoshinobu before he succeeded to the head of Tokugawa Clan in 1866.
88 HS to GS, 30 November 1866, ZBZ Ms Z II 349.
89 flour: DCB, 1 November 1866; sugar and rice: DCB, 30 March 1867; cotton: HS to GS, 16 December 1866, ZBZ Ms Z II 349; nitre: DCB, 5 November 1866; iron: HS to GS, 24 December 1869, DKH C 3 1; medicines: DCB, 10 July 1866, shoes: DCB, 9 April 1872.
90 HS to GS, 18 December 1869, DKH C 3 1; HS to GS, 16 October 1867, ZBZ Ms Z II 349.
91 HS to GS, 16 April 1867, ZBZ Ms Z II 349.
92 HS to GS, 24 February 1869, ibid. 'Prince of Bizen' would be Ikeda Akimasa, the lord of the Okayama domain.
93 See HS to GS, 23 December 1870, ZBZ Ms Z II 349.
94 Ibid.
95 HS to GS, 7 October 1871, ZBZ Ms Z II 349. On *haihan-chiken* and other drastic reforms implemented by the Meiji government during the Meiji Restoration, see: Hiroshi Mitani, 'Meiji Revolution' in *the Oxford Research Encyclopaedia of Asian History*, http://asianhistory.oxfordre.com/view/10.1093/acrefore/9780190277727.001.0001/acrefore-9780190277727-e-84 (accessed 26 June 2018).

96 Edward Schnell spoke German as his mother tongue and Dutch as a learnt language since his childhood and had already lived in Yokohama since the early 1860s, so that he could also speak (probably broken) Japanese. Fukuoka Mariko, 'Boshin sensō ni kanyo shita Shuneru kyōdai no "kokuseki" mondai' (The Issue of the 'Nationality' of the Schnell Brothers, Participants in the Boshin War), in *Boshin sensō no shiryōgaku* (Historiography of the Boshin War), ed. Hakoishi Hiroshi (Tokyo: Bensei Shuppan, 2013), 107–40.
97 DCB, 30 September, 2–6, 11, 15–18, 28 October 1866.
98 DCB, 22 March, 8. April 1867.
99 DCB, 3, 8, 28 April, 4, and especially 10 May 1867.
100 *Zoku tsūshin zenran* (General Records of Friendships, second series) (Tokyo: Yūshōdō Shuppan, 1983–88), *The Chronicle* volume 11 (1866), 'Correspondences with the Swiss Representatives' II, 579–84.
101 Most of the rifles imported and used in the late Edo period, including during the civil war (1868), were muzzleloaders, which were then becoming out of date in the West. See: Asakawa Michio, 'Boshin sensō ki ni okeru rikugun no gunbi to senpō' (Armaments and Tactics of Armies during the Boshin War), in *Boshin sensō no shin shiten* (New Perspectives on the Boshin War), ed. Nagura Tetsuzō, Hōya Tōru and Hakoishi Hiroshi, vol. 2 (Tokyo: Yoshikawa Kōbunkan, 2018) 2–26.
102 HS to GS, 16 October 1866, ZBZ Ms Z II 349.
103 On the French Minister Léon Roches and his policy towards the shogunate, see for example: Yatabe Atsuhiko, *Haiboku no gaikōkan Rosshu: Isulāmu sekau to bakumatsu Edo wo meguru yume* (The Defeated Diplomat Roches: His Dream Involving the Islamic World and Edo in the Bakumatsu Period) (Tokyo: Hakusuisha, 2014).
104 DCB, 7 November 1866. In the same entry, Brennwald refers that Favre's son was staying in the British Legation in Edo without getting permission from him, on the pretext of installing a telegraph in the legation. On another day, he records that when the Dutch representative, Dirk Graf van Polsbroek, sold two steamships to his Japanese customers, the Chamber of Commerce of Yokohama discussed to resolve a decision to protest against such 'official trading [*sic*, the term is used in English].' (DCB 19 September 1866).
105 Hayakawa Yōko, 'Boshin sensō ki no Ni'igata kō no kinō ni kansuru ichi kōsatsu' (An Examination on the Function of the Port of Niigata during the Boshin War), *Kokushi danwakai zasshi* (Journal of the Association of Narratives on National History) 20 (1979): 18–19.
106 HS to GS, 14 April 1868, ZBZ Ms Z II 349.
107 HS to GS, 14 April 1868, ibid.
108 HS to GS, 11 July 1868, ibid.

109 HS to GS, 22 August 1868, DKH C 3 1.
110 Hayakawa, 'Boshin sensō ki no Ni'igata kō no kinō ni kansuru ichi kōsatsu', 19.
111 The data are compiled by Hayakawa based on: Gaimushō kiroku (Records of the Japanese Foreign Ministry), 'Fuhanken ni okeru gaikoku fusai toriatsukai zakken (Miscellanea Concerning Foreign Liabilities by Different Domains and Prefectures in Japan)'. Some of the articles are difficult to translate from Japanese to English and are thus left untranslated.
112 Hōya Tōru, 'Kokusaihō no nakano boshin sensō, (The Boshin War Viewed through International Law)' in *Boshin sensō no shin shiten*, ed. Nagura, Hōya and Hakoishi, vol. 1, 2–24.
113 HS to GS, 12 September 1868, DKH C 3 2.
114 Ibid.
115 Probably Siber & Brennwald only reported the sum of the debt and not the illegal origins of it to the court.
116 Ōkurashō (The Finance Ministry) ed., *Meiji zenki zaisei keizai shiryō shūsei* (Collection of Records Relating to Finance and the Economy of the Early Meiji Period), vol. 9, 'Kyūhan gaikoku hosai shobunroku (Liabilities of Former Domains to Foreign Creditors)' (Tokyo: Meiji Bunken Shiryō Kankō kai, 1963), 259.
117 HS to GS, 13 June 1870, ZBZ Ms Z II 349.
118 Report by Mr. Adams (Francis O. Adams), Secretary to Her Majesty's Legation in Japan, On the Central Silk Districts of Japan; Further Report from Mr. Adams, On Silk Culture in Japan; Third Report by Mr. Adams on Silk Culture in Japan, dated August 10 1870. Presented to both Houses of Parliament by command of Her Majesty (London: Printed by Harrison and Sons, 1870–71). On a related note, the research journey of Adams was not the first one of that kind. The first was an expedition led by the Italian Minister to Japan, Conte Vittorio Sallier De La Tour, from July to August 1869, shortly before Adams. See: Pietro Savio, *La Prima Spedizione Italiana: Nell'interno del Giappone e nei Centri Sericoli* (The First Italian Expedition: In the Interior of Japan and in the Sericultural Centers) (Milano: E. Treves Editore, 1870).
119 Ishii, *Kindai Nihon to Igirisu shihon*, 182–3.
120 Hayami Michiko, ed., *Hayami Kensō shiryōshū: Tomioka seishi shochō to sono zengo ki* (Collection of Sources Related to Hayami Kensō: Director of Tomioka Silk Mill and Records Relating to His Life) (Tokyo: Bunsei Shoin, 2014), Shiryō hen: 'Hayami Kensō-ō no jiden' (Autobiography of Hayami Kensō), 9; 'Rireki Bassui' (Extracts from the Personal Records [of Hayami]), 114.
121 Ibid.
122 Maebashi Shōkō Kaigi-sho (Commercial Chamber of Maebashi), ed., *Ito no machi Maebashi o kizuita hitobito* (The People Who Founded the Silk Producing City of Maebashi) (Maebashi: Jōmō Shinbunsha, 2018), 284.

123 HS to GS, 11 July 1870, ZBZ Ms Z II 349.
124 Ibid.
125 HS to GS, 26 July 1870, ibid.; Hayami ed., *Hayami Kensō shiryōshū*, extracts from the Personal Records (of Hayami), 115.
126 HS to GS, 26 July 1870, ZBZ Ms Z II 349; Hayami ed., *Hayami Kensō shiryōshū*, 115. The hot spring is probably the Ikaho onsen.
127 Maebashi Shōkō Kaigi-sho, ed., *Ito no machi Maebashi o kizuita hitobito*, 284–5.
128 Hayami ed., *Hayami Kensō shiryōshū*, extracts from the Personal Records (of Hayami), 115.
129 Maebashi Shōkō Kaigi-sho, ed., *Ito no machi Maebashi o kizuita hitobito*, 284–5.
130 Hayami ed., *Hayami Kensō shiryōshū*, Shiryō hen: 'Hayami Kensō-ō no jiden' (Autobiography of Hayami Kensō), 9. Hayami had gone into personal debt paying part of Müller's salary in an effort to retain him.
131 Hayami ed., *Hayami Kensō shiryōshū*, extracts from the Personal Records (of Hayami), 116.
132 On Ono-gumi and its silk trade, see Miyamoto Mataji, *Ono-gumi no ki'ito bōeki to seishi gyō: ishin no gōshō Ono Zensuke ke no gyōseki* (The Silk Trade and Silk Reeling of Ono-gumi: Achievements of the Meiji Restoration Period's Great Trading House of Ono Zensuke) (Ōsaka: Ōsaka Daigaku Shuppan-kai, 1966); Miyamoto Mataji, *Ono-gumi no kenkyū* (A Study of the Ono-gumi) (Tokyo: Ōhara Shinseisha, 1970).
133 Itsukakai ed., *Okina no jikiwa: Furukawa Ichibé no keireki dan* (An Old Man's Personal Account: A Narrative of Furukawa Ichibé's Life) (Tokyo: Itsukakai, 1926), 45–6. In Siber's letters, the first clear reference to Furukawa can be found in HS to GS, 8 April 1871, ZBZ Ms Z II 349. On the keen rivalry over Furukawa between Siber and his Western competitors, see HS to GS, 8 April 1871, 26 June 1871, 3 September 1871, 5 August 1871, ZBZ Ms Z II 349.
134 HS to GS, 8 April 1871, ibid. Siber refers to the name of his friend for the first time as Furukawa in HS to GS, 26 June 1871, ibid.
135 'Ōtoru' could refer to James Walter, who, born in Liverpool in 1847, came to Japan in 1867, began working for Siber & Brennwald from 1868 on, and was to contribute substantially to the growth of the firm's silk trade in the Meiji period. See SiberHegner, Hundert Jahre im Dienste des Handels, 22; Yokohama Kaikō Shiryōkan, ed., *Brenwaldo no Bakumatsu Meiji Nippon nikki*, 91.
136 Itsukakai ed., *Okina no jikiwa*, 46; Ono Zentarō, *Ishin no gōshō: Ono-gumi shimatsu* (The Fate of the Ono-gumi: A Large Trading House of the Meiji Restoration Period), Annotated by Miyamoto Matajirō (Tokyo: Seia Shobō, 1966), 134. It is also known that four children of the owner family of the Ono-gumi studied in Europe through Siber's mediation: two of them enrolled in an

elementary school in Switzerland, while the other two studied mainly in England. The funds to stay abroad were all transferred through Siber & Brennwald (Ibid., 89–91).

137 Itsukakai ed., *Okina no jikiwa*, 46.
138 Maebashi Shōkō Kaigi-sho, ed. *Ito no machi Maebashi o kizuita hitobito*, 307
139 HS to GS, 7 October 1871, ZBZ Ms Z II 349.
140 HS to GS, 7 October 1871, ibid.
141 Itsukakai ed., *Okina no jikiwa*, 47; Nagano Yasuhiko, 'Hajimete kikaiseishi o tsutaeta Suisu jin Myurā' (A Swiss Man Müller Who Introduced Machine Silk Reeling), *Sangyō kōko gaku kenkyū* (Study of Industrial Archaeology), 1 (2014): 32–8; Maebashi Shōkō Kaigi-sho, ed. *Seishi no toshi Maebashi o kizuita hitobito*, 308.
142 See introduction of this chapter (note 3).
143 See Federico, *An Economic History of the Silk Industry*, 88–9.
144 Between the end of January and the middle of March 1874, for example, Caspar Brennwald's diary notes the export of no less than 379 bales of raw silk. See DCB, 27 January, 2 February, 16 March 1874.
145 On the origins of mechanical silk reeling, see Carlo Poni, *La seta in Italia. Una grande industria prima della rivoluzione industriale* (Silk in Italy: A Great Industry before the Industrial Revolution) (Bologna: il Mulino, 2009).
146 See entry 'Paul Ritter' in Diplomatic Documents of Switzerland, 1848–1975, dodis.ch/P19126 (accessed 18 April 2018).
147 HS to GS, 7/11 June 1866, ZBZ Ms Z II 349. For the problem of the unremunerated diplomatic activities, see also HS to GS, 11 September 1866, ZBZ Ms Z II 349.
148 HS to GS, 17 November 1867, ZBZ Ms Z II 349; HS to GS, 17 January 1867, ibid.
149 HS to GS, 1 February 1867, ibid.
150 HS to GS, 10 August 1867, ibid.
151 HS to GS, 31 August 1867, ibid. For further complaints, see HS to GS, 11 July 1868, ibid.; HS to GS, 19 November 1869, DKH C 3 1.
152 HS to GS, 2 December 1869, DKH C 3 1.
153 HS to GS, 22 August 1870, ZBZ Ms Z II 349.
154 The authors would like to thank Prof. Dr José Luis Alonso of the University of Zurich's Law Faculty for helping them to understand the nineteenth-century circumstances of the original contract.
155 See SiberHegner und Co. 1965, 16–19.
156 Ibid., 18.
157 See https://dodis.ch/R12108 (accessed 29 June 2018).

Chapter 5

1. William T. Mercer and Robert Fortune were some of the early colonists who, in their poetry and travel writings, remarked on the ghastly fate of perishing and being buried in Hong Kong. William T. Mercer, *Under the Peak, or, Jottings in Verse: Written during a Lengthened Residence in the Colony of Hongkong* (London: J.C. Hotten, 1868), 55–6; Robert Fortune, *Three Years' Wanderings in the Northern Provinces of China* (London: J. Murray, 1847), 13–15.
2. James Steven Curl's early work suggests that ostentatious displays of grief became a norm in middle- and upper-class Victorian society. The simplified understanding of upper-class extravagant funerals and lower-class pauper burial was, however, questioned in more recent works by Pat Jalland and Julie-Marie Strange, as they suggest that ostentatious funerary practices were hardly admired by all at that time. The poor in Victorian Britain also developed their own ways in mourning the dead. James Stevens Curl, *The Victorian Celebration of Death* (Stroud: Sutton, 2000); Pat Jalland, 'Victorian Death and Its Decline: 1850–1918', in *Death in England*, ed. Peter C. Jupp and Clare Gittings (Manchester: Manchester University Press, 1999), 230–55; Julie-Marie Strange, *Death, Grief and Poverty in Britain, 1870–1914* (Cambridge: Cambridge University Press, 2005).
3. As the major mercantile firm in the Canton trade, Jardine Matheson & Co. itself played a pivotal role in the outbreak of the Opium War and the founding of the colony. For more details, please refer to: Alain Le Pichon (ed.), *China Trade and Empire: Jardine, Matheson & Co. and the Origins of British Rule in Hong Kong, 1827–1843* (Oxford: Oxford University Press, 2006); Richard J. Grace, *Opium and Empire: The Lives and Careers of William Jardine and James Matheson* (Montreal: McGill-Queen's University Press, 2014).
4. Christopher Cowell, 'The Hong Kong Fever of 1843: Collective Trauma and the Reconfiguring of Colonial Space', *Modern Asian Studies* 47, no. 2 (2013): 339.
5. Chi Man Kwong, *Eastern Fortress: A Military History of Hong Kong, 1840–1997* (Hong Kong: Hong Kong University Press, 2014), 10.
6. The two graveyards were next to each other in St. Francis Square, Wan Chai. Geoffrey Robley Sayer, *Hong Kong 1841–1862: Birth, Adolescence and Coming of Age* (Hong Kong: Hong Kong University Press, [1937] 1980), 117; Hong Kong Catholic Diocesan Archives HK-DA, SIII, B36, F01., quoted from Sergio Ticozzi, *Historical Document of the Hong Kong Catholic Church* (Hong Kong: Hong Kong Catholic Diocesan Archives, 1997), 12.
7. Fortune, *Three Years' Wanderings*, 24–5.
8. Ernst Johann Eitel, a missionary and later colonial official in Hong Kong from the 1870s to the 1890s, wrote retrospectively that the 'Hong Kong Fever' from May to October 1843 carried off 24 per cent of the troops and 10 per cent of the European

civilians. Ernst Johann Eitel, *Europe in China: The History of Hongkong from the Beginning to the Year 1882* (Hong Kong: Oxford University Press, 1983 [1895]), 191.

9   Patricia Lim, *Forgotten Souls: A Social History of the Hong Kong Cemetery* (Hong Kong: Hong Kong University Press, 2011), 5–6.

10 Cowell, 'The Hong Kong Fever of 1843', 340.

11 Solomon Bard, *Garrison Memorials in Hong Kong* (Hong Kong: Antiquities and Monuments Office: Occasional Paper No. 4, 1997), 12.

12 *Hong Kong Catholic Diocesan Archives* HK-DA, SIV, B 41, F02., quoted from Ticozzi, *Historical Document of the Hong Kong Catholic Church*, 12.

13 For more on the exclusiveness of the 'Protestant Cemetery', please refer to: Bobby Tam, 'Death in Hong Kong: Managing the Dead in a Colonial City from 1841 to 1913' (MPhil diss., University of Hong Kong, Hong Kong, 2018), 114–16. For the later debate on the exclusive nature of the cemetery, please refer to: Tam, 'Death in Hong Kong', 220–5.

14 Julian Litten, *The English Way of Death: Common Funeral since 1450* (London: Robert Hale, 1991), 134.

15 For an understanding of currency and value in early colonial Hong Kong, please refer to: Christopher Munn, *Anglo-China: Chinese People and British Rule in Hong Kong, 1841–1880* (Hong Kong: Hong Kong University Press, 2009), xv. For instance, a European sailor earned about £8 ($38) per month, and a European constable of the lowest grade $19 per month.

16 Correspondence with the military authorities who object to payment of the fees charged for burial, 11 April 1849, Colonial Office Original Correspondence: Hong Kong, Series 129 (hereafter CO 129)/29, pp. 2–8. University of Hong Kong Libraries Special Collections, Hong Kong.

17 *Friend of China*, 1 February 1845, quoted from Lim, *Forgotten Souls*, 12.

18 For further information on a complete list of foreign residents in early colonial Hong Kong, and their respective occupations and employers, please consult: *The Hongkong Almanack and Directory for 1846: With an Appendix* [compiled by William Tarrant] (Hong Kong: Office of the China Mail, 1846); *The Hongkong Almanack, and Directory for the Year 1848, or Our Lord and the Twelfth of the Reign of Her Majesty Queen Victoria* [compiled by William Tarrant] (Hong Kong: D. Noronha, 1848); *The Hongkong Almanack, and Directory for the Year of Our Lord 1850, and of the Reign of Her Majesty Queen Victoria the Fourteenth* (Hong Kong: Noronha, 1849); *The Hongkong Directory with List of Foreign Residents in China* (Hong Kong: Armenian Press, 1859).

19 Lim, *Forgotten Souls*, 92.

20 Ibid., 95.

21 Before the opening of the Suez Canal and the common usage of long-distance steamships, it would take at least three months to travel from Britain to Hong

Kong. It took ninety-nine days for the fastest clippers to travel from China to Britain in the Great Tea Race of 1866. It still took more than 100 days for the clipper *Cutty Sark* to travel from China to Britain during the 1870s.

22 As evident in colonial state records of deaths before the introduction of a death registration system in 1872, the recorded deaths in the colony were simply based on burials in the Protestant and Catholic Cemetery. It is thus unlikely that a large proportion of European bodies would be sent back to Europe during the early colonial period. For more details on the large-scale industry of transporting Chinese bodies for ancestral home burial through Hong Kong, please refer to: Elizabeth Sinn, *Pacific Crossing: California Gold, Chinese Migration, and the Making of Hong Kong* (Hong Kong: Hong Kong University Press, 2015).

23 The Merchant Navy is not part of the British naval force, but refers to merchant vessels that were registered in Britain and represented British commercial interests.

24 Lim, *Forgotten Souls*, 159.

25 Ibid., 158.

26 Ibid., 211.

27 For instance, according to the Colonial Surgeon's report, only one European policeman died while fifty-four European civilians died in 1853. 'The Colonial Surgeon's Report for 1853', *Hong Kong Government Gazette* (1854), No. 32, pp. 117–19.

28 *China Mail*, 8 June 1848, quoted from Lim, *Forgotten Soul*, 212.

29 William T. Mercer, *Under the Peak, or, Jottings in Verse: Written during a Lengthened Residence in the Colony of Hongkong* (London: J.C. Hotten, 1868), 6.

30 David Arnold, *The Tropics and the Travelling Gaze: India, Landscape, and Science, 1800–1856* (Seattle: University of Washington Press, 2006), 42.

31 Xinbao Ding and Shuying Lu, *Fei wo zu yi: zhan qian Xianggang de wai ji zu qun* (Foreign Ethnic Communities in Pre-war Hong Kong) (Hong Kong: Joint Publishing, 2014), 186–7.

32 The census of 1891 recorded just ninety-one Parsees living in Hong Kong. 'Census Returns of the population of the Colony on 3 April 1881', *Hong Kong Government Gazette* (1881), No. 204.

33 Ding, *Fei wo zu yi*, 187.

34 Sek Leng Wong, 'Life and Death: Reconstructing Macau's Society in the Nineteenth Century through Historic Cemetery Walks' (MS diss., University of Hong Kong, Hong Kong, 2011), 14.

35 Ko Tim-Keung, 'A Review of Development of Cemeteries in Hong Kong: 1841–1950', *Journal of the Royal Asiatic Society Hong Kong Branch* 41 (2001): 246.

36 Excarnation through a 'Tower of Silence' was the traditional funerary practice of Zoroastrianism. Bodies would be exposed on a 'Tower of Silence' for vultures to consume. Such ancient practice was never carried out in Hong Kong. Ding, *Fei wo zu yi*, 191.

37 Ding, *Fei wo zu yi*, 192. 'Parsee Cemetery' [in Chinese], *Minority History in Hong Kong*, Lord Wilson Heritage Trust. Available online: http://www.rtedu.hk/minorityhistory/html/parsee_3.html#1
38 Ding, *Fei wo zu yi*, 169.
39 Ibid., 172–4.
40 Ibid., 177. Ko, 'A Review of Development of Cemeteries in Hong Kong: 1841–1950', 246.
41 Carl T. Smith, *A Sense of History: Studies in the Social and Urban History of Hong Kong* (Hong Kong: Hong Kong Educational Publishing, 1995), 402.
42 According to colonial records, a large proportion of policemen and soldiers were categorized as 'Indian'. The broadly defined 'Indians' in Hong Kong adhered to a diverse range of religions and many of them were Muslims.
43 Ding, *Fei wo zu yi*, 149–50.
44 'An Ordinance for Enabling Her Majesty to Resume Possession of the Mahomedan Cemetery', *Hong Kong Government Gazette* (1867), p. 181.
45 Thomas Laqueur argues that the shift in burial spaces had more to do with changes in cultural values and eschatology rather than scientific development on sanitation. Thomas Laqueur, *The Work of the Dead: A Cultural History of Mortal Remains* (Princeton: Princeton University Press, 2015), 214.
46 Lawrence Stone, *The Past and the Present* (Boston: Routledge, 1981), 247. Stone first put forward this concept in his earlier work: Lawrence Stone, *The Family, Sex and Marriage in England, 1500–1800* (London: Weidenfeld & Nicolson, 1977).
47 Philippe Ariès, *The Hour of Our Death*, trans. Helen Weaver (New York: Knopf, 1980).
48 Sarah Tarlow, 'Landscapes of Memory: The Nineteenth-Century Garden Cemetery', *European Journal of Archaeology* 3, no. 2 (2000): 217–39.
49 Henry Knollys, *English Life in China* (London: Smith, Elder & CO, 1885), 18.
50 Lim, *Forgotten Soul*, 298.
51 Ibid., 452.
52 Ibid., 453.
53 For more about the leisure and comfort of colonial lives in Hong Kong in the British popular imagination, please refer to: Daozi Huang, 'You May Go to Hong Kong for Me: British Views of a Chinese Colony' (PhD diss., University of Hong Kong, Hong Kong, 2018), 109–51.
54 For colonial policy in regulating Chinese burials and later creating Chinese burial grounds during this period, and specifically the paradox of regulation without provision, please refer to: Tam, 'Death in Hong Kong', 62–9 and 123–5.
55 For the story of how Chinese elite merchants exerted their influence through the Tung Wah Hospital, please refer to: Elizabeth Sinn, *Power and Charity: A Chinese Merchant Elite in Colonial Hong Kong* (Hong Kong: Hong Kong University Press, 2003).

56 May Holdsworth, 'Ho Tung, Sir Robert', in *Dictionary of Hong Kong Biography*, ed. May Holdsworth and Christopher Munn (Hong Kong: Hong Kong University Press, 2012), 195.
57 Steve Tsang, *A Modern History of Hong Kong* (Hong Kong: Hong Kong University Press, 2004), 49.
58 *Hong Kong Government Gazette* (1897), No. 522.
59 'Eurasian Cemetery, Inland Lot 1415 – Application from Mr. Ho Tung to Alter the Boundaries', HKRS58-1-14-44, Hong Kong Public Record Office, Hong Kong.
60 During a confrontation in removing Chinese graves in 1877, some Chinese representatives suggested to the governor that the rule restricting burial plots – not longer than 6 feet and wider than 2 feet – actually rendered burial impossible. The governor later accepted their arguments and put his veto upon the proposed rules. John Pope Hennessy, 'The Governor's Report on the Bluebook' (Section on Chinese Graves no. 116 – no. 125) in *Administrative Reports* (1880), 29 April 1881.
61 Feng-Shui, literally translated as wind and water, could be understood as Chinese geomancy. It plays an important role in determining the orientation and location of buildings and burial sites in Chinese culture.
62 May Holdsworth, 'Ho Kom-tong', in *Dictionary of Hong Kong Biography*, ed. May Holdsworth and Christopher Munn (Hong Kong: Hong Kong University Press, 2012), 190–1.
63 'Application for Burial Site within the Chinese Cemetery', HKRS58-1-17-72, Hong Kong Public Record Office, Hong Kong.
64 'Sanitary Board' in *The Hong Kong Weekly Press*, 17 April 1909, p. 314.
65 'Bye-law Made under Section 16 of the Public Health and Buildings Ordinance, 1903' *Hong Kong Government Gazette* (1909), No. 768.
66 Chinese elites, for instance, demonstrated their willingness to embrace Western medicine and supported colonial sanitary measures during and after the plague of Hong Kong in 1894. This distinctly separated them from the common Chinese who were hostile to colonial medicine. See: Sinn, *Power and Charity*, 159–83.
67 The lack of emotions or lack of emotional authenticity was a common depiction of Chinese funerary practices in the colonial discourse. The English press in China, travellers' accounts, and missionaries' writings often depicted Chinese funerary practices as frivolous rituals empty of genuine feeling to the dead. Some examples of such negative depiction in travel writings include: P.G. Laurie, *A Reminiscence of Canton* (London: Harrison and Sons, 1866), 26–9; Knollys, *English Life in China*, 14–15.
68 Brenda Yeoh, *Contesting Space in Colonial Singapore* (Singapore: Singapore University Press, 2003), 284–5.
69 Ibid., 289.
70 Ibid., 292.

71 The practice of storing remains in urns for flexible relocation of burial spots was common across southern China. Yeoh, *Contesting Space*, 292.
72 Ernst Johann Eitel, *Feng-shui or the Rudiments of Natural Science in China* (London: Trubner, 1873), 81–2.
73 *The Hong Kong Daily Press*, 15 April 1909, quoted from *The Hong Kong Weekly Press*, 17 April 1909, p. 321.
74 For instance, Charles Dickens ridiculed the Victorian extravagance of death. See: Julie-Marie Strange, *Death, Grief and Poverty in Britain, 1870–1914* (Cambridge: Cambridge University Press, 2005), 2.
75 Western funeral processions in Hong Kong and Shanghai were often reported in newspapers such as the *North China Herald, China Mail* and *Hong Kong Daily Press*. They were usually for deceased military or official figures. Even for private European citizens who were given a public funeral procession, they were publicly commemorated for their contribution to the colonial community – as in the case of Charles Richardson, one of the lives examined in this volume. Much emphasis was put on individual's sacrifice for British interests rather than their personal wealth. See: Robert Fletcher, *The Ghost of Namamugi: Charles Lenox Richardson and the Anglo-Satsuma War* (Folkestone: Renaissance Books, 2019).
76 The funeral procession of Ng Hon Tsz, another wealthy merchant who later joined the colonial administration, was accompanied by both a large Chinese and European band. The funeral was well attended by Chinese spectators as well as many colonial officials including the governor. 'The Late Hon. Mr Ng Hon Tsz' in *Hong Kong Daily Press*, 12 April 1923, p. 5.

Chapter 6

1 Colin Amodeo and the Canterbury Pilgrims and Early Settlers Association, *The Summer Ships: Being an Account of the First Six Ships Sent Out from England by the Canterbury Association in 1850–1851* (Christchurch, NZ: Caxton Press, 2001).
2 'The Charlotte Jane', *Lyttelton Times*, 11 January 1851, 2.
3 Charlotte Godley, *Letters from Early New Zealand* (Christchurch: Whitcombe and Tombs Ltd., 1951), introduction.
4 Katie Pickles, *Christchurch Ruptures* (Wellington: Bridget Williams Books, 2016), 22.
5 Henry Wigram, *The Story of Christchurch, New Zealand* (Christchurch: The Lyttelton Times Co. Ltd., 1916), forward.
6 Gordon Ogilvie, *Pioneers of the Plains: The Deans of Canterbury* (Christchurch: Shoal Bay Press, 1996), 52.

7   Sir Henry Brett, *White Wings, Volume Two: The Founding of the Provinces* (Auckland: The Brett Printing Co. Ltd., Publishers, 1928), 69; 'The Sir George Seymour', *Lyttelton Times*, 11 January 1851, Issue 1.
8   Untitled, *Maori Messenger*, 27 February 1851, 2.
9   Wigram, *The Story of Christchurch, New Zealand*, 48.
10 Ibid.
11 Amodeo et al., *The Summer Ships*, 19.
12 P.A. Thomas, 'Large Letter'd as with Thundering Shout: An Analysis of Typographic Posters Advertising Emigration to New Zealand, 1839–1875', (unpublished PhD diss., Massey University, 2014).
13 John Cookson, 'Pilgrims' Progress – Image, Identity and Myth in Christchurch', in *Southern Capital, Christchurch: Towards a City Biography*, ed. John Cookson and Graeme Dunstall (Christchurch: Canterbury University Press, 2000), 38.
14 Pickles, *Christchurch Ruptures*, 48.
15 Ibid., 48–9.
16 Cookson, 'Pilgrims' Progress', 33.
17 Pickles, *Christchurch Ruptures*, 45–6, 49–50.
18 Colin Amodeo, *Forgotten Forty-Niners* (Christchurch: Caxton Press, 2003), 185.
19 Pickles, *Christchurch Ruptures*, 49–50.
20 Untitled, *Maori Messenger*, 27 February 1851, 2.
21 Jane Deans, *Letters to My Grandchildren* (Christchurch: Cadsonbury Publications, 1995), 15.
22 Godley, *Letters from Early New Zealand*, 142. Godley's description displays the subtle gradations of the British class system. She is happy to describe Deans as gentlemanlike, but not as a gentleman.
23 Pickles, *Christchurch Ruptures*, 49.
24 Edward Ward, *The Journal of Edward Ward* (Christchurch: Pegasus Press, 1951), 214.
25 Uncatalogued magazine entry, labelled 4.4. 38, possibly from the *Bristol Evening Courier*, by regular columnist C.R. Huddleston, courtesy of Bristol Museums.
26 Ward, *The Journal of Edward Ward*, 214.
27 Amodeo et al., *The Summer Ships*, 17.
28 *Allen's Indian Mail and Register of Intelligence for British and Foreign India, China and All Parts of the East, Vol 3. Jan–Dec 1845* (London: Wm. H. Allen and Co., 1845), 172; *The Spectator* 13 (London: F.C. Westley, 1840), 238.
29 Robert Erskine Waddell, *Biographies, the Little Connection*, http://www.ornaverum.org/reference/pdf/009.pdf (accessed 7 June 2017).
30 Amodeo et al., *The Summer Ships*, 56.
31 'Immigrants Per Charlotte Jane', *Sydney Morning Herald*, 13 October 1848, 3.
32 Julius Berncastle, *A Voyage to China* (London: W. Shoberl, 1850), 265.

33 Ibid.
34 Hoh Cheung Mui and Lorna H. Mui eds., *William Melrose in China, 1854–1855* (Edinburgh: Scottish History Society, 1973), 111.
35 Berncastle, *A Voyage to China*, 266.
36 Ibid., 274–5.
37 Ibid., 271.
38 Aaron Jaffer, '"Lord of the Forecastle": Serangs, Tindals, and Lascar Mutiny, c.1780–1860', in *Mutiny and Maritime Radicalism in the Age of Revolution*, ed. Clare Anderson, Niklas Frykman, Lex Heerma van Voss, and Marcus Rediker (Cambridge: Cambridge University Press, 2013), 166–7.
39 Charles Knight ed., *The Land We Live in: A Pictorial and Literary Sketchbook of the British Empire. Vol 3* (London: Charles Knight, date not given), 276.
40 Ward, *The Journal of Edward Ward*, 17.
41 Amodeo, et al., *The Summer Ships*, 57–8.
42 Ward, *The Journal of Edward Ward*, 58.
43 Ibid., 57.
44 Ibid., 25.
45 Amodeo et al., *The Summer Ships*, 136.
46 Whitehouse, Olwyn, Entry in 'Deserters from the First Four Ships to Lyttelton in 1851', http://freepages.genealogy.rootsweb.ancestry.com/~nzbound/desert.htm (accessed 7 June 2017).
47 Ward, *The Journal of Edward Ward*, 24.
48 Ibid., 30.
49 C.C. Burton, *Dr Barker, 1819–1873: Photographer, Farmer, Physician* (Dunedin: John McIndoe, 1972), 18–19.
50 Amodeo et al., *The Summer Ships*, 45.
51 Burton, *Dr Barker, 1819–1873*, 27.
52 'The Charlotte Jane', *Lyttelton Times*, 11 January 1851, 2.
53 Johannes C. Andersen, *Old Christchurch* (Christchurch: Simpson and Williams Ltd., 1949), 60.
54 Burton, *Dr Barker, 1819–1873*, 43.
55 'Departures', *The Sydney Morning Herald*, 17 April 1851, 4.
56 *Sydney Morning Herald*, 8 April 1851, 3.
57 Mrs Pollack, *Log of the Voyage of the Charlotte Jane from Gravesend to Holdfast Bay, 19 September 1851–14 January 1852* (transcription, State Library of South Australia, Gov't of South Australia, D6419 [L]) entry for 18 December 1851.
58 *Sydney Morning Herald*, 29 January 1852, 2.
59 The Ships List, SA Passenger Lists, 1847–1886, barque Charlotte Jane, http://www.theshipslist.com/ships/australia/charlottejane1852.shtml (accessed 7 June 2017).
60 'South Australia', *The Empire*, 9 February 1852, 2.

61 'Police Court', *Adelaide Observer*, 17 July 1852, 7.
62 *South Australian Register*, 28 July 1852, 3.
63 *South Australian Register*, 27 July 1852, 2; *The Empire*, 7 June 1852, 2.
64 *South Australian Register*, 28 July 1852, 3.
65 Ibid.
66 *Adelaide Observer*, 30 April 1853, 5.
67 'For London Direct', *The Times of Adelaide*, 13 June 1853, 1.
68 'Ship "Charlotte Jane" for London' (advertisement), *The Times of Adelaide*, 13 June 1853, 1.
69 Robert Erskine Waddell, *Biographies, the Little Connection*, http://www.ornaverum.org/reference/pdf/009.pdf (accessed 7 June 2017).
70 Ibid.
71 William Alt to his aunt, Barbados, March 1854. Reference here is to the personal correspondences of William John Alt, 1853–1865: Digital versions held by Sainsbury Institute for the Study of Japanese Arts and Cultures, Norwich UK. Hereafter, each specific reference to the letters will be given as WA (for William Alt), followed by the date, place where written, the recipient (if known), and the file number of the digitized collection in this case WA08-006a.
72 Brian Burke-Gaffney, 'The Alt House: Yesterday, Today and Tomorrow', *Crossroads: A Journal of Nagasaki History and Culture* 6 (Autumn 1998): online http://www.uwosh.edu/home_pages/faculty_staff/earns/althouse.html
73 WA to Aunt, Portsmouth, February 1854 (WA08-004a).
74 WA to Aunt, Barbados, March 1854 (WA08-006a).
75 'Vessels in Harbour', *The South Australian Register*, 24 May 1854, 2.
76 'To William Russell Esq. Commander of the "Charlotte Jane"', *The South Australian Register*, 24 May 1854, 2.
77 WA to Mother, The Lizard Peninsula, November 1854 (WA08-001b).
78 WA to Mother, Port Adelaide, May 1854 (WA10-001b).
79 Ibid.
80 Advertisements and notices, *London Daily News*, 21 June 1855.
81 WA dictated note, March 1908 (WA02-002-02).
82 British Battles: The Crimean War, The National Archives (United Kingdom) https://www.nationalarchives.gov.uk/battles/crimea/
83 WA dictated note, March 1908 (WA02-002-02).
84 See message by historian Ian Welch on this humanities website, http://h-net.msu.edu/cgi-bin/logbrowse.pl?trx=vx&list=h-asia&month=1207&week=c&msg=vOmkIonYfPGqMWFz/TdhRA&user=&pw= (accessed 7 June 2017).
85 WA to Mother, Shantou, August 1857 (WA08-007a).
86 Ibid.
87 WA to Mother, Shanghai, 1857 (WA09-001b).

88 Robert Hellyer, 'Mid-Nineteenth Century Nagasaki: Western and Japanese Merchant Communities within Political and Commercial Transitions', in *Merchant Communities in Asia, 1600–1980*, ed. Lin Yu-ju and Madeleine Zelin (London: Pickering and Chatto Ltd., 2015), 164–5.
89 *The Times of London*, 1 February 1862.
90 Pickles, *Christchurch Ruptures*, 22.
91 'Vessels in Port', *Southland Times*, 25 August 1864, 2.
92 This information has not yet been verified by academic sources, so for now must just remain a strong possibility. See: Thomas Scarrow, Master Mariner: Voyage Record, *The Scarrows of Cumberland*, http://www.cumberlandscarrow.com/thomasrecord.htm (accessed 7 June 2017).
93 *Melbourne Argus*, 11 August 1864, 4.
94 *Southland Times*, 16 July 1864, 4.
95 *Southland Times*, 25 August 1864, 4; 20 September 1864, 3.
96 *Nelson Examiner* and *New Zealand Chronicle*, 21 July 1864, 3.
97 *Southland Times*, 16 July 1864, 4.
98 *The Melbourne Argus*, 11 August 1864, 4.
99 Neill Atkinson, *Trainland: How the Railways Made New Zealand* (Auckland: Random House, 2007), 27.
100 Geoffrey B. Churchman and Tony Hurst, *The Railways of New Zealand: A Journey through History* (Wellington: Transpress New Zealand, 2001), 210.
101 Atkinson, *Trainland*, 27.
102 Ibid., 28.
103 *The Melbourne Argus*, 15 February 1865, 4.
104 Ward, *The Journal of Edward Ward*, 214.
105 'Marshalls, Foreign Ships in Micronesia', Micronesian Seminar, http://www.micsem.org/pubs/articles/historical/forships/marshalls.htm (accessed 7 June 2017).
106 Wigram, *The Story of Christchurch, New Zealand*, 48.

Chapter 7

1 R.H.W. Reece, 'Earl, George Samuel Windsor (1813–1865)', *Oxford Dictionary of National Biography*, e-version, 2004, https://doi.org/10.1093/ref:odnb/59850 (accessed 23 July 2019).
2 Russell Jones, 'George Windsor Earl and "Indonesia"', *Indonesia Circle: School of Oriental & African Studies*, Newsletter 22, no. 64 (1994): 279–90.
3 The rest of this chapter, which offers a synopsis of the monograph, Ranald Noel-Paton, *An Eastern Calling: George Windsor Earl and a Vision of Empire*

(London: Ashgrove Publishing, 2018), draws on these publications, the full details of which are listed alongside material relation to Earl's personal records, in *An Eastern Calling*.

4   George Windsor Earl, *The Eastern Seas, or Voyages and Adventures in the Indian Archipelago, in 1832-33-34 ... Also an Account of the Present State of Singapore* ... (London: W.H. Allen, 1837).

5   Demetrius Charles Boulger, *The Life of Sir Stamford Raffles* (London: H. Marshall, 1897), ix.

6   James Cameron, 'The Northern Settlements: Outposts of Empire', in *The Origins of Australia's Capital Cities*, ed. Pamela Stratham (Cambridge: Cambridge University Press, 1989), 273.

7   Jim Allen, *Port Essington: The Historical Archaeology of a North Australian Nineteenth-Century Military Outpost* (Sydney: Sydney University Press, 2008), 108.

8   George Windsor Earl, *Observations on the Commercial and Agricultural Capabilities of the North Coast of New Holland and the Advantages to Be Derived from the Establishment of a Settlement in the Vicinity of Raffles Bay* (London: E. Wilson, 1836).

9   C.A. Gibson-Hill, 'George Samuel Windsor Earl', *Journal of the Malayan Branch of the Royal Asiatic Society* 32, no. 1 (185) (May 1959): 106.

10 George Windsor Earl, *Observations on the Commercial and Agricultural Capabilities of the North Coast of New Holland and the Advantages to Be Derived from the Establishment of a Settlement in the Vicinity of Raffles Bay* (London: Effingham Wilson, 1836).

11 A newspaper article describing the devastation caused by the hurricane lamented that 'what has been done during the last 18 months by one hundred men is entirely destroyed'. 'Hurricane at Port Essington', *Perth Gazette and Western Australia Journal*, 11 April 1840, 3.

12 W. Earl, 'On the Physical Structure and Arrangements of the Islands in the Indian Archipelago', *The Journal of the Royal Geographical Society* 15 (1845): 358–65.

13 G. Windsor Earl, *Enterprise in Tropical Australia* (London: Madden and Malcolm, 1846).

14 G. Windsor Earl, 'On the Aboriginal Tribes of the Northern Coast of Australia', *Journal of Royal Geographical Society* 16 (1846): 239–51.

15 George Windsor Earl, *The Native Races of the Indian Archipelago; the Papuans* (London: H. Bailliere, 1853).

16 George Windsor Earl, *A Correspondence Relating to the Discovery of Gold in Australia* (London: Pelham Richardson, 1853).

17 G. Windsor Earl, 'On the Shell-Mounds of Province Wellesley, in the Malay Peninsula', *Transactions of the Ethnological Society of London* 11 (1863): 119–29; George Windsor Earl, *Topography and Itinerary of Province Wellesley* (George

Town [Penang]: Pinang Gazette Press, 1861); George Windsor Earl, 'Handbook for Colonists in Tropical Australia', *Journal of the Indian Archipelago and Eastern Asia* 4, no. 1 (1863): 1–187.

18 G. Windsor Earl, 'On the Leading Characteristics of the Papuan, Australian, and Malayu-Polynesian Nations', Chapter II, *Journal of the Indian Archipelago and Eastern Asia* (January 1850): 1–10.
19 'Married. Alt-Earl', *The Adelaide Express*, 16 September 1864, 2.
20 Elisabeth penned a memoir chronicling her experiences in Japan and later in Britain after she, William and their children returned there to reside permanently. Elisabeth Alt, 'Some Memories of Elisabeth Christiana Fernhill Alt (née Earl)', unpublished manuscript, National Library of Australia.
21 'The Late Mr. G.W. Earl', *The Southern Australia Register*, 27 October 1865, 6.
22 Bob Reece, 'The Australasian Career of George Windsor Earl', *Journal of the Malaysian Branch of the Royal Asiatic Society* 65, no. 2 (263) (1992): 60.

Bibliography

Introduction

Alt, William John. *Personal Correspondence, 1853–1865: Digital Versions Held by Sainsbury Institute for the Study of Japanese Arts and Cultures.* Norwich, UK.

Auslin, Michael. *Negotiating with Imperialism: The Unequal Treaties and the Culture of Japanese Diplomacy.* Cambridge, MA: Harvard University Press, 2004.

Beasley, William. *Select Documents on Japanese Foreign Policy, 1853–1868.* London: Oxford University Press, 1955.

Bickers, Robert. *Settler and Expatriates: Britons over the Seas.* Oxford: Oxford University Press, 2010.

Blagg, Michele. 'Gold Refining in London: The End of the Rainbow, 1919–1922'. In *The Global Gold Market and the International Monetary System from the Late 19th Century to the Present: Actors, Networks, Power*, edited by Sandra Bott, 88–108. Houndmills, Basingstoke, UK: Palgrave Macmillan, 2013.

Brunero, Donna and Stephanie Villalta Puig. *Life in Treaty Port China and Japan.* Singapore: Palgrave Macmillan, 2018.

Cassel, Pär Kristoffer. *Grounds of Judgment: Extraterritoriality and Imperial Power in Nineteenth-Century China and Japan.* New York: Oxford University Press, 2012.

Cleall, Esme, Laura Ishiguro and Emily J. Manktelow. 'Imperial Relations: Families in the British Empire', *Journal of Colonialism and Colonial History* 14, no. 1 (2013): n.p.

Cleere, Eileen. *Avuncularism: Capitalism, Patriarchy, and Nineteenth-century English Culture.* Stanford: Stanford University Press, 2004.

Cortazzi, Hugh. *Victorians in Japan: In and around the Treaty Ports, 1987.* London: Bloomsbury Academic Collections, 2012.

Davidoff, Leonore. *Thicker than Water: Siblings and their Relations, 1780–1920.* Oxford: Oxford University Press, 2012.

Earl, George Windsor. *The Eastern Seas: Or, Voyages and Adventures in the Indian Archipelago, in 1832-33-34.* London: W.H. Allen, 1837.

Ennals, Peter. *Opening a Window to the West: The Foreign Concession at Kobe, Japan, 1868–1899.* Toronto: University of Toronto Press, 2014.

Fairbank, John. *Trade and Diplomacy on the China Coast: The Opening of the Treaty Ports, 1842–1854.* Cambridge, MA: Harvard University Press, 1953.

Fletcher, Robert S.G. *The Ghost of Namamugi: Charles Lenox Richardson and the Anglo-Satsuma War.* Amsterdam: Amsterdam University Press, 2019.

Greenberg, Michael. *British Trade and the Opening of China, 1800–1842.* Cambridge: Cambridge University Press, 1951.

Hamashita, Takeshi. 'Tribute and Treaties: Maritime Asia and Treaty Port Networks in the Era of Negotiation, 1800–1900'. In *The Resurgence of East Asia: 500, 150 and 50 Year Perspectives*, edited by Giovanni Arrighi, Takeshi Hamashita and Mark Selden, 17–47. London: Routledge, 2003.

Hellyer, Robert. *Green with Milk and Sugar – When Japan Filled America's Tea Cups*. New York: Columbia University Press, 2021.

Hellyer, Robert. 'Mid Nineteenth-Century Nagasaki: Western and Japanese Merchant Communities within Commercial and Political Transitions'. In *Merchant Communities in Asia, 1600–1980*, edited by Yuju Lin and Madeleine Zelin, 159–76. London: Pickering and Chatto, 2014.

Hoare, J.E. *Culture, Power & Politics in Treaty Port Japan, 1854–1899: Key Papers, Press and Contemporary Writings: Volume 1: Historical Perspectives*. London: Renaissance Books, 2018.

Jackson, Isabella and Robert Bickers. *Treaty Ports in Modern China: Law, Land and Power*. London: Routledge, 2016.

Laidlaw, Zoë. *Colonial Connections 1815–45: Patronage, the Information Revolution and Colonial Government*. Manchester: Manchester University Press, 2005.

Lambert, David and Alan Lester. *Colonial Lives across the British Empire*. Cambridge: Cambridge University Press, 2006.

Lester, Alan. 'Imperial Circuits and Networks: Geographies of the British Empire'. *History Compass*, 4, no. 1 (2005): 124–41.

Melancon, Glenn. *Britain's China Policy and the Opium Crisis: Balancing Drugs, Violence and National Honour, 1833–1840*. Aldershot: Ashgate, 2003.

Mountford, Benjamin and Steven Tufnell. *A Global History of Gold Rushes*. Oakland, CA: University of California Press, 2019.

Murphey, Rhoads. *The Treaty Ports and China's Modernization: What Went Wrong?* Ann Arbor, MI: University of Michigan, 1970.

Nield, Robert. *China's Foreign Places: The Foreign Presence in China in the Treaty Port Era, 1840–1943*. Hong Kong: Hong Kong University Press, 2015.

Osborn, Sherard. *The Past and Future of British Relations in China, 1860*. Cambridge: Cambridge University Press, 2014.

Phipps, Catherine L. *Empires on the Waterfront: Japan's Ports and Power, 1858–1899*. Cambridge, MA: Harvard University Asia Center, 2015.

Rogaski, Ruth. *Hygienic Modernity: Meanings of Health and Disease in Treaty-Port China*. Berkeley: University of California Press, 2004.

Roskum, Cole. *Improvised City: Architecture and Governance in Shanghai, 1843–1937*. Seattle: University of Washington Press, 2019.

So, Billy K.L. and Ramon H. Myers. *The Treaty Port Economy in Modern China: Empirical Studies of Institutional Change and Economic Performance*. Berkeley: University of California, 2011.

Sugiyama, Shinya. *Japan's Industrialization in the World Economy, 1859–1899: Export Trade and Overseas Competition*. London: Athlone Press, 1988.

Tiffen, Mary. *Friends of Sir Robert Hart: Three Generations of Carrall Women in China.* Crewkerne, UK: Tiffania Books in association with Queen's University Belfast, 2012.
Wong, J.Y. *Deadly Dreams: Opium, Imperialism and the Arrow War (1856–1860) in China.* Cambridge: Cambridge University Press, 1998.

*

Chapter 1

Primary Sources held by The National Archives, United Kingdom

FO 17 (Foreign Office: Political and Other Departments: General Correspondence before 1906, China): FO 17/85, 87, 88, 89, 420, 432, 448, 450, 451, 452, 474, 475, 476, 477, 546, 547, 548, 571, 572, 578, 579, 581.

FO 46 (Foreign Office: Political and Other Departments: General Correspondence before 1906, Japan): FO 46/2, 3, 42, 47, 52.

FO 228 (Foreign Office: Consulates and Legation, China: General Correspondence, Series I): FO 228/50, 52, 64, 76, 77, 91, 131, 146, 176.

FO 391 (Letters to Lord Hammond): FO 391/1.

FO 682 (Foreign Office: Chinese Secretary's Office, Various Embassies and Consulates, China: General Correspondence): FO 682/1977/127.

PRO 30/22/50 (Lord John Russell: Papers: China and Japan, China: legation at Peking, Japan: legation at Tokyo [Yedo] and Yokohama, China and Japan - miscellaneous Private correspondence).

Other Published Primary Sources

China. No. 1 (1870). *Despatch from Sir Rutherford Alcock Respecting a Supplementary Convention to the Treaty of Tien-tsin, Signed by Him on the 23rd of October 1869.* (Published command paper.) London: Harrison and Sons, 1870.

Parliamentary Papers, Session 1860, Vol. LXIX (Accounts and Papers: State Papers-China; Japan; Syria).

Tokyo Daigaku Shiryō Hensanjo, ed., *Bakumatsu gaikoku kankei monjo* (Collection of Documents on late-Edo Period Foreign Relations), vols. 20, 22. Tokyo: Tokyo Daigaku Shuppan-kai, 1972, 1973.

Contemporary Works

Alcock, Rutherford. *Art and Art Industries in Japan.* London: Virtue and Co., Limited, 1878.
Alcock, Rutherford. *The Capital of the Tycoon: The Three Years' Residence in Japan,* vol. 1. London: Longman Green, Longman, Roberts, & Green, 1863.

Fukuchi Genichirō. *Kaiojidan* (Reflections on the Past). Tokyo: Ozorasha, 1993 (facsimile edition of Tokyo: Min'yusha, 1894 original).

Michie, Alexander. *The Englishman in China during the Victorian Era: As Illustrated in the Career of Sir Rutherford Alcock*, 2 vols. Edinburgh: William Blackwood and Sons, 1900.

Secondary Sources

Banno Masataka. *Kindai Chūgoku gaikō-shi kenkyū* (A Study of the History of Modern Chinese Diplomacy). Tokyo: Iwanami shoten, 1970.

Banno Masataka. *Kindai Chūgoku seiji gaikō-shi* (History of Politics and Diplomacy of Modern China). Tokyo: University of Tokyo Press, 1973.

Brunero, Donna, Stephanie Villalta Puig, eds. *Life in Treaty Port China and Japan*. Basingstoke, Hampshire: Palgrave Macmillan, 2018.

Coates, P.D. *China Consuls: British Consular Officers, 1843–1943*. New York: Oxford University Press, 1988.

Cobbing, Andrew. 'A Victorian Embarrassment: Consular Jurisdiction and the Evils of Extraterritoriality'. *International History Review*, 40, no. 2 (2018): 273–91.

Cortazzi, Hugh, Ian Nish, et al. eds. *British Envoys in Japan, 1859–1972*. Kent: Global Oriental, 2004.

Fox, Grace. *Britain and Japan 1858–1883*. Oxford: Oxford University Press, 1969.

Haga Tōru. *Taikun no shisetsu* (The Tycoon's Mission). Tokyo: Chūōkōronsha, 1968.

Hillier, Andrew. 'Bridging Cultures: The Forging of the China Consular Mind'. *Journal of Imperial and Commonwealth History*, 47, no. 4 (2019): 742–72.

Hoare, J.E., ed. *Culture, Power and Politics in Treaty-Port Japan, 1854–1899: Key Papers, Press and Contemporary Writings*, 2 vols. Folkestone: Renaissance Books, 2018.

Hoare, J.E. *Japan's Treaty Ports and Foreign Settlements: The Uninvited Guests 1858–1899*. Surrey: Japan Library, 1994.

Hsu, Immanuel C.Y. 'Late Ch'ing Foreign Relations, 1866–1905'. In *Cambridge History of China, Volume 2: Late Ch'ing, 1800–1911, Part 2*, edited by John K. Fairbank and Kwang-Ching Liu, 70–141. Cambridge: Cambridge University Press, 1980.

Mitani Hiroshi. *Perii raikō* (The Arrival of Perry). Tokyo: Yoshikawa Kōbunkan, 2003.

Mössalang, Markus, and Torsten Riotte, eds. *The Diplomat's' World: A Cultural History of Diplomacy, 1815–1914*. Oxford: Oxford University Press, 2008.

Pelcovits, Nathan A. *Old China Hands*. New York: King's Crown Press, 1948.

Platt, D.C.M. *The Cinderella Service: British Consuls since 1825*. London: Longman, 1971.

Sano Mayuko. *Bakumatsu gaikō girei no kenkyū: Ōbei gaikōkan tachi no shōgun haietsu* (Diplomatic Ceremonial in the Bakumatsu Period: Western Diplomats' Castle Audiences with the Shogun). Kyoto: Shibunkaku, 2016.

Sano Mayuko. *Orukokku no Edo: Shodai Eikoku koshi ga mita Bakumatsu Nihon* (Alcock's Edo: Japan in the Bakumatsu Period as Seen by the First British Minister). Tokyo: Chūōkōron-shinsha, 2003.
Smith, George et al., *The Dictionary of National Biography: From the Earliest Times to 1900*. London: Oxford University Press, 1917.
Steeds, David and Ian Nish. *China, Japan and 19th-Century Britain*. Dublin: Irish University Press, 1977.
Wei Fei. 'The New Treaty between China and Britain in 1869 and the Sino-British Relations'. Doctoral thesis (abstract), East China Normal University, Shanghai, 2004.
Wright, Mary Clabaugh. *The Last Stand of Chinese Conservatism: The T'ung-chih Restoration, 1862–1874*. Stanford: Stanford University Press, 1957.

*

Chapter 2

Alcock, Sir Rutherford. *The Capital of the Tycoon: A Narrative of a Three Years' Residence in Japan*. London: Longman, Green, Longman, Roberts, and Green, 1863.
Auslin, Michael R. *Negotiating with Imperialism: The Unequal Treaties and the Culture of Japanese Diplomacy*. Cambridge, MA: Harvard University Press, 2004.
Beasley, William G. *Great Britain and the Opening of Japan, 1834–1858*. London: The Japan Library, 1995.
Beasley, William G. *Select Documents on Japanese Foreign Policy, 1853–1868*. London: Oxford University Press, 1955.
Burke-Gaffney, Brian. *Nagasaki: The British Experience, 1854–1945*. Kent: Global Oriental UK, 2009.
Burke-Gaffney, Brian. *The Former Nagasaki British Consulate, 1859–1955*. Nagasaki: Flying Crane Press, 2019.
Burke-Gaffney, Brian. *The Former Alt House: Biography of a Nagasaki Landmark*. Nagasaki: Flying Crane Press, 2020.
Cortazzi, Hugh, Ian Nish, Peter Lowe, James E. Hoare, eds. *British Envoys in Japan, 1859–1972*. Folkestone: Global Oriental, 2004.
Crocker, Antoinette Cheney. *Frank Woodbridge Cheney: Two Years in China and Japan*. Worcester, MA: Priv. Print. by Davis Press, 1970.
Hoare, J.E. 'Britain's Japan Consular Service, 1859–1941'. In *Britain & Japan: Biographical Portraits Vol. II*, edited by Ian Nish, 94–106. Folkestone: The Japan Library, 1997.
Hoare, J.E. *Embassies in the East*. London and New York: Routledge, 1999.
Hodgson, C. Pemberton. *A Residence at Nagasaki and Hakodate in 1859–1860*. London: Richard Bentley, 1861.
Kuwata Masaru. *Kindai ni okeru chūnichi Eikokugaikōkan* (British Diplomats in Japan, 1859–1945). Kobe: Mirume Shobo, 2003.

McKay, Alexander. *Scottish Samurai: Thomas Blake Glover, 1838–1911*. Edinburgh: Canongate Press, 1997.
Nagasaki-shi, ed. *Nagasaki shisei rokujūgonenshi* (A Sixty-Five-Year History of the Nagasaki Municipal Administration). Nagasaki: Nagasaki Shiyakusho Sōmubu Chōsa Tōkeika, 1956.
Paske-Smith, M. *Western Barbarians in Japan and Formosa in Tokugawa* Days, *1603–1868*. Kobe: J.L. Thompson and Co., 1927.
Shigefuji Takeo. *Nagasaki kyoryūchi to gaikokushōnin* (Nagasaki Foreign Settlement and Foreign Merchants). Tokyo: Kazama Shobo, 1967.
Sugiyama Shinya. *Meiji ishin to Igirisu shōnin: Tomasu Gurabā no shōgai* (The Meiji Restoration and a British Merchant: The Life of Thomas B. Glover). Tokyo: Iwanami Shoten, 1993.

*

Chapter 3

Documents:

France:
Ministère des Affaires Etrangères, correspondence politique, Japan, vol. 9, no. 262.
United Kingdom:
FO 46 (Foreign Office General Correspondence, Japan) /34, no. 61; no. 69; no. 83.
FO 46/40, Lugard to Hammond, 9 September 1863.
FO 46/43, no. 11.
FO 46/109, no. 116; no. 131.
Letter from J. Smyth to his father, 13 June 1864 from the J. Smyth collection. Courtesy of the Smyth family on deposit at the Yokohama Kaikō Shiryōkan (Yokohama Archives of History).
A Memoir of F. Davies. In the collection of the National Army Museum.
United States of America Diplomatic despatches, Japan, vol. 4, no. 24.

Periodicals:

Japan Gazette, 30 January 1875.
Japan Herald, 25 October 1862.
Japan Times, 17 November 1865; 9 March 1866; 6 April 1866.
Japan Times' Daily Advertiser, 18 Sept 1865; 9 January 1866; 22 January 1866; 6 March 1866.
Japan Weekly Mail, 6 March 1875; 2 November 1907.
North China Herald, 9 July 1864.
Yokohama Mainichi Shimbun (Yokohama Daily News), 12 June 1872; 19 December 1873.

Other sources

Black, John R. *Young Japan; Yokohama and Yedo*, vol. 1. London: Trubner, 1880.
Brandt, Max von. *Dreiunddreissig Jahre in Ost-Asien. Erinnerungen eines deutschen Diplomaten* (A German Diplomat's Thirty-Three Years in East Asia), vol. 2. Leipzig: Georg Wigand, 1901.
British Parliamentary Papers, China 27. Shannon, Ireland: Irish University Press, 1971.
Carew, Tim. *The Royal Norfolk Regiment*. London: Hamish Hamilton, 1967.
'Caspar Brennwald Diary', 26 November 1866, in the Possession of DKSH. English Translation'. In *Shiryō de tadoru Meiji-ishinki no Yokohama Eifutsu chūtongun* (Collection of Documents Related to the British and French Troops Stationed at Yokohama), edited by Yokohama Kaikō Shiryōkan, 131. Yokohama: Yokohama Kaikō Shiryōkan, 1993.
Davies, Frederick, Oyama Mizuyo, trans. 'Dai 20 rentai gungakutaiin Davies no shuki (The Memoir of F. Davies, a Military Band Member of the 20th Regiment)'. In *Shiryō de tadoru Meiji-ishinki no Yokohama Eifutsu chūtongun* (Collection of Documents Related to the British and French Troops Stationed at Yokohama), edited by Yokohama Kaikō Shiryōkan, 101–2. Yokohama: Yokohama Kaikō Shiryōkan, 1993.
Hakoishi Hiroshi. 'Kaisetsu: Meiji ishin to Fon Buranto' (An Explanation: The Meiji Restoration and Max von Brandt). In *Doitsu to Nihon o musubu mono: Nichidoku shūkō 150nen no rekishi* (Relations between Germany and Japan: 150 Years of Friendship between Germany and Japan), edited by Kokuritsu Rekishi Minzoku Hakubutsukan, 58. Sakura: National Museum of Japanese History, 2015.
Hara Kiyoshi and Nagaoka Atsushi, trans. *Doitsu kōshi no mita Meiji-ishin* (Max von Brandt, Dreiunddreissig Jahre in Ost-Asien [Thirty-three Years in East Asia]). Tokyo: Shin-jinbutsu ōraisha, 1987.
Hirose Shizuko. 'Bakumatsu ni okeru gaikoku guntai Nihon chūryū no tancho' (The Beginning of the Stationing of Foreign Troops in Japan in the Bakumatsu Period). *Ochanomizu-shigaku* (Bulletin of the Department of History, Ochanomizu University), 15 (1972): 8–42, 83.
Hunter, William. *Chronicle & Directory for China, Japan, & the Philippines for the Year 1872*. Hong Kong: 'Daily Press' Office, 1872.
Hora Tomio. *Bakumatsu-ishinki no gaiatsu to teikō* (Foreign Pressure and Japanese Resistance in the Bakumatsu and the Meiji Restoration Periods). Tokyo: Azekura-shobō, 1977.
Ishii Takashi. *Meiji ishin no kokusaiteki kankyō, zotei* (The International Contexts of the Meiji Restoration), enlarged and revised edition. Tokyo: Yoshikawa Kōbunkan, 1966.
Japan Gazette Co. Ltd., *'Japan Gazette' Yokohama semi-centennial*. Yokohama: Japan Gazette Co., 1909.
Kishi Motokazu. 'Ishinki no Yokohama chūton Igirisu guntai tettai mondai; 'Gaiatsu' to chūōshūken katei no tokushitsu' (The Withdrawal of British Troops from Yokohama

in the Meiji Restoration Period: 'Foreign Pressure' and the Process of Centralization of Power and Authority). *Nihon rekishi* (Journal of Japanese History) 377 (1979): 69–87.

Kokaze Hidemasa. 'Eifutsu chūtongun tettai-ki no kokusai kankei: fubyōdō jyōyaku taisei no saihen wo meguru Igirisu to Nihon' (The International Circumstances Surrounding the Withdrawal of British and French Troops: Relations between Britain and Japan During the Revision of the Unequal Treaty System). In *Yokohama Eifutsu chūtongun to gaikokujin kyoryūchi* (The British and French Troops Stationed in Yokohama and the Foreign Settlement), edited by Yokohama Kaikō Shiryōkan, 309–35. Tokyo: Tokyo-dō shuppan, 1999.

'Letter from N. P. Kingdon to His Mother, 12 May 1863' (transcript). In *Shiryō de tadoru Meiji-ishinki no Yokohama Eifutsu chūtongun* (Collection of Documents Related to the British and French Troops Stationed at Yokohama), edited by Yokohama Kaikō Shiryōkan,126–7. Yokohama: Yokohama Kaikō Shiryōkan, 1993.

McCabe, Patricia. *Gaijin Bochi, the Foreigners' Cemetery Yokohama, Japan*. London: Bacsa, 1994.

Morita Chūkichi, ed. *Yokohama seikō meiyo kagami* (A Directory of Successful Individuals in Yokohama). Yokohama: Yokohama shōkyō shimpō-sha, 1910

Nakatake (Hori) Kanami. 'Bakumatsu no Yokohama Igirisu chūtongun shikan no shokan: Dai 20 rentai dai 2 daitai Sumisu chūi no shokan, 1–3' (The Letters of J. Smyth, Lieutenant of the 2nd Battalion, 20th Regiment from 1863 to 1866), *Yokohama Kaikō Shiryōkan kiyō* (Yokohama Archives of History Review) 34, 36, 37 (2016, 2019, 2021).

Nakatake (Hori) Kanami. 'Moto Igirisu chūtongun heishi, Vincent-ke no haka' (The Family Tomb of Vincent, a British Soldier Stationed in Yokohama), *Kaikō no hiroba* (Brochure of the Yokohama Archives of History), 115 (February 2012): 6–7.

Nakatake (Hori) Kanami. 'Bakumatsu-ishinki no Yokohama Eifutsu chūtongun no jittai to sono eikyō: Igirisu gun wo chūsin ni' (The Conditions Surrounding the Stationing of British and French Troops in Yokohama and Their Influence – A Focus on the British Troops), *Yokohama Kaikō Shiryōkan kiyō* (Yokohama Archives of History Review) 12 (1994): 1–32.

Satow, Ernest. *A Diplomat in Japan*. Philadelphia: J. B. Lippincott, 1921.

Sims, Richard. *French Policy towards the Bakufu and Meiji Japan, 1854–95*. Richmond, Surrey: Japan Library, 1998.

Sutherland, Jonathan and Diane Canwell. *The Holy Boys: A History of the Royal Norfolk Regiment and the Royal East Anglian Regiment, 1685–2010*. Barnsley, South Yorkshire: Pen & Sword Military, 2010.

Suzuki Jun. 'Ran-shiki, Ei-shiki, Futsu-shiki: Shohan no 'heisei' dōnyū (The Introduction of Dutch-style, British-style and French-style 'Military Systems' in Various Domains)'. In *Yokohama Eifutsu chūtongun to gaikokujin kyoryūchi* (The British and French Troops Stationed in Yokohama and the Foreign Settlement), edited by Yokohama Kaikō Shiryōkan, 213–46. Tokyo: Tokyo-dō shuppan, 1999.

Yokohama Bōeki Shimpō-sha. *Yokohama kaikō sokumen shi* (Another Aspect on the History of the Opening of the Port of Yokohama). Yokohama: Yokohama Bōeki Shimpō-sha, 1909.

Yokohama Kaikō Shiryōkan, ed. *Shiryō de tadoru Meiji-ishinki no Yokohama Eifutsu chūtongun* (Collection of Documents Related to the British and French Troops Stationed at Yokohama). Yokohama: Yokohama Kaikō Shiryōkan, 1993.

Yokohama Kaikō Shiryōkan, ed. *Yokohama Eifutsu chūtongun to gaikokujin kyoryūchi* (The British and French Troops Stationed in Yokohama and the Foreign Settlement). Tokyo: Tokyo-dō shuppan, 1999.

Yokohama-shi, ed. *Yokohama shishi* (The History of Yokohama City), vol. 2 and vol. 3-2. Yokohama: Yokohama-shi, 1959, 1963.

*

Chapter 4

Asakawa Michio. 'Boshin sensō ki ni okeru rikugun no gunbi to senpō (Armaments and Tactics of Armies during the *Boshin* War)'. In *Boshin sensō no shin shiten* (New Perspectives on the Boshin War), edited by Nagura Tetsuzō, Hōya Tōru and Hakoishi Hiroshi, vol. 2, 2–26. Tokyo: Yoshikawa Kōbunkan, 2018.

Auslin, Michael. *Negotiating with Imperialism: The Unequal Treaties and the Culture of Japanese Diplomacy*. Cambridge, MA: Harvard University Press, 2006.

Bodmer, Walter. *Die Entwicklung der schweizerischen Textilwirtschaft im Rahmen der übrigen Industrien und Wirtschaftszweige* (The Development of the Swiss Textile Industry in the Context of Other Industries and Parts of the Economy). Zürich: Berichthaus, 1960.

Brennwald, Kaspar. *Bericht über den Seiden-Export von Japan* (Report on Silk Exports of Japan). Bern: Schweizerisches Handels- und Zolldepartement, 1863.

Brennwald, Kaspar. *Bericht über den Thee-Exporthandel Japans und den Exporthandel Japans im Allgemeinen* (Report on Tea Exports of Japan and the Export Trades of Japan in General). Bern: Schweizerisches Handels- und Zolldepartement, 1863.

Brennwald, Kaspar. *Notizen über die Seidenzucht in Japan* (Notes on Silk Rearing in Japan). Bern: Schweizerisches Handels- und Zolldepartement, 1864.

Brennwald, Kaspar. *Generalbericht betreffend den kommerziellen Theil der schweizerischen Abordnung nach Japan* (General Report Relating to the Commercial Section of the Swiss Delegation to Japan). Bern: J.A. Weingart, 1865.

Bartu, Friedemann. *The Fan Tree Company: Three Swiss Merchants in Asia*. Zürich: Diethelm Keller Holding Ltd., 2005.

Dai Nippon Sanshi kaichō Danshaku Matsudaira Masanao yori Tokubetsu Kai'in Siber Wolff Shōkai ate Shōjō (Certificate of Commendation from the Director of the Dainippon Silk Foundation, Baron Matsudaira Masanao, to Siber, Wolff & Co.), dated on 29 May 1903 (in possession of DKSH Holding Ltd.).

Dejung, Christof. *Die Fäden des globalen Marktes. Eine Sozial- und Kulturgeschichte des Welthandels am Beispiel der Handelsfirma Gebrüder Volkart 1851–1999* (The Threads of the Global Market. A Social and Cultural History of Global Trade Based on the Example of the Trading House: Volkart Brothers). Köln: Böhlau, 2013.

Federico, Giovanni. *An Economic History of the Silk Industry, 1830–1930*. Cambridge: Cambridge University Press, 1997.

Fukuoka Mariko. 'Boshin sensō ni kanyo shita Shuneru kyōdai no "kokuseki" mondai' (The Issue of the 'Nationality' of the Schnell Brothers, Participants in the Boshin War). In *Boshin sensō no shiryōgaku* (Historiography of the Boshin War), edited by Hakoishi Hiroshi, 107–40. Tokyo: Bensei Shuppan, 2013.

Gaimushō and Tsūshin Zenran Henshū Iinkai, ed. *Zoku tsūshin zenran* (General Records of Communications, Complete Series). Tokyo: Yūshōdō Shuppan, 1983–88.

Haller, Lea. *Transithandel. Die Rolle des Kleinstaats im globalen Kapitalismus* (Transit Trade: The Role of the Small State in Global Capitalism). Berlin: Suhrkamp, 2019.

Hayakawa Yōko. 'Boshin sensō ki no Ni'igata kō no kinō ni kansuru ichi kōsatsu' (An Examination on the Function of the Port of Niigata during the Boshin War). *Kokushi danwakai zasshi* (Journal of the Association of Narratives on the National History), 20 (1979): 13–25.

Hayami Michiko ed., *Hayami Kensō shiryōshū: Tomioka seishi shochō to sono zengo ki* (A Collection of Sources of Hayami Kensō: Director of the Tomioka Silk Mill and Records Relating to His Life). Tokyo: Bunsei Shoin, 2014.

Honegger, Silvio. *Gli Svizzeri di Bergamo. Storia della comunità svizzera di Bergamo dal Cinquecento all'inizio del Novecento* (The Swiss of Bergamo. History of the Swiss Community in Bergamo from the 16th to the 19th century). Bergamo: Edizioni Junior, 1997.

Hōya Tōru. 'Kokusaihō no naka no boshin sensō' (The Boshin War Viewed through International Law). In *Boshin sensō no shin shiten* (New Perspectives on the Boshin War), edited by Nagura Tetsuzō, Hōya Tōru and Hakoishi Hiroshi, vol. 1, 2–24. Tokyo: Yoshikawa Kōbunkan, 2018.

Ishii Kanji. *Kindai Nihon to Igirisu shihon: Jardine Matheson shōkai o chūshin ni* (Modern Japan and British Capital: The Case of Jardine Matheson and Company). Tokyo: Tokyo Daigaku Shuppan-kai, 1984.

Ishii Kanji. *Nihon sanshi gyō bunseki* (An Analysis of Japanese Silk Industry). Tokyo: Tokyo Daigaku Shuppan-kai, 1972.

Itsukakai, ed., *Okina no jikiwa: Furukawa Ichibé no keireki dan* (An Old Man's Personal Account: A Narrative of Furukawa Ichibé's Life). Tokyo: Itsukakai, 1926.

Jost, Albert. *Charles Rudolph & Co. 50 Jahre Rohseidenimport* (Charles Rudolph & Co. 50 years of Importing Raw Silk). Zürich: Desco Handels AG, 1939.

Miyamoto Mataji. *Ono-gumi no kenkyū* (A Study of the Ono-gumi). Tokyo: Ōhara Shinseisha, 1970.

Miyamoto Mataji. *Ono-gumi no ki'ito bōeki to seishi gyō: ishin no gōshō Ono Zensuke ke no gyōseki* (Silk Trade and Silk Reeling of the Ono-gumi: Achievements of the Meiji

Restoration Period's Great Trading House of Ono Zensuke). Ōsaka: Ōsaka Daigaku Shuppan-kai, 1966.

Maebashi Shōkō Kaigi-sho (Commercial Chamber of Maebashi), ed. *Ito no machi Maebashi o kizuita hitobito* (The People who Founded the Silk Producing City of Maebashi). Maebashi: Jōmō Shinbunsha, 2018.

Makimura, Yasuhiro. *Yokohama and the Silk Trade: How Eastern Japan Became the Primary Economic Region of Japan, 1843–1893*. Lanham: Lexington Books, 2017.

McMaster, John. *Jardines in Japan, 1859–1867*. Groningen: V.R.B. Offsetdrukkerij, 1966.

Mitani, Hiroshi. 'Meiji Revolution'. In *The Oxford Research Encyclopaedia of Asian History*, http://asianhistory.oxfordre.com/view/10.1093/acrefore/9780190277727.001.0001/acrefore-9780190277727-e-84 (accessed 26 June 2018).

Nagano Yasuhiko. 'Hajimete kikaiseishi o tsutaeta Suisu jin Myurā' (A Swiss Man Müller, Who Introduced Machine Silk Reeling), *Sangyō kōko gaku kenkyū* (Study of Industrial Archaeology), 1 (2014): 32–8.

Nakai Akio. *Shoki Nihon Suisu kankeishi: Suisu Renpō Monjokan no Bakumatsu Nihon bōeki shiryō* (The History of Early Swiss-Japanese Relations: Sources on Japanese Trade of the Bakumatsu Period Held in the Swiss Federal Archives). Tokyo: Kazama Shobō, 1971.

Nakai, Paul Akio. *Das Verhältnis zwischen Japan und der Schweiz. Vom Beginn der diplomatischen Beziehungen 1859 bis 1868* (The Relationship between Japan and Switzerland: From the Beginning of Diplomatic Relations in 1859 until 1868). Bern: Haupt, 1967.

Nishikawa Takeomi. *Bakumatsu Meiji no kokusai shijō to Nihon: ki'ito bōeki to Yokohama* (International Markets and Japan in Bakumatsu and Meiji Japan: The Raw Silk Trade and Yokohama). Tokyo: Yūzankaku, 1997.

Ōkurashō (The Finance Ministry of Japan), ed. *Meiji zenki zaisei keizai shiryō shūsei* (Collection of Records Relating to Finance and the Economy of the Early Meiji Period), 1931–1936, vol. 9, 'Kyūhan gaikoku hosai shobunroku' (Liabilities of Former Domains to Foreign Creditors). Tokyo: Meiji Bunken Shiryō Kankō kai, 1963.

Ono Zentarō. *Ishin no gōshō: Ono-gumi shimatsu* (The Fate of the Ono-gumi: A Large Trading House of the Meiji Restoration Period), annotated by Miyamoto Matajirō. Tokyo: Seia Shobō, 1966.

Partner, Simon. *The Merchant's Tale: Yokohama and the Transformation of Japan*. New York: Columbia University Press, 2017.

Poni, Carlo. *La seta in Italia. Una grande industria prima della rivoluzione industriale* (Silk in Italy: A Great Industry before the Industrial Revolution). Bologna: il Mulino, 2009.

Report by Mr. Adams (Francis O. Adams), Secretary to Her Majesty's legation in Japan, on the Central Silk Districts of Japan; Further Report from Mr. Adams, On Silk Culture in Japan; Third Report by Mr. Adams on Silk Culture in Japan, dated August 10 1870.

Presented to both Houses of Parliament by command of Her Majesty. London: Printed by Harrison and Sons, 1870–1.
Saitō Takio. 'Gaishō gawa kara mita Meiji zenki no Yokohama bōeki' (Trade in Yokohama Seen from the View of Western Firms). *Yokohama Kaikō Shiryōkan kiyō* (Yokohama Archives of History Review) 6 (1988): 115–34.
Savio, Pietro. *La prima spedizione italiana: nell'interno del Giappone e nei centri sericoli* (The First Italian Expedition: In the Interior of Japan and in the Sericultural Centers). Milano: E. Treves Editore, 1870.
SiberHegner und Co., ed. *Hundert Jahre im Dienste des Handels, 1865–1965* (Hundred Years in the Service of Trade). Zürich: SiberHegner Holding, 1965.
Sugiyama, Shinya. *Japan's Industrialization in the World Economy, 1859–1899: Export Trade and Overseas Competition*. London: Athlone Press, 1988.
Suzuki Yoshiyuki. *Kaiko ni miru Meiji ishin* (The Meiji Restoration Seen through Cocoons). Tokyo: Yoshikawa Kōbunkan, 2011.
Wolle, Jürg. *Expedition in fernöstliche Märkte. Die Erfolgsstory des Schweizer Handelspioniers DKSH* (Expeditions in Far Eastern Markets: The Success Story of the Swiss Trading Pioneer, DKSH). Zürich: Orell Füssli, 2009.
Yatabe Atsuhiko. *Haiboku no gaikōkan Rosshu: Isulāmu sekai to Bakumatsu Edo o meguru yume* (The Defeated Diplomat Roches: His Dream Surrounding the Islamic World and Edo in the Bakumatsu Period). Tokyo: Hakusuisha, 2014.
Yokohama Kaikō Shiryōkan (Yokohama Archives of History), ed. *Brenwaldo no Bakumatsu Meiji Nippon nikki* (Brennwald's Diary of Japan During the Bakumatsu and Meiji Periods). Tokyo: Nikkei-BP, 2015.
Yokohama-shi, ed. *Yokohama shishi* (History of Yokohama City), vol. 2: 'Kaikō ki no Yokohama' (Yokohama in the Period of the Port's Opening). Yokohama: Yokohama City, 1959.
Yokohama-shi, ed. *Yokohama shishi* (History of Yokohama City), vol. 3-I, 'Meiji zenki no Yokohama' (Yokohama in the Early Meiji Period). Yokohama: Yokohama-shi, 1961.
Yokohama-shi Furusato Rekishi Zaidan (Historical Foundation of the City of Yokohama), ed. *Yokohama: rekishi to bunka* (Yokohama: Its History and Culture: Memorial Edition on the 150-Year Anniversary of the Port's Opening). Yokohama: Yūrindō, 2009.
Yokohama-shi Furusato Rekishi Zaidan (Historical Foundation of Yokohama City) and Burenwaldo Nikki kenkyū kai (Study Group of the Brennwald's Diary), eds. *Suisu shisetsu dan ga mita Bakumatsu no Nihon: Brenwaldo nikki 1862–1867* (Japan of the Bakumatsu Period: Seen by the Swiss Mission Brennwald's Diary 1862–1867). Tokyo: Bensei Shuppan, 2020.
Zangger, Andreas. *Koloniale Schweiz. Ein Stück Globalgeschichte zwischen Europa und Südostasien (1860–1930)* (Colonial Switzerland. A Piece of Global History between Europe and Southeast Asia). Berlin: Transcript, 2014.
Zangger, Andreas. 'Schweizer Seidenhändler in Japan' (Swiss Silk Merchants in Japan). In *Kirschblüte & Edelweiss. Der Import des Exotischen* (Cherry Blossom & Edelweiss: Importing the Exotic), edited by Michaela Reichel, Hans Bjarne Thomsen, 129–44. Baden: Hier + Jetzt, 2014.

Zürcher, Walter. *Schweizer Flagge zur See. Die Geschichte der schweizerischen Hochseeschiffahrt* (The Swiss Flag at Sea: The History of Swiss High Sea Shipping). Bern: Benteli, 1986.

*

Chapter 5

Published Primary Sources:

Books

Eitel, Ernst Johann. *Europe in China: The History of Hongkong from the Beginning to the Year 1882*. Hong Kong: Oxford University Press, 1983 [1895].
Eitel, Ernst Johann. *Feng-shui or the Rudiments of Natural Science in China*. London: Trubner, 1873.
Fortune, Robert. *Three Years' Wanderings in the Northern Provinces of China*. London: J. Murray, 1847.
Knollys, Henry. *English Life in China*. London: Smith, Elder & CO, 1885.
Laurie, P.G. *A Reminiscence of Canton*. London: Harrison and Sons, 1866.
Mercer, William T. *Under the Peak or Jottings in Verse*. London: J.C. Hotten, 1868.
Ticozzi, Sergio. *Historical Documents of the Hong Kong Catholic Church*. Hong Kong: Hong Kong Catholic Diocesan Archives, 1997.

Government Publications

Administrative Reports: 1880.
The Hongkong Almanack and Directory: 1846, 1848, 1850.
Hong Kong Daily Press: 1923.
The Hongkong Directory with List of Foreign Residents in China. Hong Kong: Armenian Press, 1859.
Hong Kong Government Gazette: 1854, 1867, 1881, 1897, 1909.
The Hong Kong Weekly Press: 1909.
Newspapers

Archival Sources:

CO 129/29, pp. 2–8. Correspondence with the military authorities who object to payment of the fees charged for burial, 11 April 1849.
Colonial Office Original Correspondence: Hong Kong, Series 129 (CO 129):
Hong Kong Public Record Office, Hong Kong.

HKRS58-1-14-44.
HKRS58-1-17-72.
University of Hong Kong Libraries Special Collections, Hong Kong.

Secondary Sources:

Books and book chapters

Ariès, Philippe. *The Hour of Our Death*, translated by Helen Weaver. New York: Knopf, 1980.

Arnold, David. *The Tropics and The Travelling Gaze: India, Landscape, and Science, 1800–1856*. Seattle: University of Washington Press, 2006.

Bard, Solomon. *Garrison Memorials in Hong Kong*. Hong Kong: Antiquities and Monuments Office: Occasional Paper No. 4, 1997.

Curl, James Stevens. *The Victorian Celebration of Death*. Stroud: Sutton, 2000.

Ding, Xinbao and Shuying Lu. *Fei wo zu yi: zhan qian Xianggang de wai ji zu qun* (Foreign Ethnic Communities in Pre-war Hong Kong). Hong Kong: Joint Publishing, 2014.

Fletcher, Robert S.G. *The Ghost of Namamugi: Charles Lenox Richardson and the Anglo-Satsuma War*. Folkestone: Renaissance Books, 2019.

Grace, Richard J. *Opium and Empire: The Lives and Careers of William Jardine and James Matheson*. Montreal: McGill-Queen's University Press, 2014.

Holdsworth, May and Christopher Munn, eds. *Dictionary of Hong Kong Biography*. Hong Kong: Hong Kong University Press, 2012.

Jallard, Pat. 'Victorian Death and Its Decline: 1850–1918'. In *Death in England*, edited by Peter C. Jupp and Clare Gittings, 230–55. Manchester: Manchester University Press, 1999.

Kwong, Chi Man. *Eastern Fortress: A Military History of Hong Kong, 1840–1997*. Hong Kong: Hong Kong University Press, 2014.

Laqueur, Thomas. *The Work of the Dead: A Cultural History of Mortal Remains*. Princeton: Princeton University Press, 2015.

Le Pichon, Alain, ed. *China Trade and Empire: Jardine, Matheson & Co. and the Origins of British Rule in Hong Kong, 1827–1843*. Oxford: Oxford University Press, 2006.

Lim, Patricia. *Forgotten Souls: A Social History of the Hong Kong Cemetery*. Hong Kong: Hong Kong University Press, 2011.

Litten, Julian. *The English Way of Death: Common Funeral since 1450*. London: Robert Hale, 1991.

Munn, Christopher. *Anglo-China: Chinese People and British Rule in Hong Kong, 1841–1880*. Hong Kong: Hong Kong University Press, 2009.

Sayer, Geoffrey Robley. *Hong Kong 1841–1862: Birth, Adolescence and Coming of Age*. Hong Kong: Hong Kong University Press, [1937] 1980.

Sinn, Elizabeth. *Pacific Crossing: California Gold, Chinese Migration, and the Making of Hong Kong*. Hong Kong: Hong Kong University Press, 2015.
Sinn, Elizabeth. *Power and Charity: A Chinese Merchant Elite in Colonial Hong Kong*. Hong Kong: Hong Kong University Press, 2003.
Smith, Carl T. *A Sense of History: Studies in the Social and Urban History of Hong Kong*. Hong Kong: Hong Kong Educational Publishing, 1995.
Strange, Julie-Marie. *Death, Grief and Poverty in Britain, 1870–1914*. Cambridge: Cambridge University Press, 2005.
Stone, Lawrence. *The Past and the Present*. Boston: Routledge, 1981.
Stone, Lawrence. *The Family, Sex and Marriage in England, 1500–1800*. London: Weidenfeld & Nicolson, 1977.
Tsang, Steve. *A Modern History of Hong Kong*. Hong Kong: Hong Kong University Press, 2004.
Yeoh, Brenda. *Contesting Space in Colonial Singapore*. Singapore: Singapore University Press, 2003.

Journal articles

Cowell, Christopher. 'The Hong Kong Fever of 1843: Collective Trauma and the Reconfiguring of Colonial Space'. *Modern Asian Studies*, 47, no. 2 (2013): 329–64.
Ko, Tim-Keung. 'A Review of Development of Cemeteries in Hong Kong: 1841–1950'. *Journal of the Royal Asiatic Society Hong Kong Branch*, 41 (2001): 241–80.
Tarlow, Sarah. 'Landscapes of Memory: The Nineteenth-Century Garden Cemetery'. *European Journal of Archaeology*, 3, no. 2 (2000): 217–39.

Online

'Parsee Cemetery' [in Chinese]. Minority History in Hong Kong. Lord Wilson Heritage Trust. Available online: http://www.rtedu.hk/minorityhistory/html/parsee_3.html#1

Theses

Huang, Daozi. 'You May Go to Hong Kong for Me: British Views of a Chinese Colony'. PhD dissertation, University of Hong Kong, Hong Kong, 2018.
Tam, Bobby. 'Death in Hong Kong: Managing the Dead in a Colonial City from 1841 to 1913'. MPhil dissertation, University of Hong Kong, Hong Kong, 2018.
Wong, Sek Leng. 'Life and Death: Reconstructing Macau's Society in the 19th Century through Historic Cemetery Walks'. MS dissertation, University of Hong Kong, Hong Kong, 2011.

Chapter 6

Allen, W.H., ed. *Allen's Indian Mail and Register of Intelligence for British and Foreign India, China and All Parts of the East*, vol 3. Jan–Dec 1845. London: Wm. H. Allen and Co, 1845.

Alt, William John. *Personal Correspondence, 1853–1865*: Digital versions held by Sainsbury Institute for the Study of Japanese Arts and Cultures. Norwich, United Kingdom.

Andersen, J.C. *Old Christchurch*. Christchurch: Simpson and Williams Ltd., 1949.

Amodeo, C. and Canterbury Pilgrims and Early Settlers Association. *The Summer Ships: Being an Account of the First Six Ships Sent Out from England by the Canterbury Association in 1850–1851*. Christchurch: Caxton Press, 2001.

Amodeo, C. *Forgotten Forty-Niners*. Christchurch: Caxton Press, 2003.

Atkinson, N. *Trainland: How the Railways Made New Zealand*. Auckland: Random House, 2007.

Berncastle, J. *A Voyage to China*. London: W. Shoberl, 1850.

Brett, H. *White Wings, Volume Two: The Founding of the Provinces*. Auckland: The Brett Printing Co. Ltd., Publishers, 1928.

Burke-Gaffney, Brian. 'The Alt House: Yesterday, Today and Tomorrow'. *Crossroads: A Journal of Nagasaki History and Culture*, 6 (Autumn 1998): online http://www.uwosh.edu/home_pages/faculty_staff/earns/althouse.html

Burton, C.C. *Dr Barker, 1819–1873: Photographer, Farmer, Physician*. Dunedin: John McIndoe, 1972.

Churchman, G. and T. Hurst. *The Railways of New Zealand: A Journey through History*. Wellington: Transpress New Zealand, 2001.

Cookson, J. 'Pilgrims' Progress – Image, Identity and Myth in Christchurch'. In *Southern Capital, Christchurch: Towards a City Biography*, edited by John Cookson and Graeme Dunstall, 13–40. Christchurch: Canterbury University Press, 2000.

Deans, J. *Letters to My Grandchildren*. Christchurch: Cadsonbury Publications, 1995.

Godley, C. *Letters from Early New Zealand*. Christchurch: Whitcombe and Tombs Ltd., 1951.

Hellyer, R. 'Mid-Nineteenth Century Nagasaki: Western and Japanese Merchant Communities within Political and Commercial Transitions'. In *Merchant Communities in Asia, 1600–1980*, edited by Lin Yu-ju and Madeleine Zelin, 159–76. London: Pickering and Chatto Ltd., 2015.

Jaffer, A. '"Lord of the Forecastle": Serangs, Tindals, and Lascar Mutiny, c.1780–1860'. *International Review of Social History*, 58, no. S21 (December 2013): 153–75.

Knight, C., ed. *The Land We Live In: A Pictorial and Literary Sketchbook of the British Empire*. vol 3. London: Charles Knight, n.d.

Mui, H.-C. and L.H. Mui, eds. *William Melrose in China, 1854–1855*. Edinburgh: Scottish History Society, 1973.
Ogilvie, G. *Pioneers of the Plains: The Deans of Canterbury*. Christchurch: Shoal Bay Press, 1996.
Pickles, K. *Christchurch Ruptures*. Wellington: Bridget Williams Books, 2016.
Pollack, Mrs. *Log of the Voyage of the Charlotte Jane from Gravesend to Holdfast Bay, 19 September 1851–14 January 1852* (transcription, State Library of South Australia, Gov't of South Australia, D6419 [L]), entry for 18 December 1851.
Thomas, P.A. 'Large Letter'd as with Thundering Shout: An Analysis of Typographic Posters Advertising Emigration to New Zealand, 1839–1875'. PhD dissertation, Massey University, New Zealand, 2014.
Waddell, R.E. *Biographies, the Little Connection*. Available online: http://www.ornaverum.org/reference/pdf/009.pdf (accessed 7 June 2017).
Ward, E. *The Journal of Edward Ward*. Christchurch: Pegasus Press, 1951.
Whitehouse, O. 'Deserters from the First Four Ships to Lyttelton in 1851'. Available online: http://freepages.genealogy.rootsweb.ancestry.com/~nzbound/desert.htm (accessed 7 June 2017).
Wigram, H. *The Story of Christchurch, New Zealand*. Christchurch: The Lyttelton Times Co. Ltd., 1916.

*

Chapter 7

Allen, Jim. *Port Essington: The Historical Archaeology of a North Australian Nineteenth-Century Military Outpost*. Sydney: Sydney University Press, 2008.
Boulger, Demetrius Charles. *The Life of Sir Stamford Raffles*. London: H. Marshall, 1897.
Cameron, James. 'The Northern Settlements: Outposts of Empire'. In *The Origins of Australia's Capital Cities*, edited by Pamela Stratham, 271–91. Cambridge: Cambridge University Press, 1989.
Cameron, J.M.R, comp. and ed. *Letters from Port Essington, 1838–1845*. Darwin: Historical Society of the Northern Territory, 1999.
Cameron, John. *Our Tropical Possessions in Malayan India: Being a Descriptive Account of Singapore, Penang, Province Wellesley and Malacca, Their Peoples, Products, Commerce and Government*. London: Smith, Elder, 1865.
Crawfurd, John A. *History of the Indian Archipelago, Containing an Account of the Manners, Arts, Languages, Religions, Institutions, and Commerce of Its Inhabitants*. Edinburgh: Constable and Company, 1820.
Earl, George Windsor. 'On the Shell-Mounds of Province Wellesley, in the Malay Peninsula'. *Transactions of the Ethnological Society of London* 11 (1863): 119–29.
Earl, George Windsor. 'Handbook for Colonists in Tropical Australia'. *Journal of the Indian Archipelago and Eastern Asia*, 4, no. 1 (1863): 1–187.

Earl, George Windsor. *Topography and Itinerary of Province Wellesley*. George Town [Penang]: Pinang Gazette Press, 1861.

Earl, George Windsor. *The Native Races of the Indian Archipelago; the Papuans*. London: H. Bailliere, 1853.

Earl, George Windsor. *A Correspondence Relating to the Discovery of Gold in Australia*. London: Pelham Richardson, 1853.

Earl, George Windsor. 'On the Leading Characteristics of the Papuan, Australian, and Malayu-Polynesian Nations', Chapter II, *Journal of the Indian Archipelago and Eastern Asia*, 4 (January 1850): 1–10, 66–74, 172–81.

Earl, George Windsor. *Enterprise in Tropical Australia*. London: Madden and Malcolm, 1846.

Earl, George Windsor. 'The Physical Structure and Arrangements of the Islands in the Indian Archipelago'. *The Journal of the Royal Geographical Society*, 15 (1845): 358–65.

Earl, George Windsor. *The Eastern Seas, or Voyages and Adventures in the Indian Archipelago, in 1832-33-34… Also an Account of the Present State of Singapore…* London: W.H. Allen, 1837.

Earl, George Windsor. *Observations on the Commercial and Agricultural Capabilities of the North Coast of New Holland and the Advantages to Be Derived from the Establishment of a Settlement in the Vicinity of Raffles Bay*. London: E. Wilson, 1836.

Gibson-Hill, C.A. 'George Samuel Windsor Earl'. *Journal of the Malayan Branch of the Royal Asiatic Society*, 32, no. 1 (185) (May 1959): 105–53.

Jones, Russell. 'George Windsor Earl and "Indonesia"'. *Indonesia Circle: School of Oriental & African Studies Newsletter*, 22, no. 64 (1994): 279–90.

Jones, Russell and Indonesia Circle (University of London: School of Oriental and African Studies). *Out of the Shadows: George Windsor Earl in Western Australia; George Windsor Earl and Indonesia*. London: Indonesia Circle, School of Oriental and African Studies, 1975.

Keppel, Henry. *A Visit to the Indian Archipelago*, in H.M. Ship Maeander: With Portions of the Private Journal of Sir James Brooke, *K.C.B.* London: Richard Bentley, 1853.

Noel-Paton, Ranald. *An Eastern Calling: George Windsor Earl and a Vision of Empire*. London: Ashgrove Publishing, 2018.

Reece, R.H.W. 'Earl, George Samuel Windsor (1813–1865)'. *Oxford Dictionary of National Biography*, e-version, 2004, https://doi.org/10.1093/ref:odnb/59850

Reece, R.H.W. 'The Australasian Career of George Windsor Earl'. *Journal of the Malaysian Branch of the Royal Asiatic Society*, 65, no. 2 (263) (1992): 39–67.

Index

Adams, Francis O. 79, 98, 188 n.118
Africa 18
Alcock, Rutherford (1809–97) 4, 15, 21–3,
    34–41, 45, 47, 49, 51, 57, 59,
    61–2, 89, 146, 170 n.3, 171 n.13
  Alcock Convention 30–4, 38–9, 173
    n.53
  Art and Art Industries in Japan 174 n.73
  The Capital of the Tycoon: A Narrative
    of a Three Years' Residence in
    Japan 176 n.36
  in China (Beijing) 28, 30–8
  'First Lessons in Japanese Diplomacy'
    27–30
  to Hammond 29–30, 36
  and Harris 27
  in Japan 22–7, 29, 31
  in medical field 170 n.4
  and merchants 12, 28–9, 33–4, 37,
    39–40
  and Morrison 54–7, 176 n.33
  to Russell 31
Allen, Jim 152
Alligator, HMS, warship 153
Alonso, José Luis 190 n.154
Alt, Balser 8–9, 13
Alt & Co. 137, 175 n.24
Alt, Elisabeth (Annie) 18, 160, 169 n.41,
    202 n.20
Alt, Harry 8
Alt, William John (1840–1908) 2–5, 52,
    56, 58, 92, 146, 164, 167–8 n.15,
    168 n.26, 199 n.71
  and Annie (*see* Alt, Elisabeth (Annie))
  business activities in Nagasaki
    169 n.38
  and *Charlotte Jane* (ship) 136–9
  house in Nagasaki 175 n.24
  letters of (*see* letters/letter writing)
  in nineteenth-century China and Japan
    6–19
  tea export business 168 n.32

Anglican/Anglicanism 108, 126–7,
    129–30, 139–40
Anglin, J. R. 69
Anglo-Chinese treaty 24, 39, 41
Anglo-French troops 16, 80
Anglo-Japanese Treaty of Amity and
    Commerce (1858) 24–5, 41, 44
Anglo-Satsuma War. *See Satsuei-sensō*
Annesley, Adolphus A. 47
Ansei Five-Power Treaties 44
antagonism 28, 37, 39
anti-foreign samurai 29
Aries, Philippe, 'death of the other' 114–15
Arnold, David 111
Arnold, Robert 56
Asia 5, 18, 32, 38, 83, 87, 121, 145, 151,
    158, 162. *See also* East Asia;
    Southeast Asia
Aspinall, Cornes and Co. 11
Aspinall, William Gregson 11
Australasia 5, 18, 136, 145–6, 153
Australia 17–18, 46, 128, 143, 145–6,
    149–50, 162, 165
  Adelaide 9, 130, 135–8, 164
  Barkers Bay 152
  Cobourg Peninsula 151, 155, 157
  Gulf of Carpentaria 150–1
  New South Wales 128, 150, 156–7, 161
    discovery of gold 158, 160
  Perth 147
  Port Essington 151–56
    hurricane at 201 n.11
  Port Jackson 131, 135
  Raffles Bay 151–2, 155
  Sydney 130, 135, 153–8, 161
  Tasmania 128
  Torres Straits 151, 153, 155
  Victoria 154–5, 160–1

bakumatsu period 11, 76, 80
Barker, Alfred 134–5
Barnes, William 150–1

Barrow, John 151–2
Basler Handelsgesellschaft (André & Cie) 181 n.7
Battle of Canton (1857) 7
Beagle, HMS (ship) 153
Beasley, W.G., *Select Documents on Japanese Foreign Policy, 1853–1868* 166 n.2
Beato, Felice 23
Benson, E. S. 179 n.36
Berdan Pan (ore-crushing machine) 160–1
Berncastle, Julius 132–3
  A Voyage to China 131
Bickers, Robert 5
Blomhoff, Jan Cock 46
The Bluff Settlement 64, 77, 140
Boshin War (1868–9) 70, 75, 92, 94–6, 187 n.105
Brandt, Max A. S. von 74–5
Bremer, James Gordon 151, 153–6
Brennwald, Caspar (1838–99) 4–5, 16, 71, 84–6, 89–90, 93–4, 101–3
  diaries of Caspar Brennwald (DCB) 84, 89–90, 182 n.11, 182–3 nn.17–19, 183 n.29, 187 n.104, 190 n.144
  early life 85
  to Europe 102
  and Siber (as business partners) 87–8 (*see also* Siber & Brennwald company)
  and Swiss trading mission 84–6, 183 n.26
Britain/British 1–2, 4, 6, 10–11, 14–15, 35–6, 39, 44, 52–4, 61, 65, 79–80, 100, 105–9, 114–15, 122, 125, 132, 141, 143, 148–50, 157
  Board of Trade 34
  British Army 69, 78
  British Consul/Consulate 14–16, 21–2, 32, 34, 39, 46–7, 49, 51, 58–9, 69, 172 n.42
  British Empire 12, 17–19, 123, 130, 145–6, 151, 162, 165
  British Legation 24–5, 29, 47, 52–3, 57–8, 97, 101, 187 n.104
  British troops to Yokohama 6, 61–5, 75, 78
    withdrawal of 78–80
  British War Office 64, 68
  emigrants 5, 116, 125–6, 128
  expansion (*see* expansion of British Empire)
  expatriates 5, 56
  Foreign Office 24, 26, 28, 31–5, 37–8, 45, 47, 49–50, 64, 170 n.2, 171 n.13
  to Hong Kong in long-distance steamships 192 n.21
  imperial system 5
  mercantile communities in China 33–4, 39
  relationship with China 33–5
  Union Jack 149, 154
Britomart, HMS, warship 153–4
Brooke, James (Rajah Brooke) 150, 153
Brown, W. G. 64
Bruce, Frederic 31
Bruce, James 44
Bushby, Emma Louisa 59

California Gold Rush 90
Camus, J. J. H. 63
Canterbury Association 126, 128
cemeteries 191 n.6
  affective individualism 114–15
  burial fees policy 108–9, 112, 192 n.16
    fees for interments (1854) 110
  Catholic Cemetery 108, 113, 193 n.22
  charitable 117
  Chinese burials/graves (in Hong Kong) 16–17, 106–23, 193 n.22, 194 n.54, 195 nn.60–1, 195 n.67
  Chinese Permanent Cemetery 119–20
  Christian burials 119, 164
  churchyard burials 109, 114
  civilian burial (Death Tax) 109, 112
  death of the other 114–15
  death records 193 n.22
  emotional authenticity 120–24, 195 n.67
  Eurasian Cemetery (Chiu Yuen Cemetery) 118, 195 n.59
  European 105, 109–11, 114, 116–18, 121–4, 193 n.22
  funeral processions 123, 196 nn.75–6
  garden 105, 111, 114–15
  Happy Valley (Wong Nei Chung Valley), Hong Kong 106, 108, 113, 115–16

headstones 111, 115–16
Hong Kong Cemetery/Colonial
    Cemetery/Protestant Cemetery
    105, 108–9, 111, 113–15, 117,
    119, 192 n.13, 193 n.22
Mahomedan Cemetery 113
merchants
    elites 109–12, 116–20
    Parsee, Jewish and Muslim 112–14,
        120
    prosperity and domesticity 114–16
    unexpected death 110
military graveyards 108
mortality from epidemics 108
Parsee Cemetery 112, 193 n.36
paupers' graves (for unemployed/
    seamen) 111
practice of storing remains 196 n.71
prioritization of military and
    merchants' 107–12
private 105, 109, 115, 117–18, 120
public 109, 117
for soldiers fallen from disease 105,
    108
state cemetery 108–9, 119
tombstones 105, 107, 115, 118
transport bodies/coffins 108, 110, 118
wealth/status/race 107, 111–12,
    116–20, 122–3, 191 n.2
Western 108, 114
Charlotte Jane (ship) 2, 9, 13, 17–18, 43,
    125, 142–3
    and Alt's (William) letters on 134–7
    to Antipodes 133, 137, 139
    to Australian colonies 135, 137–8
    cargo of 132–3, 135–6, 138–9
    to Crimean Peninsula 138–9
    death of ship's cook 135
    final voyages 139–42
    and global trading networks 130–6
    Lawrence (Captain) (*see* Lawrence,
        Alexander)
    Lobbett (Captain) 140–1
    myths of the Pilgrims 126–30, 140
    in New Zealand's rail industry 140–1
    Russell (Captain) (*see* Russell,
        William)
    to Shanghai 138
    shipping of gold 135–6, 139
    to Singapore 141

steerage passengers on 134
to Victoria, Canada 139
Ward, Edward (passenger) on 133–4
China 2–3, 7, 21, 39, 54, 79, 86–7, 90, 106,
    132, 139, 143, 148, 150
Amoy 2, 21–2, 170 n.2
Beijing 6, 30–8
    distance between London and 40
    to Britain in long-distance
        steamships 192 n.21
Canton 2, 6, 15, 21, 45, 56, 112–13
Chinese geomancy 105, 121, 195 n.61
Chinese Quarter 44, 50
compradores 90
Fuzhou 2, 15, 21–2, 170 n.2
Hong Kong 6, 12, 17, 34, 49, 56, 68–9,
    74, 80, 93, 98, 105, 112–13, 143
    currency and value in 192 n.15
    death and burial in (cemeteries)
        16–17, 106–23, 193 n.22, 194
        n.54, 195 nn.60–1, 195 n.67
    economic growth after 1860s 114
    funeral processions (Western) 123,
        196 nn.75–6
    Happy Valley (Wong Nei Chung
        Valley) Cemetery 106, 108, 113,
        115–16
    Indians in 194 n.42
    Kowloon 114
    leisure and comfort of colonial lives
        in 194 n.53
    Parsees living in (census of 1891)
        193 n.32
Ningbo (Ningpo) 2, 35, 37, 106
religious sincerity of Chinese
    merchants 121–2
Shanghai 2, 4, 6–8, 10–15, 17, 44, 49,
    52, 64, 73, 77, 98, 106, 112, 123,
    196 n.75
treaty port system in 2
Western medicine for Chinese elites
    195 n.66
Xiamen (Amoy) 2
Christians/Christianity 127
    Christian burials 119, 164
    European 117, 122
Clarke, Woodthorpe 72
class system 17, 31, 105, 107, 109, 116–17
    better class of Chinese 119, 121
    lower class 118, 120, 191 n.2

middle class 107, 114, 116, 122, 128, 191 n.2
upper class 107, 114, 122, 191 n.2
Cleall, Esme 10
Cleere, Eileen 8
Coates, P. D. 40
colonial expansion 2, 4–5, 17, 22, 55, 148. *See also* expansion of British Empire
Colonial Surgeon's report (1853) 193 n.27
commerce/commercial/commercialism 2, 5, 7, 13, 15, 31–3, 35, 39, 44, 52, 54, 102, 128, 130, 148, 150–3, 156, 159, 185 n.69, 193 n.23
 chambers of 33–4, 36–7, 56
 foreign troops at Yokohama and 70–2
 maritime 5, 14, 17, 146
commodities 14, 33, 37, 52, 83, 85–6, 89–90, 100, 182 n.16
Confucius/Confucian 121–2
connections 1, 4, 7–9, 11–12, 14, 73, 87, 91, 93, 97, 137, 158
 connectors 4, 14–17
Consul/Consulate 26, 53–4, 56–8
 British 14–16, 21–2, 32, 34, 39, 46–9, 51, 58–9
 European 92
 Japan Consular Service 45–7, 59
 Nagasaki 47
 Swiss 88, 92–5, 101, 103
Countess of Harcourt (ship) 151
Cressy (ship) 133
Crimea 11, 13, 17
 Crimean War 17, 138, 169 n.36
culture 8, 44, 56, 111, 116, 123–4, 146, 174 n.6, 195 n.61
Curl, James Steven, *The Victorian Celebration of Death* 191 n.2
Cutty Sark (clipper ship) 168 n.16, 193 n.21

Dainippon Silk Foundation 100
d'Almeida, José 148–9
Daly, Dominick 164
Darwin, Charles 153
Darwin, John 5
Davidoff, Leonore 9
Davies, Frederick 68
Davies, J. R. 141
Deans, John 129

Dent & Co. 54, 62, 72, 181 n.8
deployment, military 61–2, 65, 76, 80
Devonshire Regiment 68
de Wit, Jan Karel 57
Dickens, Charles 196 n.74
diplomacy/diplomatic 5, 15, 22, 25, 33–4, 36–7, 39–41, 45, 61–2, 79, 86, 101–3
 Anglo-Chinese 41
 Anglo-Japanese 41
 British 41, 57
 British-Japanese 15, 43–4, 47–8, 57
 Chinese 41
 diplomat 2, 6, 15, 24, 30, 34, 39–40, 48, 54, 70, 74–5, 78, 80, 95, 101, 103, 146 (*see also specific diplomats*)
 Japanese 169 n.16
DKSH Holding Ltd. 83–4, 180 n.3
Dohmen, Martin 179 n.36
Duchesne de Bellecourt, Gustave 63
Dukes, Edwin Joshua 121
Dumelin, Arnold 103
Dutch. *See* Holland; The Netherlands

Earl, George Windsor Samuel 4, 17–18, 145–6, 165
 from 1835–8 149–53
 in Adelaide 164
 Allen, Jim on 152
 and Australian affairs 149
 Berdan Pan business in Australia 160–1
 and Bremer 155
 and Brooke 153
 Brown Tribes of the Moluccas, Timor and Celebes 160
 and d'Almeida 148–9
 discovery of gold in New South Wales 158–61
 early life 146
 Eastern Seas (1832–5) 147–9
 The Eastern Seas (travel book) 149, 152–3, 162
 Enterprise in Tropical Australia 157
 and family (Clara and Annie) 157–64
 (*See also* Alt, Elisabeth (Annie))
 government services
  1856–9 161–2
  1859–64 163

'A Handbook for Colonists in Tropical
        Australia' 163
    illness and death 156-7, 159-64
    to Kissa in Serwatty Island 154
    as law agent (1847-52) 17, 159, 161
    *The Native Races of the Indian
        Archipelago; the Papuans* 160
    and Pace 148
    to Penang and Province Wellesley
        163-4
    and Port Essington (1838-44) 153-6
    research works 157
    to Singapore 158-61
    to Swan River 146-7
    to Sydney 157-8
    *Topography and Itinerary of Province
        Wellesley* 163
    trading link in Borneo 148-9
    *Transactions of the Ethnological Society
        of London* 163
East Asia 1-2, 4-5, 7, 10-12, 14-18, 21-2,
        31-2, 34, 40-1, 43, 64, 73, 83,
        114
    East Asian silks 86-7, 100
    East Asian treaty port 1, 4-5, 11, 14
    migration of Britons to 5
East India Company 112-13, 146, 150,
        154, 162
East India Trade Committee 151
Eitel, Ernst Johann 121, 191-2 n.8
elites/elite merchants 109-11, 134, 157
    Chinese 116-20, 122-4, 194 n.55, 195
        n.66
    Eurasian 116-20, 123
    Japanese 91
Ellice, Edward 12
Ellice, Kinnear & Company 12
emigrants 5, 116, 125-6, 128, 133, 135,
        140
empire 2, 4-5, 13, 132, 137
    British Empire 12, 17-19, 123, 130,
        145-6, 151, 162, 165
    celestial empire 139
    Ottoman Empire 138
    Qing (*see* Qing Empire)
England 8-10, 13, 34, 46, 55, 57, 59, 64,
        126-8, 136, 138, 140, 142
    Plymouth 127, 133, 153
English Common Law 102
Essington ship 153-4

ethnic minorities 112-13
ethnography 145, 155
Europe/Europeans 2, 5-6, 18, 21, 24, 30,
        32, 38, 59, 84, 89, 91, 94, 100,
        102, 106, 110, 112, 114-16,
        120-4, 150
    cemeteries 105, 109-11, 114, 116-18,
        121-4, 193 n.22
    European Christians 117, 122
    European silk reeling systems 83, 98-9
Evans, Joseph H. 54
expansion of British Empire 4-5, 17, 22,
        146. *See also* colonial expansion
expel-the-foreigner movement 12, 16. *See
        also* jōi (expel the foreigner)
        movement
exports 16, 33, 48, 51-2, 55, 83-4, 86,
        89-90, 94. *See also* imports
    raw silk 83-4, 86, 89-90, 100, 181 n.6
    silk waste 90
    silkworm eggs 89-90, 94-5, 99, 185
        n.67
extraterritoriality 2-3, 44, 48

Favre-Brandt, James Charles 94
Fei Wei 38
Feng-Shui (Chinese geomancy) 118, 121,
        195 n.61
Field, Franklin 56
Flinders, Matthew 151
foreign affairs (*gaikoku bugyō*) 25, 31
foreigners 12, 14, 16, 25-6, 43-5, 52, 54,
        57-8, 80, 99, 179 n.36
foreign residents 52, 58, 62-3, 65-6, 71-3,
        75, 79-80, 192 n.18. *See also*
        Western residents
foreign settlements 10, 26, 44, 48, 50-6,
        61, 64, 71-2, 89, 93
    Anglican settlement 129
    Canterbury settlement 128
    Nagasaki Foreign Settlement 45, 54-9
    Tokyo Foreign Settlement 99
    Yokohama Foreign Settlement 61-2,
        64-8, 76, 80, 88
foreign ships 44, 48. *See also specific
        warships*
foreign troops at Yokohama 61, 65, 79-80
    commerce/commercial opportunities
        70-2
    and foreign settlement 65-8

and Japanese society 76–8
and Yokohama Volunteer Corps 72–6
Fortune, Robert 191 n.1
France/French 6, 16, 25, 31, 44, 46, 49, 54, 61, 64–5, 78–80, 88, 138, 149, 152
   French troops 61–2, 73, 75
      withdrawal of 78–80
   imperialism 64
   Lyon 89
Franco-Prussian War 79
Fred. Huth & Co. 86–8, 100
Furukawa Ichibé 97, 99, 189 nn.133–4

Garrison amateur theatrical companies 71, 73, 154–5
Germany 80
Gibson-Hill, C. A. 153
Gipps, George 153, 155
Gladstone, William 79
globalization 1, 125–6, 142
Glover & Co. 175 n.23
Glover, Thomas B. 52, 56, 58, 175 n.23
Godley, John Robert 126, 129
   Letters from Early New Zealand 197 n.22
gold mining 17–18, 135, 149, 158, 160
good faith 24, 30, 39, 41, 64
Gower, Abel A. J. 45, 57
gradualist policy 34, 39
The Great Circle Track method (sailing technique) 133
Green, Matthew 48, 58

Hammond, Edmund 29, 36
Hansard, Albert W. 56
Hardie-Boys, Michael 128
Harris, Townsend 2, 26–7
Hayakawa Yōko 95, 187 n.105, 188 n.111
Hayami Kensō 98–9
Hoare, J. E. 171 n.21
Hodgson, C. Pemberton 45–50
Ho Fook 117
Ho Kom-tong 117–18
Holland 65
Hora Tomio 78
Ho Tung 105, 117–19
Hsu, Immanuel C. Y. 38
Huber, Caspar 87
Humbert-Droz, Aimé 85–6

Hunziker & Company 85
Hyde Clarke & Associates 160

Immoos, Thomas 181 n.10
imperialism 1, 64
imports 33, 37, 52, 55, 86, 90–6, 101. *See also* exports
India 6, 11, 37–8, 56, 86, 111, 113, 146
   Bengal 130, 159
   Bombay 112–13, 132
   burials/graveyards 111
   Calcutta 38, 113, 146
   Government of India 38, 162
   Indians in Hong Kong 194 n.42
Indian Archipelago 148–50, 163
Indian Rebellion (Mutiny, 1857–8) 6, 13, 162
individual experiences 1–4. *See also specific individuals*
Indonesia 163
   Indonesian archipelago 150, 158
   Java 148–50
   Sumatra 148, 150, 158
Ishiguro, Laura 10
Ishii Kanji 181 n.8
Italy 90, 100, 182 n.18
   Italian silk industry 184 n.32
Iwakura Tomomi 79

Jalland, Pat, 'Victorian Death and Its Decline: 1850–1918' 191 n.2
Japan 2–3, 39, 79–80, 86–7, 181 n.9
   banto/kodzukai 90, 95, 97, 99
   Chōshū domain 14, 31, 65
   Dejima (Deshima) artificial island 43–4, 54, 57
   Edo 7, 24–7, 29, 32, 40, 45, 47, 51–2, 56–7, 89, 92–3, 101, 187 n.101
   foreign merchants in 11
   Hakodate 2, 24, 32, 48–9, 171 n.20
   Hyogo 29
   Japanese Army 69, 78
   Japanese raw silk 83–4, 90, 100, 184 n.34, 185 n.67
   Kagoshima 63
      bombardment of Kagoshima 7, 14–15
   Kanagawa 15, 24–8, 45, 89, 171 n.21
   Kobe 2, 47
   Kyushu 2, 14, 57

Maebashi domain 97–9, 101
Nagasaki 2, 4, 7, 11–16, 24, 32, 43–59, 92, 137, 139, 164
  Chinese residents of 54
  Higashiyamate (Ōura commercial district) 55–6
  Minamiyamate 55–6
  Nagasaki British Consulate 47, 174 n.6, 176 n.38, 176 n.43
  Nagasaki Foreign Settlement 45, 54–9
  Nagasaki Harbour 43, 45, 52, 55–6, 58
  Nagasaki Magistrate 43, 50–2, 55, 57
  Ōura Creek 45, 52, 55, 58
  tenryō (imperial territory) 45, 53
  Tomachi Ōura 45
Niigata 29, 75
Ōmura domain 45
Osaka 29, 57
Oshio 95, 99–100
retainers of Shimazu 2, 58
Satsuma 2, 93
Sendai domain 16, 94–7, 185 n.69
sericulture 98, 100
Shimoda (Shizuoka Prefecture) 26–7
Shinshū 76, 100
sovereignty 78–9
Swiss-Japanese weapon deal 93
Swiss trading house in 83–4, 100
Tōkaidō 7, 25, 57, 74
Tokugawa shogunate (*bakufu*) 2, 7, 24–7, 29–30, 43–5, 51–2, 56, 65, 78, 80, 83, 92–3, 185 n.67
Tokyo 92–3, 99–101
Tōzenji 25, 47, 57, 171 n.18
and Western powers 61, 86
Yokohama 2, 4, 15–17, 24–8, 32, 35, 47–8, 61, 86, 89, 101, 185 n.58
  British troops to 61–5, 68, 70, 75, 78
  commerce/commercial oppurtunities 70–2
  foreign troops at (*see* foreign troops at Yokohama)
  Lincolnshire Regiment 70
  military sanitarium 68, 80
  Royal Marines Light Infantry 63, 70, 73, 77–9
  2nd Battalion 9th Regiment 68–9
  20th Regiment at 64, 68–9, 73–4, 77
  withdrawal of British and French troops 78–80
  Yokohama Custom House 77
  Yokohama Foreign Settlement 61–2, 64–8, 76, 80, 88
  Yokohama Volunteer Corps 72–6
Japan-Britain Treaty of Amity 43–4
Japan Consular Service 45–7, 59
Jardine, Matheson & Co. 5, 44, 54, 72, 98, 101, 107–8, 116–17, 175 n.23, 181 n.8, 191 n.3
Jardine, William 116
Jaurès, Louis Jean Benjamin (French admiral) 63, 65
jōi (expel the foreigner) movement 57–8
Jones, Russell 145–6

Kagoshima, bombardment of 7, 14–15
Kanagawa bugyō (governor who controlled the Yokohama trading area) 65
Kettle, Edward T. 48, 50
Kikuchi Iyo no kami 93
Kingdon, N. P. 62
Kishi Motokazu 78–9
Knollys, Henry 115
Koide Harimano 93
Kokaze Hidemasa 79–80
Kuper, Augustus 63–5

Lady Clarke (ship) 130
Laidlaw, Zoë 4
Lambert, David 4
Laqueur, Thomas 194 n.45
Lascars 132–3
Lau Chu Pak 119, 121–2
Lawrence, Alexander 130–6. *See also Charlotte Jane* (ship)
  and Barker 134–5
  The Great Circle Track method (sailing technique) 133
  personality of 133
Lenox, John 8
Lester, Alan 4
letters/letter writing 1–3, 8–10, 12–13, 16–18, 31, 50, 54–6, 58, 62–5, 84, 87, 89–91, 95, 101–2, 136, 167–8 nn.14–15, 169 n.36, 182 n.12, 199 n.71

lex loci contractus 102
Lim, Patricia 109, 111, 115–16
Lincolnshire Regiment 70
Lindau, Rudolf 88, 101
Lockett (ship) 139
Logan, Abraham 159
Logan, James Richardson (J.R.) 159, 163
London 8, 18, 31, 34, 38–40, 47, 64, 86–8, 95, 132, 135, 150, 157
    distance between Beijing/Edo and 40
London Memorandum (1862) 30
Lord Bathurst 151
Lord Colchester 160
Lord Glenelg 152
Lord Minto 152

Mackenzie Brothers and Company 8, 11
Mackenzie, Kenneth Ross 11, 44–5, 54, 174 n.3, 175 n.23
Maebashi Silk Mill 97
Major, John 56
Malay Peninsula 158–9, 163
Manchester Chamber of Commerce 36
Manktelow, Emily 10
Maritime Customs Service 23–4
Matheson, James 116
Medina (ship) 148
Meiji Government 70, 78–9, 92, 94, 96–8
    haihan-chiken 186 n.95
Meiji Japan 83, 92
Meiji period (1868–1912) 62, 78, 84, 93, 101
Meiji Restoration (1868) 10, 16, 75–6, 78, 101, 186 n.95
    Siber & Brennwald company during 94–7
Melrose, William 132
Mercer, William T. 111, 191 n.1
Merchant Navy 110, 130, 137, 193 n.23
merchants 2, 8, 16–17, 24–5, 28–9, 33–9, 52, 105–6, 112. See also trade/traders
    British 2, 13–15, 17, 22, 28, 30, 33–4, 36–7, 39, 51, 55, 64, 72, 80, 97, 107, 110–13, 123, 132
    Chinese 51, 114, 117, 119–22, 162, 194 n.55
    European 90, 109–10, 116, 139
    foreign 11, 24, 48, 56, 71, 76–7, 101, 112–14, 123
    Japanese 26, 44, 51, 62, 71, 76, 99

Jewish 17, 113, 120
    merchant ship/shipping 2, 8–9, 14, 17, 155
    Swiss 4–5, 16, 71, 85
    transportation with families 114
    Western 2, 12–13, 16–17, 62
Meynerzhagen 87
Michie, Alexander 170 n.3
The Middle East 113
Miyagi Prefecture 16
Monkey (schooner) 148
Montgomery, Tessa 167–8 n.15
Morrison, George A. 59
Morrison, George Staunton 4, 6, 15, 43, 45–6, 49–59
Morrison, Robert 49
Mössalang, Markus 40
Müller, Caspar 97–8, 189 n.130
Municipal Council 56, 75–6
Murchison, Roderick 158, 160
Murray, Robert 135
Myburgh, Francis G. 47, 53–4, 57
Myōgyōji (Buddhist Temple) 45–8, 50, 54, 56, 58–9, 174 n.6

Namamugi Incident (1862) 16, 61–3, 72–3, 80. *See also Satsuei-sensō*
National Important Cultural Property 175 n.24, 176 n.43
navigation/navigational techniques 31, 125, 127, 130, 133, 137–8, 142, 145, 147
Neale, Edward St. John 59, 62–5
    to Foreign Secretary in London 63
Negretti & Zambra Company 55
The Netherlands 25, 27, 31, 43–4, 47, 51–2, 54, 57, 117, 148–9, 156, 171 n.20, 187 n.104
New Zealand 17, 133, 139, 140–3
    Canterbury 17, 125–30, 133, 135, 142, 146
        Anglican colony in 126
        Canterbury Plains 129
    Christchurch 125–6, 128, 139, 142
    Invercargill 140–1
    Māori 129
    Ngāi Tahu people 129
    Port of Lyttelton 125, 133–5, 142
        First Four Ships (*See Charlotte Jane* (ship))

Southland Provincial Council 141
Ng Hon Tsz, funeral procession of 196 n.76
non-ratification 34, 36–8. *See also*
    ratification
Norcock, H. J. L. 63, 71
Norfolk Regiment 68
North America 12, 18

Ogilvie, Gordon 126
Ono-gumi Ito ten/Ono-group, Japan 97,
    99–100, 189 n.132
Opium Trade 38
Opium Wars 191 n.3
    First (1839–42) 2
    Second (1856–60) 6, 11, 14, 32, 114,
    162
Orient (ship) 136
The Orient 132, 169 n.42
Oronto (barque) 153
Osborn, Sherard 6–7
Ōtani School of Shin Buddhism 45
Ōtoru 99, 189 n.135
Ottoman Empire 138
Ōuetsu Reppan Dōmei (Alliance of
    Northern Domains) 75, 94

Pace, Walter 148
pagan 122
Parker King, Philip 151
Parkes, Harry (1828–85) 21, 61, 75, 79,
    97–8, 172 n.42
Parsees 17, 112–13, 120
    'Tower of Silence' for excarnation 113,
    193 n.36
Patterson, William 130
Pelcovits, Nathan A. 34, 40
    'Old China Hands' 39
personality, individual 7, 39–40, 133
Pilgrim Fathers of America 127
Portugal 54
Postal Convention (1873) 79–80
Pruyn, R. H. 63

Qing Empire 2, 6, 11, 14–15, 24, 32, 34,
    37, 54, 121, 162
    Boxer Rising 38

race 17, 107
Raffles, Stamford 150
railway industry 33, 140–1, 157

Randolph (ship) 133
ratification 15, 34–7. *See also* non-
    ratification
reciprocity 35–7, 39, 41
Reece, R. H. W. 165
Richardson, Charles (senior) 8
Richardson, Charles Lenox (1833–62)
    2–5, 61, 73, 167 n.14, 168 n.28,
    169 n.36, 178 n.27
    business activities in Shanghai 5, 7–9,
    11, 13–14, 168 nn.28–9
    death of 2, 7, 11–12, 16, 61, 73,
    168 n.29, 196 n.75 (*see also*
    Namamugi Incident)
    'Home News' 9–10
    in nineteenth-century China and Japan
    6–19
    letters of (*see* letters/letter writing)
    and remittances 10
    and the West Indies 12
Riotte, Torsten 40
Robinson, Hercules 162
Roches, Léon 93, 187 n.103
Roebuck, HMS, British warship 50
ronin (lordless samurai) 73
Rossier, Pierre 55
Royal Asiatic Society 145, 149, 152
Royal Geographical Society (RGS) 145,
    149, 152–3, 157–8, 160
Royal Navy 43, 47, 63, 146
Russell, John 31
Russell, William 9, 12, 136–40
    Alt (William) on 137
    transfer to *Athelston* (ship) 140
Russel, Maurice 70
Russia/Russian 25, 44–5, 54, 64, 171 n.20
    Ural Mountains 158

Saigon 64, 91
Sakai Tadamasu 65
Sakamoto Ryōma 53
Sampson, HMS, British warship 24, 45, 47
Samuel & Co. 161
Sanjō Sanetomi 79
Satow, Ernest 48, 72, 172 n.42
Satsuei-sensō 7. *See also* Kagoshima,
    bombardment of
Satsuma-Chōshū alliance 16
Schnell, Edward 92, 187 n.96
Scots Presbyterian settlers 129, 140

seclusion policy 25
Second World War 52, 84
Serang 132–3
settlers 5, 126, 128, 130–1, 133–4, 140, 142, 147, 154–5. *See also* foreign settlements
   Anglican 129
   Australian 137
   Scots Presbyterian 129, 140
Shanghai 6–8, 10–14, 22–4, 44, 64, 73, 98, 112, 138–9
Shanghai Volunteers 14, 72, 178 n.27
Shimonoseki campaign (1864) 31, 65–6, 80
Shimonoseki Straits 65
shipping 8, 11, 13, 113, 132, 136, 141, 151, 153, 155–6
Siber & Brennwald company (Siber, Brennwald & Co.) 83–4, 88, 182 n.15, 188 n.115, 189 n.135
   Brennwald's negotiations over weapons (1866–7) 94
   early trading in Yokohama 89–91
   imports 91–4
      foodstuffs 91–2
      of Sendai Domain 95–6, 185 n.69
      steamers 92, 95
      textiles/cloth contracts 91
   during Meiji Restoration 94–7
   Sendai's debt to 96–7
   shipments 89
   silk trade (*see* silk trade)
   success of 100–1
   tea export 90
   weapons/military deals 92–6, 101
Siber, Gustav 87
Siber-Gysi, Gustav (1827–72) 84
SiberHegner company 83
Siber, Hermann (1842–1918) 4–5, 16, 84–95, 97–103
   and Brennwald (as business partners) 87–8 (*see also* Siber & Brennwald company)
   early life 86–7
   East Asian raw silk varieties 87
   education 184 n.35
   on Furukawa 99, 189 nn.133–4
   learning Japanese language 90
Siber, Wolff & Co. 83

silk trade 8, 14, 16, 33, 52, 55, 83, 86–7, 90, 94–5, 99–100, 181 n.6
   East Asian 86–7, 100
   European 83, 86, 98, 100–1
   Italian silk industry 184 n.32
   Japanese raw silk 83–4, 100, 184 n.34, 185 n.67
   Maebashi silk 95, 97–8, 101
   pébrine crisis (pébrine silkworm disease) 86, 89, 100, 184 n.34
   Sendai silk 95
   Siber & Brennwald (*see* Siber & Brennwald company)
   silk mills/silk-reeling filature/machines 97–100, 190 n.145
   silkworm eggs 89–90, 94–5, 99–100, 185 n.67
   Swiss raw silk trading house 83–6, 89, 97, 99–100, 180 n.5, 181 n.7
   Zurich silk industry 182 n.32
Sims, Richard 79
Singapore 17, 86, 93, 132, 140–1, 143, 148–51, 153–62
   Chinese merchants in 121
   colonial 120
Sir George Seymour (ship) 133
Smyth, James 64, 177 n.8
social class. *See* class system
soldiers 4, 48, 68, 71, 73–7, 80, 113
   cemetery for (fallen from disease) 105, 108–9
   mortality in mid-nineteenth century 177 n.11
South Africa 70
The South Australian Mining Association 135
Southeast Asia 4, 14, 17–18, 145–6, 148, 158, 165
Stamford (schooner) 148–9
Stirling, James 43
Stone, Lawrence, affective individualism 114–15
Straits of Malacca 132, 148
Strange, Julie-Marie, *Death, Grief and Poverty in Britain, 1870–1914* 191 n.2
Suez Canal 114, 192 n.21
Summer War (1866) 14
Suzuki Jun 78

Switzerland/Swiss 83, 88–9, 100–1, 103, 181 n.9
   Canton of Grisons 89
   Canton of Ticino 89
   silk trade (*see* silk trade)
   Swiss-Japanese weapon deal 92–3
   Zurich 87
      Canton of Zürich 86
      Diethelm Keller Holding (DKH) 182 n.12, 182 n.15
      Kreditanstalt bank 100
      Zentralbibliothek 84, 182 n.12
      Zurich silk industry 84, 184 n.32

Taiping Rebellion (Civil War) 10, 14, 114
Tamar, HMS, transport ship 151
Tarlow, Sarah 115
technology 97, 100–1, 114, 141
Textor & Co. 95–6
Thomas, Patricia 128
Thompson, James 130
Tianjin Massacre (1870) 79
Tindals 132
Tokugawa Yoshinobu 93
Towson, John 133
Tōzenji Affair 29
trade/traders 2, 4, 6–7, 11–12, 14–15, 17, 22, 25–6, 28, 33, 44, 51, 54–6, 58, 86, 101, 103, 155–6. *See also* exports; imports; merchants
   arms 48, 91–4
   Australasian trade route 136
   British 15, 45–6, 146, 148, 150–1, 181 n.8
   Canton 112–13, 191 n.3
   East India 130
   European 86, 89
   foreign 5, 24, 32, 48, 89, 95
   free 14, 24, 44
   global trading network (*see Charlotte Jane* (ship))
   human (for coolie business) 90
   illegal 95
   international 7
   legitimate 35
   silk (*see* silk trade)
   steamer 92, 95
   tea 12, 14, 52, 55, 86, 90–1, 132, 137, 139, 168 n.32
   weapons/military supplies 16, 92–6, 101, 187 n.101
   Western 22, 93, 181 n.8
The Treasury 152
Treaty of Nanjing (1842) 2, 6, 21, 32
Treaty of Tianjin (1858) 6, 15, 32–3, 38
treaty port(s) 1–8, 11–16, 21, 25, 29, 31–4, 36, 44, 48, 73, 106
   concession 21, 35, 39, 44, 56
Tsukiji Silk Mill 97, 99–100
Tsungli Yamen 38
Tung Wah Hospital 117, 119, 194 n.55

The United States 2, 12, 16, 25, 31, 54, 65, 79–80, 84, 90
   Americans 5, 44, 72, 113
   California 110
   US Civil War 13
urban development 121
US-Japan Treaty of Amity (1854) 26
US-Japan Treaty of Friendship and Commerce (1858) 26

van Polsbroek, Dirk Graf 187 n.104
Victorian 1, 9, 111, 122, 125, 130, 135, 191 n.2, 196 n.74
Victoria, Queen 154, 157
Vincent, Eliza 69
Vincent, Henry James 69
violence 11, 16, 61
Vulcan, HMS, ship 64
Vyse, Howard 45

Wakefield, Edward Gibbon 126, 128–9
Wakizawa Kinjirō 76
Walsh & Co. 54
Walsh, John G. 54
Walter, James. *See* Ōtoru
warships in commission 152. *See also specific warships*
Washington, John 152
Wei Yuk 119
Welch, Ian 138, 199 n.84
Wellesley, HMS, warship 156
Westerners 2–3, 7, 10, 12, 14–16, 18–19, 41, 43, 61, 72–4
Western residents 61–2. *See also* foreign residents
West Indian Regiment (1863) 9

West Indies 12
wholesale family retrenchment scheme 10
Wigram, Henry 126, 129
Winchester, Charles 57
Wirgman, Charles 57
Wittal, E. 98
Wolff, Arnold 102–3

Yeoh, Brenda 120
Yokohama Archives of History 84, 177 n.8
Yokohama Mounted Volunteers Corps 73–4
Yokohama Volunteer Rifle Corps 72–3

Zuppinger, Siber & Co. 86, 88, 100

www.ingramcontent.com/pod-product-compliance
Lightning Source LLC
Chambersburg PA
CBHW062138300426
44115CB00012BA/1972